Study Guide

Avi J. Cohen
York University

Harvey B. King
University of Regina

MACROECONOMICS
Canada in the Global Environment

Seventh Edition

Michael Parkin   Robin Bade

Pearson Canada
Toronto

ISBN-13: 978-0-321-61602-9
ISBN-10: 0-321-61602-2

Vice President, Editorial Director: Gary Bennett
Developmental Editor: Catherine Belshaw
Production Editor: Cheryl Jackson
Production Coordinator: Sarah Lukaweski

2 3 4 5   13 12 11 10

Printed and bound in Canada.

Contents

Acknowledgments

This seventh edition of the *Study Guide* has benefited from students who pointed out mistakes and ambiguities they found in using the *Study Guide*. Thanks to Tong Gao, Slava Ilyin, Mitra Malekan, Novia Ng, and Xiao Shan Tan for helping us in this area. Thanks also to Robin Bade and Michael Parkin for their dedication to the continuous improvement of the textbook, the *Study Guide*, and the teaching of economics.

Harvey King dedicates this edition to Morgan and Harrison for showing me the future, and to Tracy for all her love and patience. Avi Cohen dedicates this edition to Robert Cohen, my father, whose extraordinary qualities as a teacher make him my role model.

Harvey King
Avi Cohen
March 2009

Introduction

Before You Begin ...

Our experience has taught us that what first-year economics students want most from a *Study Guide* is help in mastering course material in order to do well on examinations. We have developed this *Study Guide* to respond specifically to that demand. Using this *Study Guide* alone, however, is not enough to guarantee that you will do well in your course. In order to help you overcome the problems and difficulties that most first-year students encounter, we have some general advice on how to study, as well as some specific advice on how to best use this *Study Guide*.

Some Friendly Advice

The study of economics requires a different style of thinking from what you may encounter in other courses. Economists make extensive use of assumptions to break down complex problems into simple, analytically manageable parts. This analytical style, while not ultimately more demanding than the styles of thinking in other disciplines, feels unfamiliar to most students and requires practice. As a result, it is not as easy to do well in economics simply on the basis of your raw intelligence and high-school knowledge as it is in many other first-year courses. Many students who come to our offices are frustrated and puzzled by the fact that they are getting A's and B's in their other courses but only a C or worse in economics. They have not recognized that the study of economics is different and requires practice. In order to avoid a frustrating visit to your instructor after your first test, we suggest you do the following.

Don't rely solely on your high-school economics. If you took high-school economics, you will have seen the material on demand and supply, which your instructor will lecture on in the first few weeks. Don't be lulled into feeling that the course will be easy. Your high-school knowledge of economic concepts will be very useful, but it will not be enough to guarantee high marks on exams. Your college or university instructors will demand much more detailed knowledge of concepts and ask you to apply them in new circumstances.

Keep up with the course material on a weekly basis. Read the appropriate chapter in the textbook before your instructor lectures on it. In this initial reading, don't worry about details or arguments you can't quite follow—just try to get a general understanding of the basic concepts

and issues. You may be amazed at how your instructor's ability to teach improves when you come to class prepared. As soon as your instructor has finished covering a chapter, complete the corresponding *Study Guide* chapter. Avoid cramming the day before or even just the week before an exam. Because economics requires practice, cramming is an almost certain recipe for failure.

Keep a good set of lecture notes. Good lecture notes are vital for focusing your studying. Your instructor will only lecture on a subset of topics from the textbook. The topics your instructor covers in a lecture should usually be given priority when studying. Also give priority to studying the figures and graphs covered in the lecture.

Instructors do differ in their emphasis on lecture notes or the textbook, so early on in the course ask which is more important in reviewing for exams—lecture notes or the textbook. If your instructor answers that both are important, then ask the following, typically economic question: at the margin, which will be more beneficial—spending an extra hour rereading your lecture notes or an extra hour rereading the textbook? This question assumes that you have read each textbook chapter twice (once before lecture for a general understanding, and then later for a thorough understanding); that you have prepared a good set of lecture notes; and that you have worked through all of the problems in the appropriate *Study Guide* chapters. By applying this style of analysis to the problem of efficiently allocating your study time, you are already beginning to think like an economist!

Use your instructor and/or teaching assistants for help. When you have questions or problems with course material, come to the office to ask questions. Remember, you are paying for your education and instructors are there to help you learn. We are often amazed at how few students come to see us during office hours. Don't be shy. The personal contact that comes from one-on-one tutoring is professionally gratifying for us as well as (hopefully) beneficial to you.

Form a study group. A very useful way to motivate your studying and to learn economics is to discuss the course material and problems with other students. Explaining the answer to a question out loud is a very effective way of discovering how well you understand the question. When you answer a question only in your head, you often skip steps in the chain of reasoning without realizing it. When you are forced to explain your reasoning aloud, gaps and mistakes quickly appear, and you (with your fellow group members) can quickly correct your reasoning. The true/false and explain questions in the *Study Guide* and the critical thinking questions at the end of each textbook chapter are good study-group material. You might also get together after having worked the *Study Guide* problems, but before looking at the answers, and help each other solve unsolved problems.

Work old exams. One of the most effective ways of studying is to work through exams your instructor has given in previous years. Old exams give you a feel for the style of question your instructor may ask, and give you the opportunity to get used to time pressure if you force yourself to do the exam in the allotted time. Studying from old exams is not cheating, as long as you have obtained a copy of the exam legally. Some institutions post old exams online; others keep them in the library, the department, or at the student union. Upper-year students who have previously taken the course are usually a good source as well. Remember, though, that old exams are a useful study aid only if you use them to understand the reasoning behind each question. If you simply memorize answers in the hopes that your instructor will repeat the identical question, you are likely to fail. From year to year, instructors routinely change the questions or change the numerical values for similar questions.

Use the MyEconLab Web site. In addition to this *Study Guide*, we believe the MyEconLab site (www.pearsoned.ca/myeconlab) is worth using for the valuable help it will provide in mastering course material and doing well on examinations. However, don't just take our word for it—ask students who have used it for their opinions. MyEconLab is an online homework and tutorial system that includes practice tests, personalized study plans, practice exercises, tutorial instruction, a powerful graphing tool, Economics in the News updates, and a virtual Office Hours feature that enables you to get help by email from Michael Parkin and Robin Bade.

Using the *Study Guide*

You should only attempt to complete a chapter in this *Guide* after you have read the corresponding textbook chapter and listened to your instructor lecture on the material. Each *Study Guide* chapter contains the following sections.

Key Concepts This first section is a one-to-two-page summary, in point form, of all key definitions, concepts, and material from the textbook chapter. The summary is organized using the same major section headings from the textbook chapter. Key terms from the textbook appear in bold. This section is designed to focus you quickly and precisely on the core material that you must master. It is an excellent study aid for the night before an exam. Think

of it as crib notes that will serve as a final check of the key concepts you have studied.

Helpful Hints When you encounter difficulty in mastering concepts or techniques, you will not be alone. Many students find certain concepts difficult and often make the same kinds of mistakes. We have seen these common mistakes often enough to have learned how to help students avoid them. The hints point out these mistakes and offer tips to avoid them. The hints focus on the most important concepts, equations, and techniques for problem solving. They also review crucial graphs that appear on every instructor's exams. We hope that this section will be very useful, since instructors always ask exam questions designed to test these possible mistakes in your understanding.

This section sometimes includes extra material that your instructor may add to the course, but is not in textbook chapters. An example is the discussion in Chapter 2 of mathematics of the slope of the production possibilities frontier. Such extra material is marked with the symbol ⓔ ("e" for "extra") and may be skipped if your instructor does not cover it.

The same symbol is used throughout the *Study Guide* to identify questions and answers based on extra material.

Self-Test This should be one of the most useful sections of this *Study Guide*. The questions are designed to give you practice and to test skills and techniques you must master to do well on exams. You are encouraged to write directly in the *Guide*. There are plenty of the multiple-choice questions (25 for each chapter) you are most likely to encounter on course tests and exams. There are also other types of questions, described below, each with a specific pedagogical purpose. Questions (and answers) based on extra material covered in the Helpful Hints are marked with the "extra" symbol ⓔ so that you can easily skip them if your instructor does not assign that material.

Before we describe the three parts of the Self-Test section, here are some tips that apply to all parts:

Use a pencil. This will allow you to erase your mistakes and have neat, completed pages from which to study. Draw graphs wherever applicable. Some questions will ask explicitly for graphs; many others will not, but will require a chain of reasoning that involves shifts of curves on a graph. *Always draw the graph.* Don't try to work through the reasoning in your head—you are much more likely to make mistakes that way. Whenever you draw a graph, even in the margins of this *Guide*, label the axes. You may think that you can keep the labels in your head, but you will be confronting many different graphs with many different variables on the axes. Avoid confusion: label. As an added incentive, remember that on exams where graphs are required, instructors will deduct marks for unlabelled axes.

Do the Self-Test questions as if they were real exam questions, which means do them without looking at the answers. This is the single most important tip we can give you. Struggling for the answers to questions that you find difficult is one of the most effective ways to learn. The athletic adage "No pain, no gain" applies equally to studying. You will learn the most from right answers you had to struggle for and from your wrong answers and mistakes. Only after you have attempted all the questions should you look at the answers. When you finally do check the answers, be sure to understand where you went wrong and why the right answer is right.

If you want to impose time pressure on yourself to simulate the conditions of a real exam, allow two minutes for each true/false and multiple-choice question. The short answer problems vary considerably in their time requirements, so it is difficult to give time estimates for them. However, we believe that such time pressure is probably not a good idea for Study Guide questions. A state of relaxed concentration is best. If you want practice with time pressure, use old exams, or use the Part Wrap Up Midterm Examinations (see description on page x).

There are many questions in each chapter, and it will take you somewhere between two and five hours to answer all of them. If you get tired (or bored), don't burn yourself out by trying to work through all of the questions in one sitting. Consider breaking up your Self-Test over two (or more) study sessions.

One other tip about the Self-Test. *Before* you jump in and do the questions, be sure to read through the Key Concepts and Helpful Hints. This will save you frustration at getting wrong answers to questions. When you do get wrong answers, you will often find an explanation of the right answers in Key Concepts or Helpful Hints.

The three parts of the Self-Test section are:

True/False and Explain These questions test basic knowledge of chapter concepts and your ability to apply the concepts. Some challenge your understanding, to see if you can identify mistakes in statements using basic concepts. These questions will quickly identify gaps in your knowledge and are useful to answer out loud in a study group. There are 15 of these questions, organized using the same major section headings from the textbook. The Test Bank that your instructor will likely use to make up tests and exams also contains true/false questions like those in the Self-Test.

When answering, identify each statement as *true* or *false*. Explain your answer in one sentence. The space underneath each question should be sufficient in every case for writing your answer.

Multiple-Choice These more difficult questions test your analytical abilities by asking you to apply concepts

to new situations, manipulate information, and solve numerical and graphical problems.

This is the most frequently used type of test and exam question, and the Self-Test contains 25 of them organized using the same major section headings from the textbook. Your instructor's Test Bank contains all of the *Study Guide* multiple-choice questions, numerous questions that closely parallel the *Study Guide* questions, plus many similar questions.

Before you answer, read each question and all five choices carefully. Many of the choices will be plausible and will differ only slightly. You must choose the one *best* answer. A useful strategy is to first eliminate any obviously wrong choices and then focus on the remaining alternatives. Be aware that sometimes the correct answer will be "none of the above." Don't get frustrated or think that you are dim if you can't immediately see the correct answer. These questions are designed to make you work to find the correct choice.

Short Answer Problems The best way to learn to do economics is to do problems. Problems are also a popular type of test and exam question—practise them as much as possible! Each Self-Test concludes with ten short answer, numerical, or graphical problems, often based on economic policy issues. In many chapters, this is the most challenging part of the Self-Test. It is also likely to be the most helpful for deepening your understanding of the chapter material. We have, however, designed the questions to teach as much as to test. We have purposely arranged the parts of each multipart question to lead you through the problem-solving analysis in a gradual and sequential fashion, from easier to more difficult parts.

Problems that require critical thinking are marked with the symbol ⊕, to alert you to the need for extra time and effort. This symbol gives you the same indication you would have on a test or exam from the number of marks or minutes allocated to a problem.

Answers The Self-Test is followed by a section that gives answers to all the questions. But do not look at any answer until you have attempted the question.

When you finally do look, use the answer to understand where you went wrong, and think about why the answer is right. Every true/false and multiple-choice answer includes a brief, point-form explanation to suggest where you might have gone wrong and the economic reasoning behind the answer. At the end of each answer are page references to the textbook, so you can read a more complete explanation.

Answers to critical thinking questions are marked with ⊕ to indicate why you might have struggled with that question! (We purposely did not mark which true/false and multiple-choice questions were critical thinking, to stay as close as possible to a real test or exam format. In an exam, all multiple-choice questions, for example, are worth the same number of marks, and you would have no idea which questions are the more difficult ones requiring critical thinking.)

The detailed answers to the short answer problems should be especially useful in clarifying and illustrating typical chains of reasoning involved in economic analysis. Answers to critical thinking problems are marked with ⊖. If the answers alone do not clear up your confusion, go back to the appropriate sections of the textbook and to Key Concepts and Helpful Hints in this *Study Guide*. If that still does not suffice, go to your instructor's or teaching assistants' office, or to your study-group members, for help and clarification.

Part Wrap Up Problem and Midterm Examination
Every few chapters, at the end of each of the ten Parts of the textbook, you will find a special multipart problem (and answer). These problems draw on material from all chapters in the Part, and emphasize policy and real-world questions (e.g., the impact of cigarette smuggling on tax revenues). They will help you integrate concepts from different chapters that may seem unrelated, but actually are. We often design exam questions similar to these problems.

Each Wrap Up also contains a Midterm Examination, consisting of four or more multiple-choice questions from each chapter in the textbook part. The midterm is set up like a real examination or test, with a scrambled order and a time limit for working the questions. Like the other multiple-choice questions, there are answers with point-form explanations as well as page references to the textbook so you can go find more complete explanations.

If you effectively combine the use of the textbook, the *Study Guide*, MyEconLab, and all other course resources, you will be well prepared for exams. Equally importantly, you will also have developed analytical skills and powers of reasoning that will benefit you throughout life and in whatever career you choose.

Do You Have Any Friendly Advice for Us?
We have attempted to make this *Study Guide* as clear and as useful as possible, and to avoid errors. No doubt, we have not succeeded entirely, and you are the only judges who count in evaluating our attempt. If you discover errors, or if you have other suggestions for improving the *Guide*, please write to us. In future editions, we will try to acknowledge the names of all students whose suggestions help us improve this supplement. Send your correspondence or email to either of us:

Professor Avi J. Cohen
Department of Economics
Vari Hall, York University
Toronto, Ontario M3J 1P3
avicohen@yorku.ca

Professor Harvey B. King
Department of Economics
University of Regina
Regina, Saskatchewan S4S 0A2
Harvey.King@uregina.ca

Should the Study of Economics Be Part of Your Future?

*By Harvey King (University of Regina) and
Robert Whaples (Wake Forest University)*

Should You Take More Economics Courses?

Soon you will learn about supply and demand, utility and profit maximization, employment and unemployment. First, however, let's take a moment to look to the future.

- Should you take more classes or maybe even major in economics?

- What about graduate school in economics?

Economists generally assume that people try to make rational choices to maximize their own well-being. The purpose of this chapter is help you make that rational maximizing choice by providing low-cost information. Let us assess the benefits and see whether they outweigh the costs of studying economics.

Benefits from Studying Economics

Knowledge, Enlightenment, and Liberation

As John Maynard Keynes, a famous British economist, said, "The ideas of economists … both when they are right and when they are wrong, are more powerful than is commonly understood. Indeed the world is ruled by little else. Practical men, who believe themselves to be quite exempt from any intellectual influences, are usually the slaves of some defunct economist." Studying economics is a liberating and enlightening experience. You don't want to be the slave of a defunct economist, do you? Liberate yourself. It's better to bring your ideas out in the open, to confront and understand them, rather than to leave them buried.

Knowledge, Understanding, and Satisfaction

Many of the most important problems in the world are economic. Studying economics gives you a practical set of tools to understand and solve them. Every day, on television and in the newspapers, we hear and read about big issues such as economic growth, inflation, unemployment, health care reform, welfare reform, the environment, and the transition away from Communism. Your introduction to economics will let you watch the news or pick up a newspaper and better understand these issues. As an added bonus, economics helps you understand smaller, more immediate concerns, such as: How much Spam should I buy? Is skipping class today a good idea? Should I put my retirement funds in government bonds or in the stock market? After all, as George Bernard Shaw put it, "Economy is the art of making the most of life." Mick Jagger, who dropped out of the London School of Economics, complains that he "can't get no satisfaction." Maybe he should have studied more economics. The economic way of thinking will help you maximize your satisfaction.

Career Opportunities

All careers are not equal. While the wages in many occupations have not risen much lately, the wages of "symbolic analysts" who "solve, identify, and broker problems by manipulating symbols" are soaring.[1] These people "simplify reality into abstract images that can be rearranged, juggled, experimented with, communicated to other specialists, and then, eventually, transformed back into reality." Their wages have been rising as the globalization of the economy increases the demand for their insights and as technological developments (especially computers) have enhanced their productivity. Economists are the quintessential symbolic analysts as we manipulate ideas about abstractions such as supply and demand, cost and benefits, and equilibrium. You can think of your training in economics as an exercise regimen, a workout for your brain.

You will use many of the concepts you will learn in introductory economics during your career, but it is the practice in abstract thinking that will really pay off. In fact, most economics majors do not go on to become economists. They enter fields that use their analytical abilities, including business, management, insurance, finance, real estate, marketing, law, education, policy analysis, consulting, government, planning, and even medicine, journalism, and the arts.

A recent survey of 100 former economics majors at one university included all of these careers. If you want to verify that economics majors graduate to successful and rewarding careers, just ask your professors or watch what happens to economics majors from your school as they graduate.

Statistics from the 2006 Canadian census show that economics majors earn a healthy salary. Table 1 shows the average yearly earnings for selected occupations, with those occupations that generally require a reasonable understanding of economic highlighted in italics.

TABLE 1	AVERAGE YEARLY EARNINGS, 2005, BOTH SEXES, SELECTED OCCUPATIONS
Occupation	**Average Yearly Earnings**
Judges	$176,719
Senior managers, financial	*$175,497*
Senior managers	$139,443
Specialist physicians	$116,560
Dentists	$102,377
Managers in financial services	*$96,798*
*Lawyers and Quebec notaries**	*$89,606*
General practitioners	$84,783
Government managers in economic analysis	*$82,474*
Financial managers in administrative services	*$80,854*
*University professors**	*$70,146*
Economists and economic policy researchers and analysts	*$67,676*
Average income, all occupations	$38,226

* Clearly, not all professors or lawyers require an understanding of economics! The point is that becoming a professor or lawyer is a high-paying option for an economics major.

Source: *Statistics Canada,* "Wage and Salary Statistics (4) in Constant (2005) Dollars, Work Activity in the Reference Year (3), Highest Certificate, Diploma or Degree (5), Age Groups (5A), Occupation - National Occupational Classification for Statistics 2006 (720B) and Sex (3) for the Paid Workers 15 Years and Over With Wages and Salaries of Canada, Provinces, Territories, 2000 and 2005 - 20% Sample Data," accessed March 1, 2009 from http://www12.statcan.gc.ca/english/census06/data/topics/RetrieveProductTable.cfm?Temporal=2006&PID=96285&GID=614135&METH=1&APATH=3&PTYPE=88971%2C97154&THEME=75&AID=&FREE=0&FOCUS=&VID=0&GC=99&GK=NA&RL=0&TPL=RETR&SUB=0&d1=0&d2=0&d3=0&d4=0&d5=231

We can also see that economics degrees do well by examining data on entry-level wages (***Source:*** *Job Futures,* Services Canada, accessed March 1, 2009, at www.jobfutures.ca). The average salary two years after graduation for a B.A. in economics is $33,200, with 91 percent employed. Although this is lower than degrees in engineering ($42,100) or computing science, it is higher than the starting salary for a B.A. in humanities (English degrees earned $29,900, French degrees $26,500), or for a B.A. in the other social sciences (psychology degrees earned $31,300, sociology degrees $30,500), or for a B.Sc. in many of the sciences (physics degrees earned $30,700, biology degrees $29,800). In addition, employment rates for economics B.A.s were higher than average, and salaries grew over the first five years at a higher-than-average rate.

You might like to consider graduate school in economics—the entry-level wage for an M.A. in economics is roughly $49,700.

The Costs of Studying Economics

Since the "direct" costs of studying economics (tuition, books, supplies) aren't generally any higher or lower than the direct costs of other courses, indirect costs will be the most important of the costs to studying economics.

Forgone Knowledge

If you study economics, you can't study something else. This forgone knowledge could be very valuable.

Time and Energy

Economics is a fairly demanding major. Although economics courses do not generally take as much time as courses in English and history (in which you have to read a lot of long books) or anatomy and physiology (in which you have to spend hours in the lab and hours memorizing things), they do take a decent amount of time. In addition, some people find the material "tougher" than most subjects because memorizing is not the key. In economics (like physics), analyzing and solving are the keys.

Grades

As Table 2 shows, grades in introductory economics courses are generally lower than grades in some other majors, including other social sciences and the humanities. On the other hand, grades in economics are similar to grades in some sciences and math.

TABLE 2	AVERAGE GRADES AND GRADE DISTRIBUTION IN INTRODUCTORY COURSES AT SEVEN ONTARIO UNIVERSITIES		
Department	**Mean Grade***	**% (A + B)**	**% (D + F)**
Music	3.02	72.1	9.7
English	2.76	64.0	9.4
French	2.69	61.1	12.4
Philosophy	2.54	57.6	15.3
Biology	2.52	54.5	19.7
Sociology	2.51	52.8	14.2
Political Science	2.49	55.6	14.1
Psychology	2.40	48.4	20.6
Physics	2.38	46.1	28.4
Mathematics	2.19	44.4	33.9
Chemistry	2.18	42.9	30.9
Economics	2.18	41.6	30.7
*A = 4, B = 3, C = 2, D = 1, F = 0.			

Source: Paul Anglin and Ronald Meng, "Evidence on Grades and Grade Inflation at Ontario's Universities," *University of Windsor Working Paper,* November 1999. Used with permission.

Caveat Emptor (Buyer Beware): Interpreting Your Grades Is Not Straightforward

High grades provide direct satisfaction to most students, but they also act as a signal about the student's ability to learn the subject material. Unfortunately, because the grade distribution is not uniform across departments, you may be confused and misled by your grades. You may think that you are exceptionally good at a subject because of a high grade, when in fact nearly everyone gets a high grade in that subject. The important point here is that you should be informed about your own school's grade distribution. Just because you got a B in economics and an A in history does not necessarily mean that your comparative advantage is in learning history rather than economics. Everyone—or virtually everyone—may receive an A in history. Earning a B or a C in economics might mean that it is the best major for you, because high grades are much harder to earn in economics. It is fun to have a high GPA in college, but maximizing GPA should not be your goal. Maximizing your overall well-being is probably your goal, and this might be obtained by trading off a tenth or so of your GPA for a more rewarding major—perhaps economics.

Potential Side Effects from Studying Economics

Studying economics has some potential side effects. We're not sure whether they are costs or benefits and will let you decide.

Changing Ideas About What Is Fair

One study compared students at the beginning and end of the semester in an introductory economics course.[2] It found that by the end of the semester, significantly more of the students thought that the functioning of the market is "fair." This was especially true for female students. The results were consistent across a range of professors who fell across the ideological spectrum.

For example, the proportion of students who regarded it as unfair to increase the price of flowers on a holiday fell almost in half. The proportion that favoured government control over flower prices, rather than market determination, fell by over 60 percent. The study argues that these responses do not reflect changes in deep values, but instead represent the discovery of previous inconsistencies and their modification in the light of new information learned during the semester.

Changing Behaviour

Many people believe that the study of economics changes students' values and behaviour. Some think that it changes them for the worse. Others disagree. In particular, it is argued that economics students become more self-interested and less likely to cooperate, perhaps because they spend so much time studying economic models, which often assume that people are self-interested. For example, one study reports experimental evidence that economics students are more likely than nonmajors to behave self-interestedly in prisoners' dilemma games and ultimatum bargaining games.[3]

This need not mean that studying economics will change you, however. Another study compares beginning freshmen and senior economics students and concludes that economics students "are already different when they begin their study of economics."[4] In other words, students signing up for economics courses are already different; studying economics doesn't change them. However, there are reasons to question both of these conclusions, because it is not clear whether these laboratory experiments using economic games reflect reality. One experiment asked students whether they would return money that had been lost. It found that economics students were more likely than others to say that they would keep the cash.

However, what people say and what they do are sometimes at odds. In a follow-up experiment, this theory was tested by dropping stamped, addressed envelopes containing $10 in cash in different campus classrooms. To return the cash, the students had only to seal the envelopes and mail them. The results were that 56 percent of the envelopes dropped in economics classes were returned, while only 31 percent of the envelopes dropped in history, psychology, and business classes were sent in.[5] Perhaps economics students are less selfish than others!

Obviously, no firm conclusions have been reached about whether or how studying economics changes students' behaviour.

Cost Versus Benefits

Suppose that you've weighed the costs and benefits of studying economics and you've decided that the benefits are greater than or equal to the costs. Obviously, then, you should continue to take economics courses. If you can't decide whether the benefits outweigh the costs, then you should probably collect more information—especially if it is good but inexpensive. In either case, read the rest of this section.

The Economics Major

The study of economics is like a tree. The introductory microeconomics and macroeconomics courses you begin with are the tree's roots. Most colleges and universities require that you master this material before you go on to any other courses. The way of thinking, the language, and the tools that you acquire in the introductory course are usually reinforced in intermediate microeconomics and macroeconomics courses before they are applied in more specialized courses that you take. The intermediate courses are the tree's trunk. Among the specialized courses that make up the branches of economics are econometrics (statistical economics), financial economics, labour economics, resource economics, international trade, industrial organization, public finance, public choice, economic history, the history of economic thought, mathematical economics, current economic issues, and urban economics. The branches of the tree vary from department to department, but these are common. It will pay to check your school calendar and discuss these courses with professors and other students.

Graduate School in Economics

Preparing for Graduate School in Economics

You can prepare for graduate school in economics by taking several math classes. This would probably include one year of calculus plus a couple of courses in probability and statistics and linear/matrix algebra. Ask your advisor about the particular courses to take at your university. In addition, the mathematical economics and econometrics courses in the economics department are essential. (*Hint:* Even if you aren't going to graduate school, these mathematical courses can be valuable to you, just as more economics courses can be valuable for nonmajors.)

If your school offers graduate level economics courses, you might want to sit in on a few to get accustomed to the flavour of graduate school.

Most graduate programs require strong grades in economics, a good score on the Graduate Record Examination (GRE) for U.S. schools, and solid letters of recommendations. It is a good idea to get to know a few professors very well and to go above and beyond what is expected so that they can write glowing letters about you.

Financing Graduate School

Unlike some other graduate and professional degree programs, you probably won't need to pile up a massive amount of debt while pursuing an M.A. or Ph.D. in economics. Most graduate programs hire their economics graduate students as teaching or research assistants. Teaching assistants begin by grading papers and running review sessions and can advance to teaching classes on their own. Research assistants generally do data collection, statistical work, and library research for professors and often jointly write papers with them. Most assistantships will pay for tuition and provide you with enough money to live on.

Where Should You Apply?

The best graduate school for you depends on a lot of things, especially your ability level, geographical location, areas of research interests, and, of course, financing. You should talk with your professors about ability level and areas of research. In addition, for U.S. schools there are informative articles that give overall departmental rankings and rankings by subfield. See especially John Tschirhart, "Ranking Economics Department in Areas of Expertise," *Journal of Economic Education*, Spring 1989, and Richard Dusansky and Clayton J. Vernon, "Rankings of U.S. Economics Departments," *Journal of Economic Perspectives*, vol. 12, no. 1 (Winter 1998), pp. 157–70.

What You Will Do in Graduate School

Most students who go on to graduate school do only an M.A. These degrees typically take one year for the non-thesis route and about two years for the thesis route. Course work will include 2–4 courses in economic theory, plus 4–6 courses in specific subfields.

Most Ph.D. programs in economics begin with a year of theory courses in macroeconomics and microeconomics. After a year you will probably take a series of tests to show that you have mastered this core theory. If you pass these tests, in the second and third year of courses you will take more specialized subjects and perhaps take lengthy examinations in a couple of subfields. After this you will be required to write a dissertation—original research that will contribute new knowledge to one of the fields of economics. These stages are intertwined with work as a teaching and/or research assistant, and the dissertation stage can be quite drawn out. In the social sciences the median time it takes for a student to complete the Ph.D. degree is about 7.5 years.[6] Be aware that a high percentage (roughly 50 percent) of students do not complete their doctoral degree.

What Is Graduate School Like?

Graduate school in economics comes as a surprise to many students. The material and approach are distinctly different from what you will learn as an undergraduate. The textbooks and journal articles you will read in graduate school are often very theoretical and abstract. A good source of information is sitting in on courses or reading the reflections of recent students. See especially *The Making of an Economist* by Arjo Klamer and David Colander (Boulder, CO: Westview Press, 1990).

The Committee on Graduate Education in Economics (COGEE) undertook an important review of graduate education in economics and reported its findings in the September 1991 issue of the *Journal of Economic Literature*. COGEE asked faculty members, graduate students, and recent Ph.D.s to rank the most important skills needed to be successful in the study of graduate economics. At the top of the list were analytical skills and mathematics, followed by critical judgment, the ability to apply theory, and computational skills. At the bottom of the list were creativity and the ability to communicate. If you are interested in economic issues but do not have the characteristics required by graduate economics departments, there are other economics-related fields to consider, such as graduate school in public policy. Many economics majors go to business schools to obtain an MBA and are often better prepared than students who have undergraduate degrees in business.

Economics Reading

If you decide to make studying economics part of your future, or if you're hungry for more economics, you should immediately begin reading the economic news and books by economists. Life is short. Why waste it watching TV?

The easiest way to get your daily recommended dose of economics is to keep up with current economic events. Here are a few sources to pick up at the newsstand, bookstore, or library over your summer or winter break.

The Globe and Mail *or* The National Post

Many undergraduates subscribe to *The Globe and Mail* or *The National Post* at low student rates. Join them! Not only are these well-written business newspapers, but they also have articles on domestic and international news, politics, the arts, travel, and sports, as well as lively editorial pages. Reading one of these papers is one of the best ways to tie the economics you are studying to the real world and to prepare for your career.

Magazines and Journals

The Economist, a weekly magazine published in England, is available at a student discount rate. Pick up a copy at your school library and you will be hooked by its informative, sharp writing. *Business Week* is also well worth the read.

Also recommended are *Challenge* magazine and *The Public Interest*, two quarterlies that discuss economic policy, as well as *Policy Options*, a bimonthly publication of the Institute for Research on Public Policy. Finally, there is the *Journal of Economic Perspectives*, which is published by the American Economic Association and written to be accessible to undergraduate economics students.

Books by Economists

Below is a list of suggested readings, compiled from asking other professors, and from our own readings.

Steven Levitt and Stephen Dubner, *Freakonomics: A Rogue Economist Explores the Hidden Side of Everything*.

Milton Friedman, *Capitalism and Freedom*.

Robert Heilbroner, *The Worldly Philosophers: The Lives, Times, and Ideas of the Great Economic Thinkers*.

Steve Landsburg, *The Armchair Economist: Economics and Everyday Life*.

Jared Diamond, *Guns, Germs, and Steel: The Fates of Human Societies*.

Diane Coyle, *Sex, Drugs and Economics: An Unconventional Introduction to Economics*.

Patrick Luciani, *Economics Myths: Making Sense of Canadian Policy Issues*.

Hernando deSoto, *The Mystery of Capital: Why Capitalism Triumphed in the West and Failed Everywhere Else*.

David Friedman, *Hidden Order: The Economics of Everyday Life*.

Adam Smith's *The Wealth of Nations* is a must-read for every student of economics. It was written in 1776, yet it is the most influential work of economics ever and its insights are still valuable.

Endnotes

1. This term is used by Robert Reich in *The Work of Nations*. The quote is from p. 178.

2. Robert Whaples, "Changes in Attitudes About the Fairness of Free Markets Among College Economics Students," *Journal of Economic Education*, vol. 26, no. 4 (Fall 1995).

3. Robert H. Frank, Thomas Gilovich, and Dennis T. Regan, "Does Studying Economics Inhibit Cooperation?" *Journal of Economic Perspectives*, vol. 7, no. 2 (Spring 1993), pp. 159–171.

4. John R. Carter and Michael D. Irons, "Are Economists Different, and If So, Why?" *Journal of Economic Perspectives*, vol. 5, no. 2 (Spring 1991), pp. 171–177.

5. "Economics Students Aren't Selfish, They're Just Not Entirely Honest," *Wall Street Journal*, January 18, 1995, B1.

6. See Ronald Ehrenberg, "The Flow of New Doctorates," *Journal of Economic Literature*, vol. 30, June 1992, pp. 830–875. If breaks in school attendance are included, this climbs to 10.5 years. Of course, some students attend only part time, and most have some kind of employment while completing their degrees.

Chapter 1
What Is Economics?

Definition of Economics

All economic questions arise from **scarcity**.

♦ Because wants exceed the resources available to satisfy them, we cannot have everything we want and must make choices.

• Choices depend on **incentives**—rewards that encourage actions and penalties that discourage action.

♦ **Economics** is the social science that studies the choices people make to cope with scarcity.

• **Microeconomics** studies choices of individuals and businesses.

• **Macroeconomics** studies national and global economies.

Two Big Economic Questions

Two questions summarize the scope of economics:

♦ How do choices determine *what*, *how*, and *for whom* **goods and services** are produced, and in what quantities?

♦ How can choices made in the pursuit of self-interest also promote the social interest?

The **factors of production** used to produce goods and services are

♦ **land** (shorthand for all natural resources), which earns **rent**.

♦ **labour** (includes **human capital**—knowledge and skills from education, training, experience), which earns **wages**.

♦ **capital** (machinery), which earns **interest**.

♦ **entrepreneurship**, which earns **profit**.

Choices made in **self-interest** are best for the person making them. Choices that are in the **social interest** are best for society as a whole.

♦ Markets often provide incentives so that the pursuit of our self-interest also promotes the social interest; but self-interest and social interest sometimes conflict.

♦ Economic principles allow us to understand when self-interest promotes the social interest, when they conflict, and policies to reduce those conflicts.

The Economic Way of Thinking

A choice is a **tradeoff**—we give up one thing to get something else—and the **opportunity cost** of any action is the highest-valued alternative forgone. Opportunity cost is the single most important concept for making choices.

Economic tradeoffs:

♦ "guns" versus "butter" tradeoffs (between any pair of goods).

♦ "what," "how," and "for whom" tradeoffs.

♦ the **big tradeoff**—between equality and efficiency. Government redistribution using taxes and transfers weaken incentives, so a more equally shared pie results in a smaller pie.

We make choices in small steps, or at the **margin**, and choices are influenced by incentives.

♦ Economic choices are made by comparing the *additional* benefit—**marginal benefit**—and *additional* cost—**marginal cost**—of a small increase in an activity. If marginal benefit exceeds marginal cost, we choose to increase the activity.

♦ By choosing only activities that bring greater benefits than costs, we use our scarce resources in the way that makes us as well off as possible.

♦ Given a change in incentives—rewards and penalties for particular actions—we can predict how choices will change by looking for changes in marginal benefit and marginal cost.

Economists assume that it is human nature for all people—consumers, producers, politicians, public servants—to pursue their self-interest. Incentives are key for reconciling self-interest and the social interest. Economists identify incentive systems and institutions (like a legal system protecting personal security and private property) that result in self-interested choices leading to the social interest.

Economics as Social Science and Policy Tool

Economics, as a social science, distinguishes between

- *positive* statements—statements about what *is*, that can be tested by checking them against the facts.

- *normative* statements—statements about what *ought* to be, that depend on values and cannot be tested.

Economics attempts to understand the economic world and is concerned with positive statements. Economists try to discover positive statements that are consistent with observed facts by

- unscrambling cause and effect.

- creating **economic models**—simplified description of the economic world including only features needed for purpose of explanation.

- testing economic models, comparing predictions with the facts, using

  - natural experiments—where one factor is different in real world; other things are equal.

  - statistical investigations—correlations between variables.

  - economic experiments—putting people in decision-making situations and changing one variable to see response.

Economics is a useful toolkit for making decisions about

- personal economic policy

- business economic policy

- government economic policy

For any *normative* policy objective, economics provides a method of evaluating alternative solutions—evaluate marginal benefits and marginal costs to find solution with greatest gain.

HELPFUL HINTS

1 The definition of economics (explaining the choices we make using limited resources to try to satisfy unlimited wants) leads us directly to two important economic concepts—choice and opportunity cost. If wants exceed resources, we cannot have everything we want and therefore must make *choices* among alternatives. In making a choice, we forgo other alternatives, and the *opportunity cost* of any choice is the highest-valued alternative forgone.

2 Marginal analysis is a fundamental tool economists use to predict people's choices. The key to understanding marginal analysis is to focus on *additional*, rather than total, benefits and costs. For example, to predict whether or not Taejong will eat a fourth Big Mac, the economist compares Taejong's *additional* benefit or satisfaction from the fourth Big Mac with its *additional* cost. The total benefits and costs of all four Big Macs are not relevant. Only if the marginal benefit exceeds the marginal cost will Taejong eat a fourth Big Mac.

3 In attempting to understand how and why something works (e.g., an airplane, a falling object, an economy), we can try to use description or theory. A description is a list of facts about something. But it does not tell us which facts are essential for understanding how an airplane works (the shape of the wings) and which facts are less important (the colour of the paint).

   Scientists use theory to abstract from the complex descriptive facts of the real world and focus only on those elements essential for understanding. Those essential elements are fashioned into models—highly simplified representations of the real world.

   In physics and some other natural sciences, if we want to understand the essential force (gravity) that causes objects to fall, we use theory to construct a simple model, and then test it by performing a controlled experiment. We create a vacuum to eliminate less important forces like air resistance.

   Economic models are also attempts to focus on the essential forces (competition, self-interest) operating in the economy, while abstracting from less important forces (whims, advertising, altruism). Unlike physicists, economists cannot easily perform controlled experiments to test their models. As a result, it is difficult to conclusively prove or disprove a theory and its models. Economists rely on naturally occurring experiments, statistical investigations of correlations between variables, and artificial laboratory economic experiments about choices.

4   Models are like maps, which are useful precisely because they abstract from real-world detail. A map that reproduced all of the details of the real world (street lamps, fireplugs, electric wires) would be useless. A useful map offers a simplified view, which is carefully selected according to the purpose of the map. Remember that economic models are not claims that the real world is as simple as the model. Models claim to capture the simplified effect of some real force operating in the economy. Before drawing conclusions about the real economy from a model, we must be careful to consider whether, when we reinsert all of the real-world complexities the model abstracted from, the conclusions will be the same as in the model.

5   The most important purpose of studying economics is not to learn what to think about economics but rather *how* to think about economics. The "what"—the facts and descriptions of the economy—can always be found in books. The value of an economics education is the ability to think critically about economic problems and *to understand how* an economy works. This understanding of the essential forces governing how an economy works comes through the mastery of economic theory and model-building.

S E L F - T E S T

True/False and Explain

Definition of Economics

1   Economics explains how we use unlimited resources to satisfy limited wants.

2   Economics studies the choices people make to cope with scarcity and the institutions that influence and reconcile choices.

Two Big Economic Questions

3   In economics, the definition of "land" includes nonrenewable resources but excludes renewable resources.

4   In economics, the definition of "capital" includes financial assets like stocks and bonds.

5   Entrepreneurs bear the risks arising from the business decisions they make.

6   "How do choices determine *what*, *how*, and *for whom* goods and services are produced?" is one of the big economic questions.

7   "When do choices made in the pursuit of the social interest also promote self-interest?" is one of the big economic questions.

8   Choices made in the pursuit of self-interest always promote the social interest.

The Economic Way of Thinking

9   When the opportunity cost of an activity increases, the incentive to choose that activity increases.

10   Tradeoffs and opportunity costs are the key concepts for understanding the economic way of thinking.

11   Economists assume that it is human nature for all people to act selfishly.

Economics as Social Science and Policy Tool

12 A positive statement is about what is, while a normative statement is about what will be.

13 Economists test positive statements about how the world works to weed out those that are wrong.

14 The main economics policy tool is to compare total costs and total benefits to find the solution with the greatest gain.

15 Economics is a useful policy tool for governments and businesses, but not for individuals.

Multiple-Choice

Definition of Economics

1 The fact that human wants cannot be fully satisfied with available resources is called the problem of
  a opportunity cost.
  b scarcity.
  c normative economics.
  d what to produce.
  e who will consume.

2 The problem of scarcity exists
  a only in economies with government.
  b only in economies without government.
  c in all economies.
  d only when people have not optimized.
  e now, but will be eliminated with economic growth.

3 Scarcity differs from poverty because
  a resources exceed wants for the rich.
  b wants exceed resources even for the rich.
  c the rich do not have to make choices.
  d the poor do not have any choices.
  e the poor do not have any wants.

4 The branch of economics that studies the choices of individual households and firms is called
  a macroeconomics.
  b microeconomics.
  c positive economics.
  d normative economics.
  e home economics.

5 Microeconomics studies all of the following *except* the
  a decisions of individual firms.
  b effects of government safety regulations on the price of cars.
  c global economy as a whole.
  d prices of individual goods and services.
  e effects of taxes on the price of beer.

Two Big Economic Questions

6 The two big economic questions
  a arise from scarcity.
  b summarize the scope of economics.
  c describe choices we make.
  d examine incentives that influence choices.
  e are all of the above.

7 The first big economic question about goods and services includes all of the following *except*
  a *what* to produce.
  b *why* produce.
  c *how* to produce.
  d *what* quantities to produce.
  e *who* gets what is produced.

8 The trends over the past 60 years in what we produce show that _____ has expanded and _____ has shrunk.
  a manufacturing; services
  b manufacturing; agriculture
  c agriculture; services
  d agriculture; manufacturing
  e services; agriculture

9 All of the following are resources *except*
  a natural resources.
  b tools.
  c entrepreneurship.
  d government.
  e land.

10 The knowledge and skill obtained from education and training is
  a labour.
  b human capital.
  c physical capital.
  d entrepreneurship.
  e technological know-how.

11 Which statement about incomes earned by factors of production is *false*?
- **a** Land earns rent.
- **b** Natural resources earn rent.
- **c** Labour earns wages.
- **d** Capital earns profit.
- **e** Entrepreneurship earns profit.

12 When boats fish in international waters, that is certainly a(n)
- **a** self-interested choice.
- **b** altruistic choice.
- **c** globalization choice.
- **d** factor of production choice.
- **e** choice in the social interest.

The Economic Way of Thinking

13 When the government chooses to use resources to build a dam, those resources are no longer available to build a highway. This illustrates the concept of
- **a** a market.
- **b** macroeconomics.
- **c** opportunity cost.
- **d** a "how" tradeoff.
- **e** the big tradeoff.

14 The big tradeoff is between
- **a** taxes and transfers.
- **b** equality and efficiency.
- **c** current consumption and a higher future standard of living.
- **d** guns and butter.
- **e** personal security and private property.

15 Renata has the chance to either attend an economics lecture or play tennis. If she chooses to attend the lecture, the value of playing tennis is
- **a** greater than the value of the lecture.
- **b** not comparable to the value of the lecture.
- **c** equal to the value of the lecture.
- **d** the opportunity cost of attending the lecture.
- **e** zero.

16 Which of the following sayings best describes opportunity cost?
- **a** "Make hay while the sun shines."
- **b** "Money is the root of all evil."
- **c** "Boldly go where no one has gone before."
- **d** "There's no such thing as a free lunch."
- **e** "Baseball has been very good to me."

17 Marginal benefit is the
- **a** total benefit of an activity.
- **b** additional benefit of a decrease in an activity.
- **c** additional benefit of an increase in an activity.
- **d** opportunity cost of a decrease in an activity.
- **e** opportunity cost of an increase in an activity.

18 Monika will choose to eat a seventh pizza slice if
- **a** the marginal benefit of the seventh slice is greater than its marginal cost.
- **b** the marginal benefit of the seventh slice is less than its marginal cost
- **c** the total benefit of all seven slices is greater than their total cost.
- **d** the total benefit of all seven slices is less than their total cost.
- **e** she is training to be a Sumo wrestler.

19 Economists assume that
- **a** self-interested actions are all selfish actions.
- **b** consumers and producers pursue their self-interest while politicians and public servants pursue the social interest.
- **c** incentives are key in reconciling self-interest and the social interest.
- **d** all people pursue the social interest.
- **e** human nature changes as incentives change.

Economics as Social Science and Policy Tool

20 A positive statement is
- **a** about what ought to be.
- **b** about what is.
- **c** always true.
- **d** capable of evaluation as true or false by observation and measurement.
- **e** **b** and **d**.

21 Which of the following is a positive statement?
- **a** Low rents will restrict the supply of housing.
- **b** High interest rates are bad for the economy.
- **c** Housing costs too much.
- **d** Owners of apartment buildings ought to be free to charge whatever rent they want.
- **e** Government should control the rents that apartment owners charge.

22 A normative statement is a statement regarding
- **a** what is usually the case.
- **b** the assumptions of an economic model.
- **c** what ought to be.
- **d** the predictions of an economic model.
- **e** what is.

23 Which of the following statements is/are normative?
a Scientists should not make normative statements.
b Warts are caused by handling toads.
c As compact disc prices fall, people will buy more of them.
d If income increases, sales of luxury goods will fall.
e None of the above.

24 Which of the following statements is *false*? An economic model
a is tested by comparing predictions with the facts.
b is difficult to test because of the simultaneous operation of many factors.
c tests only positive economic statements.
d can be tested using natural and economic experiments
e includes all aspects of the economic world.

25 The common element to making personal, business and government policy decisions is to evaluate
a total benefits and total costs to find greatest gain.
b marginal benefits and marginal costs to find greatest gain.
c marginal benefits and marginal costs to find highest marginal benefit.
d marginal benefit and marginal cost to find lowest marginal costs.
e average benefit and average costs to find greatest gain.

Short Answer Problems

1 What is meant by scarcity, and why does the existence of scarcity mean that we must make choices?

2 "If all people would only economize, the problem of scarcity would be solved." Agree or disagree, and explain why.

3 Ashley, Doug, and Mei-Lin are planning to travel from Halifax to Sydney. The trip takes one hour by airplane and five hours by train. The air fare is $100 and train fare is $60. They all have to take time off from work while travelling. Ashley earns $5 per hour in her job, Doug $10 per hour, and Mei-Lin $12 per hour.

Calculate the opportunity cost of air and train travel for each person. Assuming they are all economizers, how should each of them travel to Sydney?

4 Suppose the government builds and staffs a hospital in order to provide "free" medical care.
a What is the opportunity cost of the free medical care?
b Is it free from the perspective of society as a whole?

5 Branko loves riding the bumper cars at the amusement park, but he loves the experience a little less with each successive ride. In estimating the benefit he receives from the rides, Branko would be willing to pay $10 for his first ride, $7 for his second ride, and $4 for his third ride. Rides actually cost $5 apiece for as many rides as Branko wants to take. This information is summarized in Table 1.1.

TABLE **1.1**

Ride	1st	2nd	3rd
Marginal benefit	10	7	4
Marginal cost	5	5	5

a If Branko chooses by comparing total benefit and total cost, how many rides will he take?
b If Branko chooses by comparing marginal benefit and marginal cost, how many rides will he take?
c Is Branko better off by choosing according to total or marginal benefit and cost? Explain why.

6 Assume Branko's benefits are the same as in Short Answer Problem 5. Starting fresh, if the price of a bumper car ride rises to $8, how many rides will Branko now take? Explain why.

7 Indicate whether each of the following statements is positive or normative. If it is normative (positive), rewrite it so that it becomes positive (normative).
a The government ought to reduce the size of the deficit in order to lower interest rates.
b Government imposition of a tax on tobacco products will reduce their consumption.

8 Perhaps the biggest economic questions is how can we organize our lives so that when each of us makes choices in our self-interest, these choices also promote the social interest. When Nike builds a factory in Malaysia and pays workers far less than North American wages, it is acting in its own corporate self-interest. What questions do you need to ask to decide if this is also in the social interest?

9 Suppose we examine a model of plant growth that predicts that, given the amount of water and sunlight, the application of fertilizer stimulates plant growth.

   a How might you test the model?

   b How is the test different from what an economist could do to test an economic model?

🕮 **10** Suppose your friend, who is a history major, claims that economic models are useless because they are so unrealistic. He claims that since the models leave out so many descriptive details about the real world, they can't possibly be useful for understanding how the economy works. How would you defend your decision to study economics?

ANSWERS

True/False and Explain

1 **F** Limited resources and unlimited wants. (2)

2 **T** This is the full definition of economics—the institutional aspect is often omitted for brevity. (2)

3 **F** "Land" includes all natural resources, whether nonrenewable (oil) or renewable (forests). (3)

4 **F** "Capital" only consists of physical equipment like tools and buildings used in production. (4)

5 **T** Entrepreneurs earn profits in return for bearing the risks of organizing labour, land, and capital. (4)

6 **T** See text discussion. (3–4)

7 **F** When do choices made in the pursuit of self-interest also promote the social interest? (5)

8 **F** Markets often provide incentives so that pursuit of self-interest also promotes social interest, but self-interest and social interest sometimes conflict. (5–7).

9 **F** Incentive decreases because activity is now more expensive. (9)

10 **T** Scarcity requires choice, choice involves tradeoffs, and tradeoffs involve opportunity cost. (8–10)

11 **F** Economists assume people act in their self-interest, but self-interested actions are not necessarily selfish actions, if what makes you happy is to help others. (10)

12 **F** Normative statements are about what *ought* to be. (11)

13 **T** Test *positive* statements. (11)

14 **F** Compare *marginal* benefits and *marginal* costs. (12)

15 **F** Useful for personal, business, government policy. (12)

Multiple-Choice

1 **b** Definition. (2)

2 **c** With infinite wants and finite resources, scarcity will never be eliminated. (2)

3 **b** Poverty is a low level of resources. But wants exceed resources for everyone, necessitating choice. (2)

4 **b** Definition. (2)

5 **c** Macroeconomic topic. (2)

6 **e** Economics explains choices created by scarcity and incentives that help reconcile self-interest and social interest. (3–7)

7 **b** *Why* is not part of first big question. (3–4)

8 **e** Services have expanded; agriculture and manufacturing have shrunk. See Text Figure 1.1. (3)

9 **d** Government is a social institution. (3–4)

10 **b** Definition. (3)

11 **d** Capital earns interest. (4)

🕮 **12** **a** Certainly in fishing company's self-interest; not altruistic or in social interest depending on benefits and costs. (5–7)

13 **c** Highway is forgone alternative. (8–10)

14 **b** Greater equality (using taxes and transfers) reduces efficiency by weakening incentives. **c**, **d**, are other tradeoffs, **e** nonsense. (8–10)

15 **d** Choosing lecture means its value > tennis. Tennis = (highest-valued) forgone alternative to lecture. (8–10)

16 **d** Every choice involves a cost. (9)

17 **c** Definition; **e** is marginal cost, **b** and **d** are nonsense. (10)

18 **a** Choices are made at the margin, when marginal benefit exceeds marginal cost. (10)

19 **c** Assume human nature given and all people pursue self-interest. When self-interested choices not in social interest, there are wrong incentives. (10)

20 **e** Definition. (11)

21 **a** While **a** may be evaluated as true or false, other statements are matters of opinion. (11)

22 **c** Key word for normative statements is *ought*. (11)

23 **a** Key word is *should*. Even statement **b** is positive. (11)

24 **e** Includes only relevant aspects and ignores others. (11)

25 **b** See text discussion. (12)

Short Answer Problems

1 Scarcity is the universal condition that human wants always exceed the resources available to satisfy them. The fact that goods and services are scarce means that individuals cannot have all of everything they want. It is therefore necessary to choose among alternatives.

2 Disagree. If everyone economized, then we would be making the best possible use of our resources and would be achieving the greatest benefits or satisfaction possible, given the limited quantity of resources. But this does not mean that we would be satisfying all of our limitless needs. The problem of scarcity can never be "solved" as long as people have infinite needs and finite resources for satisfying those needs.

3 The main point is that the total opportunity cost of travel includes the best alternative value of travel time as well as the train or air fare. The total costs of train and air travel for Ashley, Doug, and Mei-Lin are calculated in Table 1.2.

TABLE 1.2

Traveller		Train	Plane
Ashley			
(a)	Fare	$ 60	$100
(b)	Opportunity cost of travel time at $5/hr	$ 25	$ 5
	Total cost	**$ 85**	**$105**
Doug			
(a)	Fare	$ 60	$100
(b)	Opportunity cost of travel time at $10/hr	$ 50	$ 10
	Total cost	**$110**	**$110**
Mei-Lin			
(a)	Fare	$ 60	$100
(b)	Opportunity cost of travel time at $12/hr	$ 60	$ 12
	Total cost	**$120**	**$112**

On the basis of the cost calculation in Table 1.2, Ashley should take the train, Mei-Lin should take the plane, and Doug could take either.

4 **a** Even though medical care may be offered without charge ("free"), there are still opportunity costs. The opportunity cost of providing such health care is the highest-valued alternative use of the resources used in the construction of the hospital, and the highest-valued alternative use of the resources (including human resources) used in the operation of the hospital.

   b These resources are no longer available for other activities and therefore represent a cost to society.

5 a If Branko rides as long as total benefit is greater than total cost, he will take 3 rides.

Total benefit (cost) can be calculated by adding up the marginal benefit (cost) of all rides taken. Before taking any rides, his total benefit is zero and his total cost is zero. The first ride's marginal benefit is $10, which when added to 0 yields a total benefit of $10. The first ride's marginal cost is $5, which when added to zero yields a total cost of $5. Total cost is greater than total benefit, so Branko takes the first ride. For the first and second rides together, total benefit is $17, which is greater than total cost of $10. For all 3 rides together, total benefit is $21, which is greater than total cost of $15.

b If Branko compares the marginal benefit of each ride with its marginal cost, he will only take 2 rides. He will take the first ride because its marginal benefit ($10) is greater than its marginal cost ($5). After the first ride, he will still choose to take the second ride because its marginal benefit ($7) is greater than its marginal cost ($5). But he will quit after the second ride. The third ride would add a benefit of $4, but it costs $5, so Branko would be worse off by taking the third ride.

c The marginal rule for choosing will make Branko better off. It would be a mistake to pay $5 for the third ride when it is only worth $4 to Branko. He would be better off taking that final $5 and spending it on something (the roller coaster?) that gives him a benefit worth at least $5.

You will learn much more about applying marginal analysis to choices like Branko's in Chapters 2 and 5.

6 If the price of a bumper car rises to $8, Branko now takes only 1 ride. He will take the first ride because its marginal benefit ($10) is greater than its marginal cost ($8). After the first ride, he will quit. The marginal benefit of the second ride ($7) is now less than its marginal cost ($8).

7 a The given statement is normative. The following is positive: If the government reduces the size of the deficit, interest rates will fall.

b The given statement is positive. The following is normative: The government ought to impose a tax on tobacco products.

8 Questions must identify benefits and costs that need to be compared. Some of the many possible questions are: Even though the Malaysian workers earn less than North Americans, are they better off or worse off with these jobs? As consumers in North America, are we better off or worse off with shoes being produced more cheaply in Malaysia? Are workers in North America better off or worse off with the Malaysian Nike plant? How do we define the social interest when people from many countries are involved?

You don't yet have enough information to answer these questions, but economics provides a way of thinking about them that makes it easier to come to a well-reasoned conclusion.

9 a The prediction of the model can be tested by conducting the following controlled experiment and carefully observing the outcome. Select a number of plots of ground of the same size that have similar characteristics and are subject to the same amount of water and sunlight. Plant equal quantities of seeds in all the plots. In some of the plots apply no fertilizer and in some of the plots apply (perhaps varying amounts of) fertilizer. When the plants have grown, measure the growth of the plants and compare the growth of the fertilized plots and the unfertilized plots. If plant growth is greater in fertilized plots, we provisionally accept the model and the theory on which it is based. If plant growth is not greater in fertilized plots, we discard the theory (model), or modify its assumptions. Perhaps the effective use of fertilizer requires more water.

Then construct a new model that predicts that, given more water (and the same amount of sunlight), fertilized plants will grow larger than equivalently watered unfertilized plants. Test that model and continue modifying assumptions until predictions are consistent with the facts.

b Economists cannot easily perform such controlled experiments and instead must change one assumption at a time in alternative models and compare the results. Then differences in outcomes can only be tested against variations in data that occur naturally in the economy, using statistical investigations. This is a more difficult and less precise model-building and testing procedure than exists for the controlled fertilizer experiment.

For some limited choices, economists also perform laboratory-like experiments, changing one factor at a time, just as in the plant experiment.

10 A brief answer to your friend's challenge appears in Helpful Hint **3**. Models are like maps, which are useful precisely because they abstract from real-world detail. A useful map offers a simplified view, which is carefully selected according to the purpose of the map. No mapmaker would claim that the world is as simple as her map, and economists do not claim that the real economy is as simple as their models. What economists claim is that their models isolate the simplified effect of some real forces (like optimizing behaviour) operating in the economy, and yield predictions that can be tested against real-world data.

Another way to answer your friend would be to challenge him to identify what a more realistic model or theory would look like. You would do well to quote Milton Friedman (a Nobel Prize winner in economics) on this topic: "A theory or its 'assumptions' cannot possibly be thoroughly 'realistic' in the immediate descriptive sense.... A completely 'realistic' theory of the wheat market would have to include not only the conditions directly underlying the supply and demand for wheat but also the kind of coins or credit instruments used to make exchanges; the personal characteristics of wheat-traders such as the color of each trader's hair and eyes, ... the number of members of his family, their characteristics,... the kind of soil on which the wheat was grown,... the weather prevailing during the growing season;... and so on indefinitely. Any attempt to move very far in achieving this kind of 'realism' is certain to render a theory utterly useless." From Milton Friedman, "The Methodology of Positive Economics," in *Essays in Positive Economics* (Chicago: University of Chicago Press, 1953), p. 32.

Chapter 1
Appendix: Graphs in Economics

Graphing Data

Graphs represent quantity as a distance. On a two-dimensional graph,

♦ horizontal line is *x-axis*.

♦ vertical line is *y-axis*.

♦ intersection (0) is the *origin*.

Main types of economic graphs:

♦ **Time-series graph**—shows relationship between time (measured on *x*-axis) and other variable(s) (measured on *y*-axis). Reveals variable's level, direction of change, speed of change, and **trend** (general tendency to rise or fall).

♦ **Cross-section graph**—shows level of a variable across different groups at a point in time.

♦ **Scatter diagram**—shows relationship between two variables, one measured on *x*-axis, the other measured on *y*-axis. Correlation between variables does not necessarily imply causation.

Misleading graphs often break the axes or stretch/compress measurement scales to exaggerate or understate variation. Always look closely at the values and labels on axes before interpreting a graph.

Graphs Used in Economic Models

Graphs showing relationships between variables fall into four categories:

♦ **Positive (direct) relationship**—variables move together in same direction: upward-sloping.

♦ **Negative (inverse) relationship**—variables move in opposite directions: downward-sloping.

♦ Relationships with a maximum/minimum:

• Relationship slopes upward, reaches a maximum (zero slope), and then slopes downward.

• Relationship slopes downward, reaches a minimum (zero slope), and then slopes upward.

♦ Unrelated (independent) variables—one variable changes while the other remains constant; graph is vertical or horizontal straight line.

The Slope of a Relationship

Slope of a relationship is change in value of variable on *y*-axis divided by change in value of variable on *x*-axis.

♦ Δ means "change in."

♦ Formula for slope is $\Delta y/\Delta x$ = rise/run.

♦ Straight line (**linear relationship**) has constant slope.

• A positive, upward-sloping relationship has a positive slope.

• A negative, downward-sloping relationship has a negative slope.

♦ Curved line has varying slope, which can be calculated

• *at a point*—by drawing straight line tangent to the curve at that point and calculating slope of the line.

• *across an arc*—by drawing straight line across two points on the curve and calculating slope of the line.

Graphing Relationships Among More Than Two Variables

Relationships among more than two variables can be graphed by holding constant the values of all variables except two. This is done by making a ***ceteris paribus*** assumption—"other things remain the same."

HELPFUL HINTS

1 Throughout the text, relationships among economic variables will almost invariably be represented and analyzed graphically. An early, complete understanding of graphs will greatly facilitate your mastery of the economic analysis of later chapters. Avoid the common mistake of assuming that a superficial understanding of graphs will be sufficient.

2 If you have limited experience with graphical analysis, this appendix is crucial to your ability to understand later economic analysis. You will likely find significant rewards in occasionally returning to this appendix for review. If you are experienced in constructing and using graphs, this appendix may be "old hat." Even so, you should skim it and work through the Self-Test in this *Study Guide*.

3 Slope is a *linear* concept since it is a property of a straight line. For this reason, the slope is constant along a straight line but is different at different points on a curved (nonlinear) line. For the slope of a curved line, we actually calculate the slope of a straight line. The text presents two alternatives for calculating the slope of a curved line: (1) slope at a point and (2) slope across an arc. The first of these calculates the slope of the *straight line* that just touches (is tangent to) the curve at a point. The second calculates the slope of the *straight line* formed by the arc between two points on the curved line.

4 A straight line on a graph can also be described by a simple equation (see Text Mathematical Note, pages 26–27). The general form for the equation of a straight line is

$$y = a + bx$$

If you are given such an equation, you can graph the line by finding the *y*-intercept (where the line intersects the vertical *y*-axis), finding the *x*-intercept (where the line intersects the horizontal *x*-axis), and then connecting those two points with a straight line:

To find the *y*-intercept, set $x = 0$.
$$y = a + b(0)$$
$$y = a$$
To find the *x*-intercept, set $y = 0$.
$$0 = a + bx$$
$$x = -a/b$$

Connecting these two points (($x = 0$, $y = a$) and ($x = -a/b$, $y = 0$)) or (0, a) and ($-a/b$, 0) allows you to graph the straight line. For any straight line with the equation of the form $y = a + bx$, the slope of the line is b. Figure A1.1 illustrates a line where b is a *negative* number, so there is a *negative* relationship between the variables x and y.

FIGURE **A1.1**

To see how to apply this general equation, consider this example:

$$y = 6 - 2x$$

To find the *y*-intercept, set $x = 0$.
$$y = 6 - 2(0)$$
$$y = 6$$
To find the *x*-intercept, set $y = 0$.
$$0 = 6 - 2x$$
$$x = 3$$

Connecting these two points, (0, 6) and (3, 0), yields the line in Figure A1.2.

FIGURE **A1.2**

The slope of this line is −2. Since the slope is negative, there is a negative relationship between the variables x and y.

SELF-TEST

True/False and Explain

Graphing Data

I   A time-series graph shows the level of a variable across different groups at a point in time.

2   A graph with a break in the axes must be misleading.

3   If a scatter diagram shows a clear relationship between variables x and y, then x must cause y.

Graphs Used in Economic Models

4   If the graph of the relationship between two variables slopes upward (to the right), the graph has a positive slope.

5   The graph of the relationship between two variables that are in fact unrelated is always vertical.

6   In Figure A1.3, the relationship between y and x is first negative, reaches a minimum, and then becomes positive as x increases.

7   In Figure A1.3, the value of x is a minimum at point b.

The Slope of a Relationship

8   In Figure A1.3, the slope of the curve is increasing as we move from point b to point c.

9   In Figure A1.3, the slope of the curve is approaching zero as we move from point a to point b.

10   The slope of a straight line is calculated by dividing the change in the value of the variable measured on the horizontal axis by the change in the value of the variable measured on the vertical axis.

11   For a straight line, if a small change in y is associated with a large change in x, the slope is large.

12 For a straight line, if a large change in *y* is associated with a small change in *x*, the line is steep.

13 The slope of a curved line is not constant.

Graphing Relationships Among More Than Two Variables

14 *Ceteris paribus* means "other things change."

15 Relationships between three variables can be displayed on a two-dimensional graph.

Multiple-Choice

Graphing Data

1 Figure A1.4 is a time-series graph. The horizontal axis measures _____ and the vertical axis measures _____.
   a time; the variable of interest
   b time; slope
   c the variable of interest in one year; the variable of interest in another year
   d the variable of interest; time
   e slope; time

FIGURE **A1.4**

2 The tendency for a variable to rise or fall over time is called its
   a slope.
   b trend.
   c *y*-coordinate.
   d level.
   e correlation.

3 Which type of graph can mislead?
   a Time-series graphs only
   b Cross-section graphs only
   c Scatter diagrams only
   d Graphs with correlations between variables only
   e Any of the above

Graphs Used in Economic Models

4 From the data in Table A1.1, it appears that
   a *x* and *y* have a negative relationship.
   b *x* and *y* have a positive relationship.
   c there is no relationship between *x* and *y*.
   d there is first a negative and then a positive relationship between *x* and *y*.
   e there is first a positive and then a negative relationship between *x* and *y*.

TABLE **A1.1**

Year	x	y
2004	6.2	143
2005	5.7	156
2006	5.3	162

5 If variables *x* and *y* move up and down together, they are said to be
   a positively related.
   b negatively related.
   c conversely related.
   d unrelated.
   e trendy.

6 The relationship between two variables that move in opposite directions is shown graphically by a line that is
   a positively sloped.
   b relatively steep.
   c relatively flat.
   d negatively sloped.
   e curved.

The Slope of a Relationship

7 In Figure A1.5 the relationship between x and y as x increases is
  a positive with slope decreasing.
  b negative with slope decreasing.
  c negative with slope increasing.
  d positive with slope increasing.
  e positive with slope first increasing then decreasing.

FIGURE **A1.5**

8 What is the slope across the arc between b and c in Figure A1.5?
  a 1/2
  b 2/3
  c 1
  d 2
  e 3

9 In Figure A1.5, consider the slopes of arc ab and arc bc. The slope at point b is difficult to determine exactly, but it must be
  a greater than 5/2.
  b about 5/2.
  c between 5/2 and 1.
  d about 1.
  e less than 1.

10 In Table A1.2, suppose that w is the independent variable measured along the horizontal axis. The slope of the line relating w and u is
  a positive with a decreasing slope.
  b negative with a decreasing slope.
  c positive with an increasing slope.
  d negative with a constant slope.
  e positive with a constant slope.

TABLE **A1.2**

w	2	4	6	8	10
u	15	12	9	6	3

11 Refer to Table A1.2. Suppose that w is the independent variable measured along the horizontal axis. The slope of the line relating w and u is
  a +3.
  b −3.
  c −2/3.
  d +3/2.
  e −3/2.

12 In Figure A1.6, if household income increases by $1,000, household expenditure will
  a increase by $1,333.
  b decrease by $1,333.
  c remain unchanged.
  d increase by $1,000.
  e increase by $750.

FIGURE **A1.6**

13 In Figure A1.6, if household income is zero, household expenditure is
  a 0.
  b −$4,000.
  c $4,000.
  d $8,000.
  e impossible to determine from the graph.

14 In Figure A1.6, if household expenditure is $28,000, household income is
   a $36,000.
   b $32,000.
   c $28,000.
   d $25,000.
   e none of the above.

15 At all points along a straight line, slope is
   a positive.
   b negative.
   c constant.
   d zero.
   e none of the above.

16 What is the slope of the line in Figure A1.7?
   a 2
   b 1/2
   c 3
   d 1/3
   e −3

FIGURE **A1.7**

17 If the line in Figure A1.7 were to continue down to the x-axis, what would the value of x be when y is zero?
   a 0
   b 2
   c 2/3
   d −2/3
   e −3/2

18 If the equation of a straight line is $y = 6 + 3x$, the slope is
   a −3 and the y-intercept is 6.
   b −3 and the y-intercept is −2.
   c 3 and the y-intercept is 6.
   d 3 and the y-intercept is −2.
   e 3 and the y-intercept is −6.

19 If the equation of a straight line is $y = 8 − 2x$, then the slope is
   a −2 and the x-intercept is −4.
   b −2 and the x-intercept is 4.
   c −2 and the x-intercept is 8.
   d 2 and the x-intercept is −4.
   e 2 and the x-intercept is 4.

Graphing Relationships Among More Than Two Variables

20 To graph a relationship among more than two variables, what kind of assumption is necessary?
   a normative
   b positive
   c linear
   d independence of variables
   e *ceteris paribus*

21 Given the data in Table A1.3, holding income constant, the graph relating the price of strawberries (vertical axis) to the purchases of strawberries (horizontal axis)
   a is a vertical line.
   b is a horizontal line.
   c is a positively sloped line.
   d is a negatively sloped line.
   e reaches a minimum.

TABLE **A1.3**

Weekly Family Income ($)	Price per Box of Strawberries ($)	Number of Boxes Purchased per Week
300	$1.00	5
300	$1.25	3
300	$1.50	2
400	$1.00	7
400	$1.25	5
400	$1.50	4

22 Given the data in Table A1.3, suppose family income decreases from $400 to $300 per week. Then the graph relating the price of strawberries (vertical axis) to the purchases of strawberries (horizontal axis) will
   a become negatively sloped.
   b become positively sloped.
   c shift rightward.
   d shift leftward.
   e no longer exist.

23 Given the data in Table A1.3, holding price constant, the graph relating family income (vertical axis) to the purchases of strawberries (horizontal axis) is a

a   vertical line.

b   horizontal line.

c   positively sloped line.

d   negatively sloped line.

e   positively or negatively sloped line, depending on the price that is held constant.

24 In Figure A1.8, x is

a   positively related to y and negatively related to z.

b   positively related to both y and z.

c   negatively related to y and positively related to z.

d   negatively related to both y and z.

e   greater than z.

FIGURE **A1.8**

25 In Figure A1.8, a decrease in the value of z will cause, *ceteris paribus*,

a   a decrease in the value of x.

b   an increase in the value of x.

c   an increase in the value of y.

d   no change in the value of y.

e   no change in the value of x.

Short Answer Problems

1 Consider the data in Table A1.4.

a   Draw a time-series graph for the interest rate.

b   Draw a time-series graph for the inflation rate.

c   Draw a scatter diagram for the inflation rate (horizontal axis) and the interest rate (vertical axis).

d   Would you describe the general relationship between the inflation rate and the interest rate as positive, negative, or unrelated?

TABLE **A1.4**

Year	Inflation Rate (%)	Interest Rate (%)
1970	5.4	6.4
1971	3.2	4.3
1972	3.4	4.1
1973	8.3	7.0
1974	11.8	7.9
1975	6.7	5.8
1976	4.9	5.0
1977	6.5	5.3
1978	8.6	7.2
1979	12.3	10.0

2 Draw a graph of variables x and y that illustrates each of the following relationships:

a x and y move up and down together.

b x and y move in opposite directions.

c   as x increases y reaches a maximum.

d   as x increases y reaches a minimum.

e x and y move in opposite directions, but as x increases y decreases by larger and larger increments for each unit increase in x.

f y is unrelated to the value of x.

g x is unrelated to the value of y.

3 What does it mean to say that the slope of a line is $-2/3$?

4 Compute the slopes of the lines in Figure A1.9(a) and (b).

FIGURE **A1.9**

(a)

(b)

5 Draw each of the following:

a a straight line with slope −10 and passing through the point (2, 80).

b a straight line with slope 2 and passing through the point (6, 10).

6 The equation for a straight line is $y = 4 - 2x$.

a Calculate the y-intercept; the x-intercept; the slope.

b Draw the graph of the line.

7 Explain two ways to measure the slope of a curved line.

8 Use the graph in Figure A1.10 to compute the slope

a across the arc between points a and b.

b at point b.

c at point c, and explain your answer.

FIGURE **A1.10**

9 How do we graph a relationship among more than two variables using a two-dimensional graph?

10 In Table A1.5 on the following page, x represents the number of umbrellas sold per month, y represents the price of an umbrella, and z represents the average number of rainy days per month.

a On the same diagram, graph the relationship between x (horizontal axis) and y (vertical axis) when $z = 4$, when $z = 5$, and when $z = 6$.

b On average, it rains six days per month. This implies a certain average relationship between monthly umbrella sales and umbrella price. Suppose that the "greenhouse effect" reduces the average monthly rainfall to four days per month. What happens to the graph of the relationship between umbrella sales and umbrella prices?

c On a diagram, graph the relationship between x (horizontal axis) and z (vertical axis) when $y = \$10$ and when $y = \$12$. Is the relationship between x and z positive or negative?

d On a diagram, graph the relationship between y (horizontal axis) and z (vertical axis) when $x = 120$ and when $x = 140$. Is the relationship between y and z positive or negative?

TABLE **A1.5**

Umbrellas Sold per Month (x)	Price per Umbrella (y)	Average Number of Rainy Days per Month (z)
120	$10	4
140	$10	5
160	$10	6
100	$12	4
120	$12	5
140	$12	6
80	$14	4
100	$14	5
120	$14	6

ANSWERS

True/False and Explain

1 F Definition of a cross-section graph. Time-series graph shows relationship between time (on x-axis) and other variable(s) (on y-axis). (16)

2 F Breaks in the axes may be misleading, or may bring information into clearer view. (18)

3 F x and y are correlated, but correlation does not guarantee causation. (18)

4 T Upward-sloping curves/lines have positive slopes. (18–19)

5 F Graph of unrelated variables may be vertical or horizontal. (21)

6 T Arc ab would have negative slope, arc bc positive slope. (20–24)

7 F Value of y is minimum at point b. (20–21)

8 T Curve becomes steeper, meaning Δy increasing faster than Δx, so slope increasing. (22–24)

9 T At b, tangent has slope = 0, since $\Delta y = 0$ along horizontal line through b. (22–24)

10 F Slope = (Δ variable on vertical (y) axis)/(Δ variable on horizontal (x) axis). (22–23)

11 F Large slope means large Δy associated with small Δx. (22–23)

12 T Steep line has large slope, meaning large Δy associated with small Δx. (22–23)

13 T Slope of straight line is constant. (22–23)

14 F "Other things remain the same." Only variables being studied are allowed to change. (24)

15 T See Text Figure A1.12. A *ceteris paribus* assumption holds one variable constant, allowing other two variables to be plotted in two dimensions. (24–25)

Multiple-Choice

1 a Time is measured on the x-axis and the variable in which we are interested on the y-axis. (16)

2 b Definition. (16)

3 e Any type of graph can mislead with breaks in the axes or stretched/compressed measurement scales. (18)

4 a Higher values x (6.2) associated with lower values y (143). (18–20)

5 a Definition. (18–20)

6 d Graph may be steep, flat, or curved, but must have negative slope. (19–20)

7 a Slope of arc ab = +2.5. Slope of arc bc = +1. (22–24)

8 c $\Delta y = 3(8 - 5)$; $\Delta x = 3(6 - 3)$. (23–24)

9 c 5/2 is slope of ab, while 1 is slope of bc. (23–24)

10 d As w increases, u decreases. $\Delta u/\Delta w$ is constant. (22–24)

11 e Between any two points, $\Delta u = 3$, $\Delta w = -2$. (22–24)

12 e Slope ($\Delta y/\Delta x$) = 3/4. If Δx (Δ household income) = $1,000, then Δy (Δ household expenditure) = $750 = ¾ of $1,000. (22–24)

13 c Where the line intersects the household expenditure (y) axis. (22–24)

14 b From $28,000 on vertical (expenditure) axis, move across to line, then down to $32,000 on horizontal (income) axis. (22–24)

15 c Along straight line, slope may or may not be **a**, **b**, or **d**. (22–23)

16 c Between any two points, $\Delta y = 3$ and $\Delta x = 1$. (22–23)

17 **d** Equation of line is $y = 2 + 3x$. Solve for x-intercept (set $y = 0$). (22–24, 26–27)

18 **c** Use formula $y = a + bx$. Slope = b, y-intercept = a. (22–24, 26–27)

19 **b** Use formula $y = a + bx$. Slope = b, x-intercept = $-a/b$. (22–24, 26–27)

20 **e** Must hold constant other variables to isolate relationship between two variables. (24–25)

21 **d** Look either at data in top 3 rows (income = 300) or data in bottom 3 rows (income = 400). Higher price associated with lower purchases. (24–25)

22 **d** At each price, fewer boxes will be purchased. (24–25)

23 **c** For $P = 1$, two points on line are (5 boxes, $300) and (7 boxes, $400). Same relationship for other prices. (24–25)

24 **c** Increased y causes decreased x holding z constant. Increased z causes increased x holding y constant. (24–25)

25 **a** Decreased z causes decreased x holding y constant. Decreased z causes decreased y holding x constant. (24–25)

Short Answer Problems

1 **a** A time-series graph for the interest rate is given in Figure A1.11(a).

b A time-series graph for the inflation rate is given in Figure A1.11(b).

c The scatter diagram for the inflation rate and the interest rate is given in Figure A1.11(c).

d From the graph in Figure A1.11(c), we see that the relationship between the inflation rate and the interest rate is generally positive (upward-sloping).

FIGURE **A1.11**

(a)

(b)

(c)

2 Figures A1.12(a) through (g) illustrate the desired graphs.

FIGURE **A1.12**

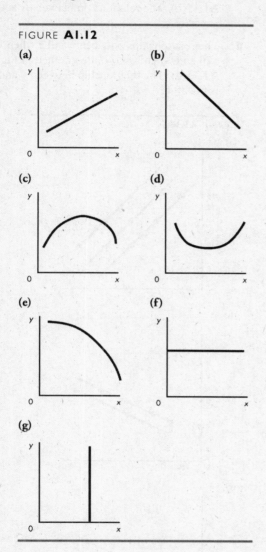

y-coordinate decreases by 10 for every 1 unit increase in the *x*-coordinate, for example, (5, 50). The slope between the two points is −30/3 = −10.

b The requested straight line is graphed in Figure A1.13(b). First plot the point (6, 10). Then pick a second point whose *y*-coordinate decreases by 2 for every 1 unit decrease in the *x*-coordinate, for example, (5, 8). The slope between the two points is −2/−1 = 2.

FIGURE **A1.13**

(a)

(b)

3 The negative sign in the slope of −2/3 means that there is a negative relationship between the two variables. The value of 2/3 means that when the variable measured on the vertical axis decreases by 2 units (the rise or Δy), the variable measured on the horizontal axis increases by 3 units (the run or Δx).

4 To find the slope, pick any two points on a line and compute $\Delta y/\Delta x$. The slope of the line in Figure A1.9(a) is −2/3, and the slope of the line in Figure A1.9(b) is 1/2.

5 a The requested straight line is graphed in Figure A1.13(a). First plot the point (2, 80). Then pick a second point whose

6 a To find the *y*-intercept, set $x = 0$.
$$y = 4 - 2(0)$$
$$y = 4$$
To find the *x*-intercept, set $y = 0$.
$$0 = 4 - 2x$$
$$x = 2$$
The slope of the line is −2, the value of the "*b*" coefficient on *x*.

b The graph of the line is shown in Figure A1.14.

FIGURE **A1.14**

FIGURE **A1.14**

7 The slope of a curved line can be measured at a point or across an arc. The slope at a point is measured by calculating the slope of the straight line that is tangent to (just touches) the curved line at the point. The slope across an arc is measured by calculating the slope of the straight line that forms the arc.

8 a The slope across the arc between points a and b is $-3/2$.

b The slope at point b is $-3/4$.

c The slope at point c is zero because it is a minimum point. Nearby a minimum point the slope changes from negative to positive and must pass through zero, or no slope, to do so.

9 To graph a relationship among more than two variables, we hold all of the variables but two constant, and graph the relationship between the remaining two. Thus, we can graph the relationship between any pair of variables, given the constant values of the other variables.

10 a The relationships between x and y for $z = 4$, 5, and 6 are graphed in Figure A1.15(a).

b If the average monthly rainfall drops from 6 days to 4 days, the curve representing the relationship between umbrella sales and umbrella prices will shift from the curve labelled $z = 6$ to $z = 4$.

c The relationships between x and z when y is \$10 and when y is \$12 are graphed in Figure A1.15(b). The relationship between x and z is positive.

d The relationships between y and z when $x = 120$ and when $x = 140$ are graphed in Figure A1.15(c). The relationship between y and z is positive.

FIGURE **A1.15**

(a)

(b)

(c)

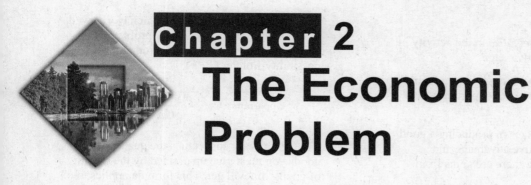

Chapter 2
The Economic Problem

Production Possibilities and Opportunity Cost

The production possibility frontier (*PPF*)

- ♦ is the boundary between unattainable and attainable production possibilities.

- ♦ shows maximum combinations of outputs (goods and services) that can be produced with given resources and technology.

PPF characteristics:

- ♦ points on *PPF* represent **production efficiency**—outputs produced at the lowest possible cost.

- ♦ points inside *PPF* are inefficient—attainable, but not maximum combinations of outputs; they represent unused or misallocated resources.

- ♦ points on *PPF* are preferred to points inside *PPF*.

- ♦ points outside *PPF* are unattainable.

- ♦ choosing among efficient points on *PPF* involves an **opportunity cost** (highest-valued opportunity foregone) and a *tradeoff*.

*PPF*s are generally bowed outward (concave), reflecting increasing opportunity costs as more of a good is produced.

- ♦ *PPF* is bowed outward because resources are not equally productive in all activities (nonhomogeneous). Resources most suitable for a given activity are the first to be used.

- ♦ Bowed-out-shaped *PPF* represents increasing opportunity cost—opportunity cost of good increases as its quantity produced increases.

- ♦ In moving between two points on *PPF* more good *X* can be obtained only by producing less good *Y*.

Opportunity cost on *PPF* of additional *X* is amount of *Y* forgone.

- ♦ No opportunity cost in moving from point inside *PPF* to point on *PPF*.

Using Resources Efficiently

To choose among points on *PPF*, compare

- ♦ **marginal cost**—opportunity cost of producing one more unit of a good.

  - • marginal cost curve slopes upwards because of *increasing opportunity cost*.

- ♦ **marginal benefit**—benefit (measured in willingness to forgo other goods) from consuming one more unit of a good. Depends on a person's **preferences**—likes and dislikes.

  - • **marginal benefit curve** slopes downwards because of *decreasing marginal benefit*.

We choose a point on *PPF* of **allocative efficiency** where

- ♦ outputs produced at lowest possible cost, and in quantities providing greatest possible benefit

- ♦ marginal benefit = marginal cost.

Economic Growth

Economic growth is the expansion of production possibilities—an outward shift of *PPF*.

- ♦ *PPF* shifts from changes in resources or technology.

- ♦ **Capital accumulation** and **technological change** shift *PPF* outward—economic growth.

- ♦ Opportunity cost of increased goods and services in future (economic growth through capital accumulation and technological progress) is decreased consumption today.

Gains from Trade

Production increases if people *specialize* in the activity in which they have a comparative advantage.

♦ Person has **comparative advantage** in producing a good if she can produce at lower opportunity cost than anyone else.

♦ When each person specializes in producing a good at which she has comparative advantage and exchanges for other goods, there are gains from trade.

♦ Specialization and exchange allow consumption (not production) at points outside *PPF*.

♦ Person has **absolute advantage** in producing a good if, using the same quantity of resources, she can produce more than anyone else.

   • Absolute advantage is irrelevant for specialization and gains from trade.

   • Even a person with an absolute advantage in producing all goods gains by specializing in activity in which she has a comparative advantage and trading.

♦ **Dynamic comparative advantage** results from specializing in an activity, **learning-by-doing**, and over time becoming the producer with the lowest opportunity cost.

Economic Coordination

Gains from trade and specialization require coordination. Decentralized coordination through markets depends on the social institutions of

♦ **firms**—hire and organize factors of production to produce and sell goods and services. Firms coordinate much economic activity, but the efficient size of a firm is limited.

♦ **markets**—coordinating buying and selling decisions through price adjustments.

♦ **property rights**—governing ownership, use, and disposal of resources, goods, and services.

♦ **money**—any generally acceptable means of payment; makes trading more efficient.

HELPFUL HINTS

I This chapter reviews the absolutely critical concept of opportunity cost—the best alternative forgone—that was introduced in Chapter 1. Opportunity cost is a *ratio*. A very helpful

formula for opportunity cost, which works well in solving problems, especially problems that involve moving up or down a production possibility frontier (*PPF*), is:

$$\text{Opportunity Cost} = \frac{\text{Give Up}}{\text{Get}}$$

Opportunity cost equals the quantity of goods you must give up divided by the quantity of goods you will get. This formula applies to all *PPF*s, whether they are bowed out as in Text Figure 2.1 or linear as in Text Figure 2.7. To illustrate, look again at the bowed-out *PPF*.

FIGURE 2.1   Production Possibilities Frontier

First, consider an example of moving down the *PPF*. In moving from *C* to *D*, what is the opportunity cost of an additional pizza? This economy must give up 3 colas (12 − 9) to get 1 pizza (3 − 2). Substituting into the formula, the opportunity cost is:

$$\frac{3 \text{ colas}}{1 \text{ pizza}} = 3 \text{ colas per pizza}$$

Next, consider an example of moving up the *PPF*. In moving from *D* to *C*, what is the opportunity cost of an additional cola? We must give up 1 pizza (3 − 2) to get 3 colas (12 − 9). Substituting into the formula, the opportunity cost is:

$$\frac{1 \text{ pizza}}{3 \text{ colas}} = \frac{1}{3} \text{ pizza per colas}$$

Opportunity cost is always measured in the units of the forgone good.

2 Opportunity cost can also be related to the slope of the *PPF*. As we move down between any two points on the *PPF*, the opportunity cost of an additional unit of the good on the horizontal axis is:

$$|\text{slope of } PPF|$$

The slope of the *PPF* is negative, but economists like to describe opportunity cost in terms of a positive quantity of forgone goods. Therefore, we must use the absolute value of the slope to calculate the desired positive number.

As we move up between any two points on the *PPF*, the opportunity cost of an additional unit of the good on the vertical axis is:

$$\left|\frac{1}{\text{slope of } PPF}\right|$$

This is the *inverse* relation we saw between possibilities *C* and *D*. The opportunity cost of an additional pizza (on the horizontal axis) between *C* and *D* is 3 colas. The opportunity cost of an additional cola (on the vertical axis) between *D* and *C* is 1/3 pizza.

3 All points on a *PPF* achieve production efficiency in that they fully employ all resources. But how do we pick a point on the *PPF* and decide *what* combination of goods we want? The *PPF* provides information about resources and *costs*. But choosing what goods we want also requires information about *benefits*.

This choice, like all economic choices, is made at the margin. To decide what goods we want, compare the marginal cost (*MC*) and marginal benefit (*MB*) of different combinations. Marginal cost is the opportunity cost of producing one more unit. The marginal cost of producing more of any good increases as we move along the *PPF*. Marginal benefit is the benefit received from consuming one more unit. Marginal benefit decreases as we consume more of any good.

If the marginal cost of a good exceeds the marginal benefit, we decrease production of the good. If the marginal benefit exceeds the marginal cost, we increase production. When marginal cost equals marginal benefit for every

good, we have chosen the goods that we value most highly. The decision rule of *MB* = *MC* yields an *efficient* allocation of resources.

Text Figure 2.4 is crucial for explaining all economic decisions. Make sure you spend time on it even though it may be hard to fully understand. You will understand Text Figure 2.4 better after we spend time in future chapters elaborating the concepts of marginal cost and marginal benefit.

4 The colas and pizza production possibility frontier assumes that resources are *not* equally productive in all activities. Resources with such differences are also called nonhomogeneous resources. As a result of this assumption, opportunity cost increases as we increase the production of either good. In moving from possibility *C* to *D*, the opportunity cost per unit of pizza is 3 colas. But in increasing pizza production from *D* to *E*, the opportunity cost per unit of pizza increases to 4 colas. In producing the first 1 (million) pizzas, we use the resources best suited to pizza production. As we increase pizza production, however, we must use resources that are less well suited to pizza production—hence increasing opportunity cost. A parallel argument accounts for the increasing opportunity cost of increasing cola production.

It is also possible to construct an even simpler model of a *PPF* that assumes resources are equally productive in all activities, or homogeneous resources. As a result of this assumption, opportunity cost is constant as we increase production of either good. Constant opportunity cost means that the *PPF* will be a straight line (rather than bowed out). As you will see in some of the following exercises, such a simple model is useful for illustrating the principle of comparative advantage, without having to deal with the complications of increasing opportunity cost.

5 The text defines absolute advantage as a situation where one person is more productive than another in the producing one or more goods. We can also define *absolute advantage in the production of one good*. In comparing the productivity of two persons, this narrower concept of absolute advantage can be defined in terms of either greater output of the good per unit of resource inputs or fewer resource inputs per unit of output. It is useful to understand these definitions of absolute advantage only to demonstrate that absolute advantage has no role

in explaining specialization and trade. The gains from trade depend only on differing comparative advantages. People have a comparative advantage in producing a good if they can produce it at lower opportunity cost than others.

6 This chapter gives us our first chance to develop and use economic models. It is useful to think about the nature of these models in the context of the general discussion of models in Chapter 1. For example, one model in this chapter is a representation of the production possibilities in the two-person and two-good world of Liz and Joe. The model abstracts greatly from the complexity of the real world in which there are billions of people and numerous different kinds of goods and services. The model allows us to explain a number of phenomena that we observe in the world such as specialization and exchange.

The production possibilities model also has some implications or predictions. For example, countries that devote a larger proportion of their resources to capital accumulation will have more rapidly expanding production possibilities. The model can be subjected to "test" by comparing these predictions to the facts we observe in the real world.

S E L F - T E S T

True/False and Explain

Production Possibilities and Opportunity Cost
Refer to the production possibility frontier (*PPF*) in Figure 2.2 for Questions **1** to **4**.

I Point *a* is not attainable.

2 The opportunity cost of increasing the production of good 2 from 7 to 8 units is 4 units of good 1.

FIGURE **2.2**

3 Point *c* is not attainable.

4 In moving from point *b* to point *d*, the opportunity cost of increasing the production of good 2 equals the absolute value of the slope of the *PPF* between *b* and *d*.

Using Resources Efficiently

5 The marginal cost of the 4th pizza is the cost of producing all 4 pizzas.

6 The marginal benefit of good *X* is the amount of good *Y* a person is willing to forgo to obtain one more unit of *X*.

7 The principle of decreasing marginal benefit states that the more we have of a good, the *less* we are willing to pay for an additional unit of it.

8 All points on a *PPF* represent both production efficiency and allocative efficiency.

Economic Growth

9 Economic growth, by shifting out the *PPF*, eliminates the problem of scarcity.

10 In a model where capital resources can grow, points on the *PPF* that have more consumption goods yield faster growth.

Gains from Trade

11 With specialization and trade, a country can produce at a point outside its *PPF*.

12 Canada has no incentive to trade with a cheap-labour country like Mexico.

13 Nadim definitely has a comparative advantage in producing skateboards if he can produce more than Elle.

Economic Coordination

14 The incentives for specialization and exchange do not depend on property rights but only on differing opportunity costs.

15 Price adjustments coordinate decisions in goods markets but not in factor markets.

Multiple-Choice

Production Possibilities and Opportunity Cost

1 If Harold can increase production of good *X* without decreasing the production of any other good, he
  a is producing on his *PPF*.
  b is producing outside his *PPF*.
  c is producing inside his *PPF*.
  d must have a linear *PPF*.
  e must prefer good *X* to any other good.

2 The bowed-out (concave) shape of a *PPF*
  a is due to the equal usefulness of resources in all activities.
  b is due to capital accumulation.
  c is due to technological change.
  d reflects the existence of increasing opportunity cost.
  e reflects the existence of decreasing opportunity cost.

3 The economy is at point *b* on the *PPF* in Figure 2.3. The opportunity cost of producing one more unit of *X* is
  a 1 unit of *Y*.
  b 20 units of *Y*.
  c 1 unit of *X*.
  d 8 units of *X*.
  e 20 units of *X*.

FIGURE **2.3**

4 Refer to the *PPF* in Figure 2.3 on the previous page. Which of the following statements is *false*?

   a Resources are not equally productive in all activities.

   b Points inside the frontier represent unemployed resources.

   c Starting at point *a*, an increase in the production of good *Y* will shift the frontier out.

   d The opportunity cost of producing good *Y* increases as production of *Y* increases.

   e Shifts in preferences for good *X* or good *Y* will not shift the frontier.

5 Refer to Figure 2.4, which shows the *PPF* for an economy without discrimination operating at maximum efficiency. If discrimination against women workers is currently occurring in this economy, the elimination of discrimination would result in a(n)

   a movement from *a* to *b*.

   b movement from *b* to *c*.

   c movement from *a* to *c*.

   d outward shift of the *PPF*.

   e inward shift of the *PPF*.

FIGURE **2.4**

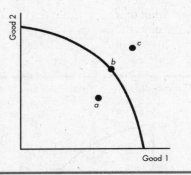

Suppose a society produces only two goods—hockey sticks and maple leaves. Three alternative combinations on its *PPF* are given in Table 2.1. Use the information in Table 2.1 to answer Questions **6** and **7**.

TABLE **2.1** PRODUCTION POSSIBILITIES

Possibility	Units of Hockey Sticks	Units of Maple Leaves
a	3	0
b	2	3
c	0	9

6 In moving from combination *c* to combination *b*, the opportunity cost of producing one additional hockey stick is

   a 2 maple leaves.

   b 1/2 maple leaves.

   c 6 maple leaves.

   d 1/6 maple leaves.

   e 3 maple leaves.

7 According to this *PPF*

   a resources are equally productive in all activities.

   b a combination of 3 hockey sticks and 9 maple leaves is attainable.

   c a combination of 3 hockey sticks and 9 maple leaves would not employ all resources.

   d the opportunity cost of producing hockey sticks increases as more hockey sticks are produced.

   e the opportunity cost of producing hockey sticks decreases as more hockey sticks are produced.

Using Resources Efficiently

8 The marginal benefit curve for a good

   a shows the benefit a firm receives from producing one more unit.

   b shows the amount a consumer is willing to pay for one more unit.

   c is upward-sloping.

   d is bowed out.

   e is none of the above.

9 With increasing production of food, its marginal benefit

   a increases and marginal cost increases.

   b increases and marginal cost decreases.

   c decreases and marginal cost increases.

   d decreases and marginal cost decreases.

   e decreases and marginal cost is constant.

10 Suppose the *PPF* for skirts and pants is a straight line. As the production of skirts increases, the marginal benefit of skirts

   a increases and marginal cost is constant.

   b is constant and marginal cost increases.

   c decreases and marginal cost decreases.

   d decreases and marginal cost increases.

   e decreases and marginal cost is constant.

11 With allocative efficiency, for each good produced, marginal
   a benefit equals marginal cost.
   b benefit is at its maximum.
   c benefit exceeds marginal cost by as much as possible.
   d cost exceeds marginal benefit by as much as possible.
   e cost is at its minimum.

Economic Growth

12 The *PPF* for wine and wool will shift if there is a change in
   a the price of resources.
   b the unemployment rate.
   c the quantity of resources.
   d preferences for wine and wool.
   e all of the above.

13 A movement *along* a given *PPF* will result from
   a technological change.
   b change in the stock of capital.
   c change in the labour force.
   d all of the above.
   e none of the above.

14 The opportunity cost of pushing the *PPF* outward is
   a capital accumulation.
   b technological change.
   c reduced current consumption.
   d the gain in future consumption.
   e all of the above.

15 In general, the higher the proportion of resources devoted to technological research in an economy, the
   a greater will be current consumption.
   b faster the *PPF* will shift outward.
   c faster the *PPF* will shift inward.
   d closer it will come to having a comparative advantage in the production of all goods.
   e more bowed out the shape of the *PPF* will be.

16 Refer to the *PPF* in Figure 2.5. A politician who argues that "if our children are to be better off, we must invest now for the future" is recommending a current point like
   a *a.*
   b *b.*
   c *c.*
   d *d.*
   e *e.*

FIGURE **2.5**

17 Refer to the *PPF* in Figure 2.5. The statement that "unemployment is a terrible waste of human resources" refers to a point like
   a *a.*
   b *b.*
   c *c.*
   d *d.*
   e *e.*

Gains from Trade

In an eight-hour day, Andy can produce either 24 loaves of bread or 8 kilograms of butter. In an eight-hour day, Rolfe can produce either 8 loaves of bread or 8 kilograms of butter. Use this information to answer Questions **18** and **19**.

18 Which of the following statements is *true*?
   a Andy has an absolute advantage in butter production.
   b Rolfe has an absolute advantage in butter production.
   c Andy has an absolute advantage in bread production.
   d Andy has a comparative advantage in butter production.
   e Rolfe has a comparative advantage in bread production.

19 Andy and Rolfe
   a can gain from exchange if Andy specializes in butter production and Rolfe specializes in bread production.
   b can gain from exchange if Andy specializes in bread production and Rolfe specializes in butter production.
   c cannot gain from exchange.
   d can exchange, but only Rolfe will gain.
   e can exchange, but only Andy will gain.

20 Mexico and Canada produce both oil and apples using labour only. A barrel of oil is produced with 4 hours of labour in Mexico and 8 hours of labour in Canada. A bushel of apples is produced with 8 hours of labour in Mexico and 12 hours of labour in Canada. Canada has
   a an absolute advantage in oil production.
   b an absolute advantage in apple production.
   c a comparative advantage in oil production.
   d a comparative advantage in apple production.
   e none of the above.

21 In Portugal, the opportunity cost of a bale of wool is 3 bottles of wine. In England, the opportunity cost of 1 bottle of wine is 3 bales of wool. Given this information,
   a England has an absolute advantage in wine production.
   b England has an absolute advantage in wool production.
   c Portugal has a comparative advantage in wine production.
   d Portugal has a comparative advantage in wool production.
   e no trade will occur.

22 To gain from comparative advantage, countries must not only trade, they must also
   a save.
   b invest.
   c engage in research and development.
   d engage in capital accumulation.
   e specialize.

23 Learning-by-doing is the basis of
   a absolute comparative advantage.
   b dynamic comparative advantage.
   c intellectual property rights.
   d financial property rights.
   e none of the above.

Economic Coordination

24 Trade is organized using the social institutions of
   a firms.
   b property rights.
   c money.
   d markets.
   e all of the above.

25 Markets
   1 enable buyers and sellers to get information.
   2 are defined by economists as geographical locations where trade occurs.
   3 coordinate buying and selling decisions through price adjustments.
   a 1 only
   b 3 only
   c 1 and 3 only
   d 2 and 3 only
   e 1, 2, and 3

Short Answer Problems

1 Why is a *PPF* negatively sloped? Why is it bowed out?

2 Suppose that an economy has the *PPF* shown in Table 2.2.

TABLE **2.2** PRODUCTION POSSIBILITIES

Possibility	Maximum Units of Butter per Week	Maximum Units of Guns per Week
a	200	0
b	180	60
c	160	100
d	100	160
e	40	200
f	0	220

   a On graph paper, plot these possibilities, label the points, and draw the *PPF*. (Put guns on the *x*-axis.)

   b If the economy moves from possibility *c* to possibility *d*, the opportunity cost *per unit of guns* will be how many units of butter?

   c If the economy moves from possibility *d* to possibility *e*, the opportunity cost *per unit of guns* will be how many units of butter?

   d In general terms, what happens to the opportunity cost of guns as the output of guns increases?

   e In general terms, what happens to the opportunity cost of butter as the output of butter increases? What do the results in parts **d** and **e** imply about resources?

f If (instead of the possibilities given) the *PPF* were a straight line joining points *a* and *f*, what would that imply about opportunity costs and resources?

g Given the original *PPF* you have plotted, is a combination of 140 units of butter and 130 units of guns per week attainable? Would you regard this combination as an efficient one? Explain.

h Given the original *PPF*, is a combination of 70 units of butter and 170 units of guns per week attainable? Does this combination achieve productive efficiency? Explain.

3 If the following events occurred (each is a separate event, unaccompanied by any other event), what would happen to the *PPF* in Short Answer Problem **2**?

a A new, easily exploited, energy source is discovered.

b A large number of skilled workers immigrate into the country.

c The output of butter increases.

d A new invention increases output per person in the butter industry but not in the guns industry.

e A new law is passed compelling workers, who could previously work as long as they wanted, to retire at age 60.

4 The Borg produce only two goods—cubes and transwarp coils—and want to decide where on their *PPF* to operate. Table 2.3 shows the marginal benefit and marginal cost of cubes, measured in the number of transwarp coils per cube.

TABLE **2.3**

Borg Cubes	Marginal Benefit	Marginal Cost
1	12	3
2	10	4
3	8	5
4	6	6
5	4	7
6	2	8

a If the Borg are efficient (and they are!), what quantity of cubes will they produce?

b If the Borg were to produce one more cube than your answer in **a**, why would that choice be inefficient?

5 Suppose the country of Quark has historically devoted 10 percent of its resources to the production of new capital goods. Use *PPF* diagrams like Text Figures on pages 38–39 to compare the consequences (costs and benefits) of each of the following:

a Quark continues to devote 10 percent of its resources to the production of capital goods.

b Quark begins now to permanently devote 20 percent of its resources to the production of capital goods.

6 Lawyers earn $200 per hour while secretaries earn $15 per hour. Use the concepts of absolute and comparative advantage to explain why a lawyer who is a better typist than her secretary will still specialize in doing only legal work and will trade with the secretary for typing services.

7 France and Germany each produce both wine and beer, using a single, homogeneous input—labour. Their production possibilities are:

• France has 100 units of labour and can produce a maximum of 200 bottles of wine or 400 bottles of beer.

• Germany has 50 units of labour and can produce a maximum of 250 bottles of wine or 200 bottles of beer.

a Complete Table 2.4.

TABLE **2.4**

	Bottles Produced by 1 Unit of Labour		Opportunity Cost of 1 Additional Bottle	
	Wine	Beer	Wine	Beer
France				
Germany				

Use the information in part **a** to answer the following questions.

ⓔ **b** Which country has an absolute advantage in wine production?

ⓔ **c** Which country has an absolute advantage in beer production?

d Which country has a comparative advantage in wine production?

e Which country has a comparative advantage in beer production?

f If trade is allowed, describe what specialization, if any, will occur.

ⓔ **8** Tova and Ron are the only two remaining inhabitants of the planet Melmac. They spend their 30-hour days producing widgets and woggles, the only two goods needed for happiness on Melmac. It takes Tova 1 hour to produce a widget and 2 hours to produce a woggle, while Ron takes 3 hours to produce a widget and 3 hours to produce a woggle.

a For a 30-hour day, draw an individual *PPF* for Tova, then for Ron.

b What does the shape of the *PPF*s tell us about opportunity costs? about resources?

c Assume initially that Tova and Ron are each self-sufficient. Define self-sufficiency. Explain what the individual consumption possibilities are for Tova, then for Ron.

d Who has an absolute advantage in the production of widgets? of woggles?

e Who has a comparative advantage in the production of widgets? of woggles?

f Suppose Tova and Ron each specialize in producing only the good in which she or he has a comparative advantage (one spends 30 hours producing widgets, the other spends 30 hours producing woggles). What will be the total production of widgets and woggles?

g Suppose Tova and Ron exchange 7 widgets for 5 woggles. On your *PPF* diagrams, plot the new point of Tova's consumption, then of Ron's consumption. Explain how these points illustrate the gains from trade.

9 The Netsilik and Oonark families live on the Arctic coast, west of Hudson Bay. They often go fishing and hunting for caribou together. During an average working day, the Netsiliks can, at most, either catch 6 kilograms of fish or kill 6

caribou. The Oonarks can either catch 4 kilograms of fish or kill 4 caribou.

a Assuming linear *PPF*s, draw each family's *PPF* on the same diagram. Put fish on the horizontal axis and caribou on the vertical axis.

b Complete Table 2.5.

TABLE **2.5**

	Opportunity Cost of 1 Additional	
	Fish (kg)	Caribou
Netsiliks		
Oonarks		

---

c Which family has a comparative advantage in catching fish? in hunting caribou?

d Can specialization and trade increase the total output of fish and caribou produced by the two families? Explain.

10 Explain the interdependence that exists between households and firms in Text Figure 2.7 on page 45.

ANSWERS

True/False and Explain

1 **F** Attainable but not an efficient point. (32–33)

2 **T** Moving from *b* to *d*, production good 1 decreases by 4 units. (33–34)

3 **T** Outside *PPF*. (32–33)

4 **T** See Helpful Hint **2**. (33–34)

5 **F** Marginal cost is *additional* cost of producing the 4th pizza alone. (35)

6 **T** Marginal benefit is also the amount a person is willing to pay for one more unit, but payment in money ultimately represents an opportunity cost in goods forgone. (36)

7 T The more we have of a good, the smaller is the marginal benefit and hence the willingness to pay for it. (36)

8 F All points represent productive efficiency (efficient use of resources). But allocative efficiency only occurs at the single point (combination of goods) that we prefer above all others (where $MB = MC$). (37)

9 F Cost of growth is forgone current consumption. (38)

10 F Points with more capital goods yield faster growth. (38–39)

11 F Can *consume* at point outside *PPF*. (41–42)

12 F Mutually beneficial trade depends on comparative advantage, not absolute advantage. (40–43)

13 F Nadim has absolute advantage in skateboard production, but without information about opportunity costs, we don't know if he has comparative advantage. (43)

14 F Property rights are prerequisite for specialization and exchange. (44)

15 F Price adjustments coordinate buying and selling decisions in all markets. (44–45)

Multiple-Choice

1 c For 0 opportunity cost, must be unemployed resources. (32–33)

2 d **a** would be true if *un*equal resources; **b** and **c** shift *PPF*. (34)

3 b To increase quantity X to 9, must decrease quantity Y from 20 to 0. (33–34)

4 c Increased production Y moves up *along PPF*. (32–34)

5 a Discrimination causes underemployment of resources. Women not allowed to produce up to full abilities. (32–34)

6 e Give up 6 maple leaves to get 2 hockey sticks: 6/2 = 3 maple leaves per hockey stick. (33–34)

7 a Constant opportunity cost means resources equally productive for producing all goods—see Helpful Hint **4**. (32–34)

8 b Benefits apply to consumers; curve is downward-sloping. (36)

9 c Principles of diminishing marginal benefit and increasing marginal cost. (35–37)

10 e Diminishing marginal benefit, but linear *PPF* means constant opportunity and marginal costs. (35–37)

11 a Whenever $MB \neq MC$, efficiency improves by reallocating resources to produce more goods with high marginal benefits, causing a decrease in their marginal benefit and increase in marginal cost. (37)

12 c Only changes in resources or technology shift *PPF*. (38)

13 e **a**, **b**, and **c** all shift *PPF*. (38–39)

14 c **a** and **b** cause outward shift *PPF*, not opportunity cost; **d** effect of outward shift *PPF*. (38–39)

15 b Technological change shifts *PPF* outward at cost of current consumption. (38–39)

16 a Producing more capital goods now, shifts *PPF* outward in future. (38–39)

17 d Points inside *PPF* represent unemployed resources, whether labour, capital, or land. (32, 38–39)

18 c Andy produces 3 loaves bread per hour; Rolfe produces 1 loaf per hour—see Helpful Hint **5**. (40–43)

19 b Andy has comparative advantage (lower opportunity cost) bread, Rolfe has comparative advantage butter production. (40–43)

20 d Opportunity cost oil in bushels of apples—Canada 2/3, Mexico 1/2. Opportunity cost apples in barrels of oil—Canada 3/2, Mexico 2. (40–43)

21 c Opportunity cost wine in bales of wool—Portugal 1/3, England 3. Opportunity cost wool in bottles of wine—Portugal 3, England 1/3. (40–43)

22 e Gains from trade require specialization based on comparative advantage. **a–d** may increase productivity and absolute advantage, not necessarily comparative advantage. (40–43)

23 b Definition. (43)

24 e All 4 institutions required for gains from trade and specialization through decentralized coordination. (44)

25 c 2 is the ordinary meaning of markets, not the economist's definition. (43–44)

Short Answer Problems

1 The negative slope of the *PPF* reflects opportunity cost: in order to have more of one good, some of the other must be forgone. It is bowed out because the existence of resources not equally productive in all activities creates increasing opportunity cost as we increase the production of either good.

2 a The graph of the *PPF* is given in Figure 2.6.

FIGURE **2.6**

b In moving from *c* to *d*, in order to gain 60 units of guns, we must give up 160 − 100 = 60 units of butter. The opportunity cost per unit of guns is

$$\frac{60 \text{ units butter}}{60 \text{ units guns}} = 1 \text{ unit butter per unit of guns}$$

c In moving from *d* to *e*, in order to gain 40 units of guns, we must give up 100 − 40 = 60 units of butter. The opportunity cost per unit of guns is

$$\frac{60 \text{ units butter}}{40 \text{ units guns}} = 1.5 \text{ unit butter per unit of guns}$$

d The opportunity cost of producing more guns increases as the output of guns increases.

e Likewise, the opportunity cost of producing more butter increases as the output of butter increases. Increasing opportunity costs imply that resources are not equally productive in gun and butter production; that is, they are nonhomogeneous.

f Opportunity costs would always be constant, regardless of the output of guns or butter. The opportunity cost per unit of guns would be

$$200/220 = 10/11 \text{ units of butter}$$

The opportunity cost per unit of butter would be

$$220/200 = 1.1 \text{ units of guns}$$

Constant opportunity costs imply that resources are equally productive in gun and butter production; that is, they are homogeneous.

g This combination is outside the *PPF* and therefore is not attainable. Since the economy cannot produce this combination, the question of efficiency is irrelevant.

h This combination is inside the *PPF* and is attainable. It is inefficient because the economy could produce more of either or both goods without producing less of anything else. Therefore some resources are not fully utilized.

3 a Assuming that both goods require energy for their production, the entire *PPF* shifts out to the northeast as in Figure 2.7(a).

b Assuming that both goods use skilled labour in their production, the entire *PPF* shifts out to the northeast.

c The *PPF* does not shift. An increase in the output of butter implies a movement along the *PPF* to the left, not a shift of the *PPF* itself.

d The new invention implies that for every level of output of guns, the economy can now produce more butter. The *PPF* swings to the right, but remains anchored at point *f* as in Figure 2.7(b).

e   The entire *PPF* shifts in toward the origin.

FIGURE **2.7**

(a)

(b)

FIGURE **2.8**

4 a   At the efficient quantity of output, marginal benefit = marginal cost. The Borg will produce 4 cubes (*MB* = *MC* = 4 transwarp coils/cube).

b   At 5 cubes, marginal benefit = 4 and marginal cost = 7. Since *MC* > *MB*, the Borg could get better use from their resources by shifting production out of cubes and into transwarp coils.

5 a   The situation for Quark is depicted by Figure 2.8. Suppose Quark starts on *PPF*₁. If it continues to devote only 10 percent of its resources to the production of new capital goods, it is choosing to produce at a point like *a*. This will shift the *PPF* out in the next period, but only to the curve labelled 2 (where, presumably, Quark will choose to produce at point *b*).

b   Starting from the same initial *PPF*, if Quark now decides to increase the resources devoted to the production of new capital to 20 percent, it will be choosing to produce at a point like *c*. In this case, next period's *PPF* will shift further—to curve 3, and a point like *d*, for example.

Thus in comparing points *a* and *c*, we find the following costs and benefits: point *a* has the benefit of greater present consumption but at a cost of lower future consumption; point *c* has the cost of lower present consumption, but with the benefit of greater future consumption.

6   The lawyer has an absolute advantage in producing both legal and typing services relative to the secretary. Nevertheless, she has a comparative advantage in legal services, and the secretary has a comparative advantage in typing. To demonstrate these comparative advantages, we can construct Table 2.6 of opportunity costs.

TABLE **2.6**

	Opportunity Cost of 1 Additional Hour ($)	
	Legal Services	**Typing**
Lawyer	200	200
Secretary	>200	15

Consider first the lawyer's opportunity costs. The lawyer's best forgone alternative to providing 1 hour of legal services is the $200 she could earn by providing another hour of legal services. If she provides 1 hour of typing, she is also forgoing $200 (1 hour) of legal services.

What would the secretary have to forgo to provide 1 hour of legal services? He would have to spend 3 years in law school, forgoing 3 years of income in addition to the tuition he must pay. His opportunity cost is a very large number, certainly greater than $200. If he provides 1 hour of typing, his best forgone alternative is the $15 he could have earned at another secretarial job.

Thus Table 2.6 shows that the lawyer has a lower opportunity cost (comparative advantage) of providing legal services, and the secretary has a lower opportunity cost (comparative advantage) of providing typing services. It is on the basis of comparative advantage (not absolute advantage) that trade will take place from which both parties gain.

7 a The completed table is shown here as Table 2.4 Solution.

TABLE **2.4** SOLUTION

	Bottles Produced by 1 Unit of Labour		Opportunity Cost of 1 Additional Bottle	
	Wine	Beer	Wine	Beer
France	2	4	2.0 beer	0.50 wine
Germany	5	4	0.8 beer	1.25 wine

b Germany, which can produce more wine (5 bottles) per unit of input, has an absolute advantage in wine production.

c Neither country has an absolute advantage in beer production, since beer output (4 bottles) per unit of input is the same for both countries.

d Germany, with the lower opportunity cost (0.8 beer), has a comparative advantage in wine production.

e France, with the lower opportunity cost (0.5 wine), has a comparative advantage in beer production.

f The incentive for trade depends only on differences in comparative advantage. Germany will specialize in wine production and France will specialize in beer production.

8 a The individual *PPF*s for Tova and Ron are given by Figure 2.9(a) and (b) respectively.

FIGURE **2.9**

b The linear shape of the *PPF*s tells us that opportunity costs are constant along each frontier and that resources are homogeneous.

These linear *PPF*s with constant opportunity costs abstract from the complexity of the real world. The world generally has increasing opportunity costs, but that fact is not essential for understanding the gains from trade, which is the objective of this problem. Making the model more complex by including increasing opportunity costs would not change our results, but it would make it more difficult to see them.

c Individuals are self-sufficient if they consume only what they produce. This means there is no trade. Without trade, Tova's (maximum) consumption possibilities are exactly the same as her production possibilities—points along her *PPF*. Ron's (maximum) consumption possibilities are likewise the points along his *PPF*.

d Tova has an absolute advantage in the production of both widgets and woggles. Her absolute advantage can be defined either in terms of greater output per unit of inputs or fewer inputs per unit of output. A comparison of the *PPF*s in Figure 2.9 shows that, for given inputs of 30 hours, Tova produces a greater output of widgets than Ron (30 versus 10) and a greater output of woggles than Ron (15 versus 10). The statement of the problem tells us equivalently that, per unit of output, Tova uses fewer inputs than Ron for both widgets (1 hour versus 3 hours) and woggles (2 hours versus 3 hours). Since Tova has greater productivity than Ron in the production of all goods (widgets and woggles), we say that overall she has an absolute advantage.

e Tova has a comparative advantage in the production of widgets, since she can produce them at lower opportunity cost than Ron (1/2 woggle versus 1 woggle). On the other hand, Ron has a comparative advantage in the production of woggles, since he can produce them at a lower opportunity cost than Tova (1 widget versus 2 widgets).

f Tova will produce widgets and Ron will produce woggles, yielding a total production between them of 30 widgets and 10 woggles.

g After the exchange, Tova will have 23 widgets and 5 woggles (point *T*). Ron will have 7 widgets and 5 woggles (point *R*). These new post-trade consumption possibility points lie outside Tova's and Ron's respective pre-trade consumption (and production) possibilities. Hence trade has yielded gains that allow the traders to improve their consumption possibilities beyond those available with self-sufficiency.

9 a The *PPF*s of the Netsiliks and Oonarks are shown in Figure 2.10.

FIGURE **2.10**

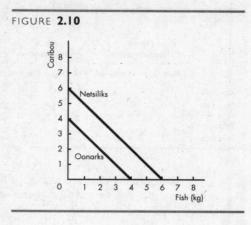

b The completed table is shown here as Table 2.5 Solution.

TABLE **2.5** SOLUTION

	Opportunity Cost of 1 Additional	
	Fish (kg)	Caribou
Netsiliks	1 caribou	1 kg fish
Oonarks	1 caribou	1 kg fish

c Neither family has a comparative advantage in catching fish, since the opportunity cost of fish is the same (1 caribou) for each family. Similarly, neither family has a comparative advantage in hunting caribou, since the opportunity cost of a caribou is the same (1 kilogram of fish) for each family.

d Gains from specialization and trade are due to the existence of comparative advantage. In this case, no family has a comparative advantage in either fishing or hunting, so there are no gains from specialization and trade.

To illustrate the absence of gains, suppose that initially each family devoted half of its time to each activity. Then suppose that the Netsiliks specialized completely in catching fish and the Oonarks specialized completely in hunting caribou. Production before and after specialization is shown in Table 2.7.

TABLE **2.7**

	Before Specialization		After Specialization	
	Fish (kg)	Caribou	Fish (kg)	Caribou
Netsiliks	3	3	6	0
Oonarks	2	2	0	4
Total Production	5	5	6	4

Compare the total production of both commodities before and after specialization.

Specialization has increased the total production of fish by 1 kilogram, but it has also led to a decrease in the total production of caribou by 1. There are no clear gains in consumption from specialization and trade.

10 Firms depend on households for the supply of factors of production. In exchange, households depend on firms for income. Households use that income to buy goods and services from firms, while firms depend on the money they get from household purchases to purchase more factors of production in the next period and renew the circular flow.

Part 1 Wrap Up
Understanding the Scope of Economics

PROBLEM

The economy is a mechanism that allocates scarce resources among competing uses. But how do those allocation decisions get made? In the Canadian economy, markets are the primary institutions that coordinate individual decisions through price adjustments.

Suppose, for simplicity, the Canadian economy produced only two outputs—child-care services and televisions. The production possibility frontier (*PPF*) for the economy appears in Figure P1.1 below. The economy is operating at point *a*, producing Q^0_{cc} units of child-care services and Q^0_{tv} televisions.

FIGURE **P1.1**

a What does the bowed-out (concave) shape of the *PPF* imply about resources? opportunity costs?

b As more women enter the labour force, there is increased demand for child-care services. As a result, the price and quantity of child-care services both increase. At the same time, the demand for televisions falls (perhaps to save money to pay for the additional child-care services). As a result, the price and quantity of televisions both decrease.

On the *PPF* in Figure P1.1, label as point *b* a new combination of child-care services and televisions reflecting the changes in demand.

c Explain how the economy came to produce these new quantities in response to the changing demands of households.

d What determines the distance of the *PPF* from the origin? What determines the precise point on the *PPF* at which the economy operates? What is the true cost of moving from point *a* to point *b* on the *PPF*?

MIDTERM EXAMINATION

You should allocate 30 minutes for this examination (15 questions, 2 minutes per question). For each question, choose the one *best* answer.

1 A *PPF* shows that
  a there is a limit to the production of any one good.
  b to produce more of one good, we must produce less of another good.
  c there are limits to total production with given resources and technology.
  d all of the above are true.
  e none of the above is true.

2 The graph showing the level of a variable across different groups at a point in time is a
  a linear graph.
  b time-series graph.
  c cross-section graph.
  d misleading graph.
  e scatter diagram.

Suppose a society produces only two goods—guns and butter. Three alternative combinations on its *PPF* are given in Table P1.1. Use the information in Table P1.1 to answer Questions **3** and **4**.

TABLE **P1.1** PRODUCTION POSSIBILITIES

Possibility	Units of Butter	Units of Guns
a	8	0
b	6	1
c	0	3

3 In moving from combination *b* to combination *c*, the opportunity cost of producing *one* additional unit of guns is
   a 2 units of butter.
   b 1/2 unit of butter.
   c 6 units of butter.
   d 1/6 unit of butter.
   e 3 units of butter.

4 According to this *PPF*
   a a combination of 6 butter and 1 gun would not employ all resources.
   b a combination of 0 butter and 4 guns is attainable.
   c resources are equally productive in all activities.
   d the opportunity cost of producing guns increases as more guns are produced.
   e the opportunity cost of producing guns decreases as more guns are produced.

5 Which of the following is a normative statement?
   a Pollution is an example of an external cost.
   b Pollution makes people worse off.
   c Firms that pollute should be forced to shut down.
   d Pollution imposes opportunity costs on others.
   e None of the above.

6 The graph of the relationship between two variables that are negatively related
   a is horizontal.
   b slopes upward to the right.
   c is vertical.
   d slopes downward to the right.
   e is linear.

7 In Figure P1.2, the slope of the line is
   a 1.50.
   b 1.25.
   c 1.00.
   d 0.75.
   e 0.50.

FIGURE **P1.2**

8 Other things being equal, which of the following statements is correct?
   1 If unemployment increases, the opportunity cost of attending university decreases.
   2 If men generally earn more than women in the labour market, the opportunity cost of attending university is higher for men than for women.
   a 1 only
   b 2 only
   c 1 and 2
   d Neither 1 nor 2
   e Impossible to judge without additional information

9 The economy is at point *b* on the *PPF* in Figure 1.3. The opportunity cost of increasing the production of *Y* to 50 units is
   a 2 units of *X*.
   b 6 units of *X*.
   c 8 units of *X*.
   d 20 units of *Y*.
   e 30 units of *Y*.

FIGURE **P1.3**

10 Because productive resources are scarce, we must give up some of one good in order to acquire more of another. This is the essence of the concept of

a   specialization.
b   monetary exchange.
c   comparative advantage.
d   absolute advantage.
e   opportunity cost.

11 The scarcity of resources implies that the *PPF* is

a   bowed inward (convex).
b   bowed outward (concave).
c   positively sloped.
d   negatively sloped.
e   linear.

12 If additional units of any good can be produced at a constant opportunity cost, the *PPF* is

a   bowed inward (convex).
b   bowed outward (concave).
c   positively sloped.
d   perfectly horizontal.
e   linear.

13 Marginal cost is the

a   total cost of an activity.
b   additional benefit of a decrease in an activity.
c   additional benefit of an increase in an activity.
d   opportunity cost of a decrease in an activity.
e   opportunity cost of an increase in an activity.

14 If variables *x* and *y* move in opposite directions, they are said to be

a   positively related.
b   negatively related.
c   intimately related.
d   unrelated.
e   siblings.

15 *Ceteris paribus* is a Latin term meaning

a   "Unscrambling cause and effect."
b   "Correlation shows causation."
c   "Causation shows correlation."
d   "Other relevant things remain the same."
e   "Your place or mine."

ANSWERS

Problem

a   The bowed-out shape of the *PPF* implies that resources are not equally productive in all activities; they are nonhomogeneous. With nonhomogeneous resources, there are increasing opportunity costs as production increases of either child-care services or televisions.

b   See Figure P1.1 Solution.

FIGURE **P1.1** SOLUTION

c   The increased demand for child-care services puts upward pressure on the price of child-care services, making it more profitable to produce them. The higher price serves as a signal to firms to shift additional resources to producing child-care services.

Those additional resources come from the television market. The decreased demand for televisions puts downward pressure on the price of televisions, making it less profitable to produce them. The lower price serves as a signal to firms to shift resources to more profitable uses (in child care).

Thus the market economy responds to the changing demands of households by reallocating resources into child-care services from television production. Prices are the signals that coordinate the demand decisions of households with the resource allocation decisions of firms. The market—operating through a combination of price signals, self-interest, and competition— acts like an "invisible hand" to guide resources to the uses that households desire.

d   The distance of the *PPF* from the origin is determined by the quantities of resources and the technology in the economy. The *PPF* shows maximum combinations of outputs (goods and services) that can be produced with given resources and technology.

The precise point on the *PPF* at which the economy operates (e.g., the combination at point *a* of child-care services and televisions) is determined by the demands of households.

The true cost of moving from point *a* to point *b* is the televisions that must be forgone as scarce resources are shifted to produce more child-care services. In other words, the true cost of additional child-care is an opportunity cost—forgone televisions.

Midterm Examination

1   d   **a** and **b** show scarcity, **c** shows opportunity cost. (32–34)

2   c   Definition. Example is a bar chart. (16–18)

3   e   Give up 6 butter to get 2 guns: 6/2 = 3 butter per gun. (32–34)

4   d   Opportunity cost gun between *a* and *b* = 2 butter; between *b* and *c* = 3 butter. *a* on *PPF*, *b* outside *PPF*. (32–34)

5   c   **a** is a true statement (definition); **d** and **b** are positive statements that can be tested. (11–12)

6   d   As *x* increases, *y* decreases. (18–20)

7   d   For example, using points (0, 4) and (16, 16): $\Delta y = 12$ (16 − 4), $\Delta x = 16$ (16 − 0). (22–24)

8   c   Unemployment decreases expected average income from working. Higher opportunity cost for men may not be fair, but is a fact. (10)

9   a   To move from *b* to *a*, quantity *X* decreases from 8 to 6. (33–34)

10   e   Definition. (33–34)

11   d   Scarcity implies opportunity cost, which involves a negative relationship—to get more of *X* you must give up *Y*. (32–34)

12   e   Constant opportunity cost yields constant slope *PPF*. (34)

13   e   Definition; **c** is marginal benefit, **b** and **d** are nonsense. (10, 35)

14   b   Definition. (19–20)

15   d   Definition. (24)

Chapter 3
Demand and Supply

Markets and Prices

Competitive market—many buyers and sellers so no one can influence prices.

Relative price of a good is

♦ its *opportunity cost*—the other goods that must be forgone to buy it.

♦ ratio of its **money price** to the money price of another good.

♦ determined by demand and supply.

Demand

The **quantity demanded** of a good is the amount consumers plan to buy during a given time period at a particular price. The **law of demand** states: "Other things remaining the same, the higher the price of a good, the smaller is the quantity demanded." Higher price reduces quantity demanded for two reasons:

♦ *substitution effect*—with an increase in the relative price of a good, people buy less of it and more of substitutes for the good.

♦ *income effect*—with an increase in the relative price of a good and unchanged incomes, people have less money to spend on all goods, including the good whose price increased.

The **demand curve** represents the inverse relationship between quantity demanded and price, *ceteris paribus*. The demand curve also is a willingness-and-ability-to-pay curve, which measures marginal benefit.

♦ A change in price causes movement along the demand curve. This is called a **change in the quantity demanded**. The higher the price of a good, the lower the quantity demanded.

♦ A shift of the demand curve is called a **change in demand**. The demand curve shifts from changes in

• prices of related goods.

• expected future prices.

• income.

• expected future income and credit.

• population.

• preferences.

♦ Increase in demand—demand curve shifts rightward.

♦ Decrease in demand—demand curve shifts leftward.

♦ For an increase in

• price of a **substitute**—demand shifts rightward.

• price of a **complement**—demand shifts leftward.

• expected future prices—demand shifts rightward.

• income (**normal good**)—demand shifts rightward.

• income (**inferior good**)—demand shifts leftward.

• expected future income or credit (**normal good**)—demand shifts rightward.

• expected future income or credit (**inferior good**)—demand shifts leftward

• population—demand shifts rightward.

• preferences—demand shifts rightward.

Supply

The **quantity supplied** of a good is the amount producers plan to sell during a given time period at a particular price. The **law of supply** states: "Other things remaining the same, the higher the price of a good, the greater is the quantity supplied." Higher price increases quantity supplied because marginal cost increases with increasing quantities. Price must rise for producers to be willing to increase production and incur higher marginal cost.

The **supply curve** represents the positive relationship between quantity supplied and price, *ceteris paribus*. The supply curve is also a minimum-supply-price curve, showing the lowest price at which a producer is willing to sell another unit.

- ◆ A change in price causes movement along the supply curve. This is called a **change in the quantity supplied**. The higher the price of a good, the greater the quantity supplied.

- ◆ A shift of the supply curve is called a **change in supply**. The supply curve shifts from changes in

  - • prices of factors of production.
  - • prices of related goods produced.
  - • expected future prices.
  - • number of suppliers.
  - • technology.
  - • state of nature.

- ◆ Increase in supply—supply curve shifts rightward.

- ◆ Decrease in supply—supply curve shifts leftward.

- ◆ For an increase in

  - • prices of factors of production—supply shifts leftward.
  - • price of a *substitute in production*—supply shifts leftward.
  - • price of a *complement in production*—supply shifts rightward.
  - • expected future prices—supply shifts leftward.
  - • number of suppliers—supply shifts rightward.
  - • technology—supply shifts rightward.
  - • state of nature—supply shifts rightward.

Market Equilibrium

The **equilibrium price** is where the demand and supply curves intersect, where quantity demanded equals quantity supplied.

- ◆ Above the equilibrium price, there is a surplus (quantity supplied > quantity demanded), and price will fall.

- ◆ Below the equilibrium price, there is a shortage (quantity demanded > quantity supplied), and price will rise.

- ◆ Only in equilibrium is there no tendency for the price to change. The **equilibrium quantity** is the quantity bought and sold at the equilibrium price.

Predicting Changes in Price and Quantity

For a single change *either* in demand *or* in supply, *ceteris paribus*, when

- ◆ demand increases, P rises and Q increases.
- ◆ demand decreases, P falls and Q decreases.
- ◆ supply increases, P falls and Q increases.
- ◆ supply decreases, P rises and Q decreases.

When there is a simultaneous change *both* in demand *and* supply, we can determine the effect on either price or quantity. But without information about the relative size of the shifts of the demand and supply curves, the effect on the other variable is ambiguous. *Ceteris paribus*, when

- ◆ both demand and supply increase, P may rise/fall/remain constant and Q increases.

- ◆ both demand and supply decrease, P may rise/fall/remain constant and Q decreases.

- ◆ demand increases and supply decreases, P rises and Q may rise/fall/remain constant.

- ◆ demand decreases and supply increases, P falls and Q may rise/fall/remain constant.

H E L P F U L   H I N T S

I   When you are first learning about demand and supply, think of specific examples to help you understand how to use the concepts. For example, in analysing complementary goods, think about hamburgers and french fries; in analysing substitute goods, think of hamburgers and hot dogs. This will reduce the "abstractness" of the economic theory and make concepts easier to remember.

2 The statement that "price is determined by demand and supply" is a shorthand way of saying that price is determined by all of the factors affecting demand (prices of related goods, expected future prices, income, expected future income and credit, population, preferences) and all of the factors affecting supply (prices of factors of production, prices of related goods produced, expected future prices, number of suppliers, technology, state of nature). The benefit of using demand and supply curves is that they allow us to systematically sort out the influences on price of each of these separate factors. Changes in the factors affecting demand shift the demand curve and move us up or down the given supply curve. Changes in the factors affecting supply shift the supply curve and move us up or down the given demand curve.

Any demand and supply problem requires you to sort out these influences carefully. In so doing, *always draw a graph*, even if it is just a small graph in the margin of a true/false or multiple-choice problem. Graphs are a very efficient way to "see" what happens. As you become comfortable with graphs, you will find them to be effective and powerful tools for systematically organizing your thinking.

Do not make the common mistake of thinking that a problem is so easy that you can do it in your head, without drawing a graph. This mistake will cost you dearly on examinations. Also, when you do draw a graph, be sure to label the axes. As the course progresses, you will encounter many graphs with different variables on the axes. It is easy to become confused if you do not develop the habit of labelling the axes.

3 Another very common mistake among students is failing to *distinguish* correctly between *a shift in a curve* and *a movement along a curve*. This distinction applies both to demand and to supply curves. Many questions in the Self-Test are designed to test your understanding of this distinction, and you can be sure that your instructor will test you heavily on this. The distinction between "shifts in" versus "movements along" a curve is crucial for systematic thinking about the factors influencing demand and supply, and for understanding the determination of equilibrium price and quantity.

Consider the example of the demand curve. The quantity of a good demanded depends on its own price, the prices of related goods, expected future prices, income, expected future income

and credit, population, and preferences. The term "demand" refers to the relationship between the price of a good and the quantity demanded, holding constant all of the other factors on which the quantity demanded depends. This demand relationship is represented graphically by the demand curve. Thus, the effect of a change in price on quantity demanded is already reflected in the slope of the demand curve; the effect of a change in the price of the good itself is given by a movement along the demand curve. This is referred to as a **change in quantity demanded**.

On the other hand, if one of the other factors affecting the quantity demanded changes, the demand curve itself will shift; the quantity demanded *at each price* will change. This shift of the demand curve is referred to as a **change in demand**. The critical thing to remember is that a change in the price of a good will not shift the demand curve; it will only cause a movement along the demand curve. Similarly, it is just as important to distinguish between shifts in the supply curve and movements along the supply curve.

To confirm your understanding, consider the effect (draw a graph!) of an increase in household income on the market for energy bars. First note that an increase in income affects the demand for energy bars and not supply. Next we want to determine whether the increase in income causes a shift in the demand curve or a movement along the demand curve. Will the increase in income increase the quantity of energy bars demanded even if the price of energy bars does not change? Since the answer to this question is yes, we know that the demand curve will shift rightward. Note further that the increase in the demand for energy bars will cause the equilibrium price to rise. This price increase will be indicated by a movement along the supply curve (an increase in the quantity supplied) and will not shift the supply curve itself.

Remember: It is shifts in demand and supply curves that cause the market price to change, not changes in the price that cause demand and supply curves to shift.

4 When analysing the shifts of demand and supply curves in related markets (for substitute goods like beer and wine), it often seems as though the feedback effects from one market to the other can go on endlessly. To avoid confusion, stick to the rule that each curve (demand and supply) for a given market can shift a maximum of *once*. (See Short Answer Problems **4** and **6** for further explanation and examples.)

5 The relationships between price and quantity demanded and supplied can be represented in three equivalent forms: demand and supply schedules, curves, and equations. Text Chapter 3 illustrates schedules and curves, but demand and supply equations are also powerful tools of economic analysis. The Mathematical Note to Chapter 3 (pages 78–79) provides the general form of these equations. The purpose of this Helpful Hint and the next is to further explain the equations and how they can be used to determine the equilibrium values of price and quantity.

Figure 3.1 presents a simple demand and supply example in three equivalent forms: (a) schedules, (b) curves, and (c) equations. The demand and supply schedules in (a) are in the same format as Text Figure 3.7. The price-quantity combinations from the schedules are plotted on the graph in (b), yielding linear demand and supply curves. What is new about this example is the representation of those curves by the equations in (c).

If you recall (Chapter 1 Appendix) the formula for the equation of a straight line $(y = a + bx)$, you can see that the demand equation is the equation of a straight line. Instead of y, P is the dependent variable on the vertical axis, and, instead of x, Q_D is the independent variable on the horizontal axis. The intercept on the vertical axis a is +5, and the slope b is –1. The supply equation is also linear and graphed in the same way, but with Q_S as the independent variable. The supply curve intercept on the vertical axis is +1, and the slope is +1. The negative slope of the demand curve reflects the law of demand, and the positive slope of the supply curve reflects the law of supply.

You can demonstrate the equivalence of the demand schedule, curve, and equation by substituting various values of Q_D from the schedule into the demand equation, and calculating the associated prices. These combinations of quantity demanded and price are the coordinates (Q_D, P) of the points on the demand curve. You can similarly demonstrate the equivalence of the supply schedule, curve, and equation.

FIGURE **3.1**

(a) Demand and Supply Schedules

Price ($)	Q_D	Q_S	Shortage (–)/ Surplus (+)
1	4	0	–4
2	3	1	–2
3	2	2	0
4	1	3	+2
5	0	4	+4

(b) Demand and Supply Curves

(c) Demand and Supply Equations

Demand: $P = 5 - 1Q_D$
Supply: $P = 1 + 1Q_S$

The demand and supply equations are very useful for calculating the equilibrium values of price and quantity. As the schedules and curves both show, two things are true in equilibrium: (1) the price is the same for consumers (the highest price they are willing to pay for the last unit) and producers (the lowest price they are willing to accept for the last unit) and (2) the quantity demanded equals the quantity supplied, so that there are no surpluses or shortages. In terms of the demand and supply equations, this means that, *in equilibrium*,

(1) The price in both equations is the same. We will denote the equilibrium price as P^*.

(2) $Q_D = Q_S$ = the equilibrium quantity bought and sold. We will denote the equilibrium quantity as Q^*.

In equilibrium, the equations become

Demand: $P^* = 5 - 1Q^*$

Supply: $P^* = 1 + 1Q^*$

These equilibrium equations constitute a simple set of simultaneous equations. Since there are two equations (demand and supply) and two unknowns (P^* and Q^*), we can solve for the unknowns.

Begin the solution by setting demand equal to supply:

$$5 - 1Q^* = 1 + 1Q^*$$

Collecting like terms, we find

$$4 = 2Q^*$$

$$2 = Q^*$$

Once we have Q^* (equilibrium quantity), we can solve for the equilibrium price using either the demand or the supply equations. Look first at demand:

$$P^* = 5 - 1Q^*$$

$$P^* = 5 - 1(2)$$

$$P^* = 5 - 2$$

$$P^* = 3$$

Alternatively, substituting Q^* into the supply equation yields the same result:

$$P^* = 1 + 1Q^*$$

$$P^* = 1 + 1(2)$$

$$P^* = 1 + 2$$

$$P^* = 3$$

Once you have solved for Q^*, the fact that substituting it into either the demand or the supply equation yields the correct P^* provides a valuable check on your calculations. If you make a mistake in your calculations, when you substitute Q^* into the demand and supply equations, you will get two different prices. If that happens, you know to recheck your calculations. If you get the same price when you substitute Q^* into the demand and supply equations, you know your calculations are correct.

6 Economists have developed the convention of graphing quantity as the independent variable (on the horizontal x-axis) and price as the dependent variable (on the vertical y-axis), and the foregoing equations reflect this. Despite this convention, economists actually consider real-world prices to be the independent variables and quantities the dependent variables. In that case, the equations would take the form

Demand: $Q_D = 5 - 1P$
Supply: $Q_S = -1 + 1P$

You can solve these equations for yourself to see that they yield exactly the same values for P^* and Q^*. (*Hint:* First solve for P^* and then for Q^*.) Whichever form of the equations your instructor may use, the technique for solving the equations will be similar and the results identical.

S E L F - T E S T

True/False and Explain

Markets and Prices

1 In a competitive market, every single buyer and seller influences price.

2 The relative price of a good is the other goods that must be forgone to buy it.

3 A good's relative price can fall even when its money price rises.

Demand

4 The law of demand tells us that as the price of a good rises, demand decreases.

5 The demand curve is a willingness-and-ability-to-pay curve that measures marginal cost.

6 Hamburgers and fries are complements. If Burger Bar reduces the price of fries, the demand for hamburgers increases.

7 A decrease in income always shifts the demand curve leftward.

Supply

8 A supply curve shows the maximum price at which the last unit will be supplied.

9 If A and B are substitutes, an increase in the price of A always shifts the supply curve of B leftward.

10 When a cow is slaughtered for beef, its hide becomes available to make leather. Thus beef and leather are substitutes in production.

11 If the price of beef rises, there will be an increase in both the supply of leather and the quantity of beef supplied.

Market Equilibrium

12 When the actual price is above the equilibrium price, a shortage occurs.

Predicting Changes in Price and Quantity

13 If the expected future price of a good increases, there will always be an increase in equilibrium price and a decrease in equilibrium quantity.

14 Suppose new firms enter the steel market. *Ceteris paribus*, the equilibrium price of steel will always fall and the quantity will rise.

15 Suppose the demand for PCs increases while the cost of producing them decreases. The equilibrium quantity of PCs will rise and the price will always fall.

Multiple-Choice

Markets and Prices

1 A relative price is
  a the ratio of one price to another.
  b an opportunity cost.
  c a quantity of a "basket" of goods and services forgone.
  d determined by demand and supply.
  e all of the above.

Demand

2 If an increase in the price of good A causes the demand curve for good B to shift leftward,
  a A and B are substitutes in consumption.
  b A and B are complements in consumption.
  c A and B are complements in production.
  d B is an inferior good.
  e B is a normal good.

3 Which of the following could *not* cause an increase in demand for a commodity?
  a an increase in income
  b a decrease in income
  c a decrease in the price of a substitute
  d a decrease in the price of a complement
  e an increase in preferences for the commodity

4 Some sales managers are talking shop. Which of the following quotations refers to a movement along the demand curve?
  a "Since our competitors raised their prices our sales have doubled."
  b "It has been an unusually mild winter; our sales of wool scarves are down from last year."
  c "We decided to cut our prices, and the increase in our sales has been remarkable."
  d "The Green movement has sparked an increase in our sales of biodegradable products."
  e none of the above.

5 If Hamburger Helper is an inferior good, then, *ceteris paribus*, a decrease in income will cause
   a a leftward shift of the demand curve for Hamburger Helper.
   b a rightward shift of the demand curve for Hamburger Helper.
   c a movement up along the demand curve for Hamburger Helper.
   d a movement down along the demand curve for Hamburger Helper.
   e none of the above.

6 A decrease in quantity demanded is represented by a
   a rightward shift of the supply curve.
   b rightward shift of the demand curve.
   c leftward shift of the demand curve.
   d movement upward and to the left along the demand curve.
   e movement downward and to the right along the demand curve.

7 Which of the following "other things" are *not* held constant along a demand curve?
   a income
   b prices of related goods
   c the price of the good itself
   d preferences
   e all of the above

Supply

8 The fact that a decline in the price of a good causes producers to reduce the quantity of the good supplied illustrates
   a the law of supply.
   b the law of demand.
   c a change in supply.
   d the nature of an inferior good.
   e technological improvement.

9 A shift of the supply curve for rutabagas will be caused by
   a a change in preferences for rutabagas.
   b a change in the price of a related good that is a substitute in consumption for rutabagas.
   c a change in income.
   d a change in the price of rutabagas.
   e none of the above.

10 If a factor of production can be used to produce either good *A* or good *B*, then *A* and *B* are
   a substitutes in production.
   b complements in production.
   c substitutes in consumption.
   d complements in consumption.
   e normal goods.

11 Which of the following will shift the supply curve for good *X* leftward?
   a a decrease in the wages of workers employed to produce *X*
   b an increase in the cost of machinery used to produce *X*
   c a technological improvement in the production of *X*
   d a situation where quantity demanded exceeds quantity supplied
   e all of the above

12 Some producers are chatting over a beer. Which of the following quotations refers to a movement along the supply curve?
   a "Wage increases have forced us to raise our prices."
   b "Our new, sophisticated equipment will enable us to undercut our competitors."
   c "Raw material prices have skyrocketed; we will have to pass this on to our customers."
   d "We anticipate a big increase in demand. Our product price should rise, so we are planning for an increase in output."
   e "New competitors in the industry are causing prices to fall."

13 If an increase in the price of good *A* causes the supply curve for good *B* to shift rightward,
   a *A* and *B* are substitutes in consumption.
   b *A* and *B* are complements in consumption.
   c *A* and *B* are substitutes in production.
   d *A* and *B* are complements in production.
   e *A* is a factor of production for making *B*.

Market Equilibrium

14 If the market for Twinkies is in equilibrium,
   a Twinkies must be a normal good.
   b producers would like to sell more at the current price.
   c consumers would like to buy more at the current price.
   d there will be a surplus.
   e equilibrium quantity equals quantity demanded.

15 The price of a good will tend to fall if
   a there is a surplus at the current price.
   b the current price is above equilibrium.
   c the quantity supplied exceeds the quantity demanded at the current price.
   d all of the above are true.
   e none of the above is true.

16 A surplus can be eliminated by
    a increasing supply.
    b government raising the price.
    c decreasing the quantity demanded.
    d allowing the price to fall.
    e allowing the quantity bought and sold to fall.

17 A shortage is the amount by which quantity
    a demanded exceeds quantity supplied.
    b supplied exceeds quantity demanded.
    c demanded increases when the price rises.
    d demanded exceeds the equilibrium quantity.
    e supplied exceeds the equilibrium quantity.

Predicting Changes in Price and Quantity

18 Which of the following will definitely cause an increase in the equilibrium price?
    a an increase in both demand and supply
    b a decrease in both demand and supply
    c an increase in demand combined with a decrease in supply
    d a decrease in demand combined with an increase in supply
    e none of the above

19 Coffee is a normal good. A decrease in income will
    a increase the price of coffee and increase the quantity demanded of coffee.
    b increase the price of coffee and increase the quantity supplied of coffee.
    c decrease the price of coffee and decrease the quantity demanded of coffee.
    d decrease the price of coffee and decrease the quantity supplied of coffee.
    e cause none of the above.

20 An increase in the price of Pepsi (a substitute for coffee) will
    a increase the price of coffee and increase the quantity demanded of coffee.
    b increase the price of coffee and increase the quantity supplied of coffee.
    c decrease the price of coffee and decrease the quantity demanded of coffee.
    d decrease the price of coffee and decrease the quantity supplied of coffee.
    e cause none of the above.

21 A technological improvement lowers the cost of producing coffee. At the same time, preferences for coffee decrease. The *equilibrium quantity* of coffee will
    a rise.
    b fall.
    c remain the same.
    d rise or fall depending on whether the price of coffee falls or rises.
    e rise or fall depending on the relative shifts of demand and supply curves.

22 Since 1980, there has been a dramatic increase in the number of working mothers. On the basis of this information alone, we can predict that the market for child-care services has experienced a(n)
    a increase in demand.
    b decrease in demand.
    c increase in quantity demanded.
    d decrease in quantity supplied.
    e increase in supply.

23 If *A* and *B* are complementary goods (in consumption) and the cost of a factor of production used in the production of *A* decreases, the price of
    a both *A* and *B* will rise.
    b both *A* and *B* will fall.
    c *A* will fall and the price of *B* will rise.
    d *A* will rise and the price of *B* will fall.
    e *A* will fall and the price of *B* will remain unchanged.

24 The demand curve for knobs is $P = 75 - 6Q_D$ and the supply curve for knobs is $P = 35 + 2Q_S$. What is the equilibrium price of a knob?
    a $5
    b $10
    c $40
    d $45
    e None of the above

25 The demand curve for tribbles is $P = 300 - 6Q_D$. The supply curve for tribbles is $P = 20 + 8Q_S$. If the price of a tribble was set at $120, the tribble market would experience
    a equilibrium.
    b excess demand causing a rise in price.
    c excess demand causing a fall in price.
    d excess supply causing a rise in price.
    e excess supply causing a fall in price.

Short Answer Problems

I Explain the difference between wants and demands.

2 The price of PCs has continued to fall even in the face of increasing demand. Explain.

€¢ **3** A tax on crude oil would raise the cost of the primary resource used in the production of gasoline. A proponent of such a tax has claimed that it will not raise the price of gasoline using the following argument. While the price of gasoline may rise initially, that price increase will cause the demand for gasoline to decrease, which will push the price back down. What is wrong with this argument?

4 Brussels sprouts and carrots are substitutes in consumption and, since they can both be grown on the same type of land, substitutes in production too. Suppose there is an increase in the demand for brussels sprouts. Trace the effects on price and quantity traded in both the brussels sprout and the carrot market. (Keep in mind Helpful Hint **4**.)

5 The information given in Table 3.1 is about the behaviour of buyers and sellers of fish at the market on a particular Saturday.

TABLE **3.I**   DEMAND AND SUPPLY
SCHEDULES FOR FISH

Price (per fish)	Quantity Demanded	Quantity Supplied
$0.50	280	40
$1.00	260	135
$1.50	225	225
$2.00	170	265
$2.50	105	290
$3.00	60	310
$3.50	35	320

a On graph paper, draw the demand curve and the supply curve. Be sure to label the axes. What is the equilibrium price?

b We will make the usual *ceteris paribus* assumptions about the demand curve so that it does not shift. List six factors that we are assuming do not change.

c We will also hold the supply curve constant by assuming that six factors do not change. List them.

d Explain briefly what would happen if the price was initially set at $3.

e Explain briefly what would happen if the price was initially set at $1.

f Explain briefly what would happen if the price was initially set at $1.50.

6 The market for wine in Canada is initially in equilibrium with supply and demand curves of the usual shape. Beer is a close substitute for wine; cheese and wine are complements. Use demand and supply diagrams to analyse the effect of each of the following (separate) events on the equilibrium price and quantity in the Canadian wine market. Assume that all of the *ceteris paribus* assumptions continue to hold except for the event listed. For both equilibrium price and quantity you should indicate in each case whether the variable rises, falls, remains the same, or moves ambiguously (may rise or fall).

a The income of consumers falls (wine is a normal good).

b Early frost (state of nature) destroys a large part of the world grape crop.

c A new churning invention reduces the cost of producing cheese.

d A new fermentation technique is invented that reduces the cost of producing wine.

e A new government study is published that links wine drinking and increased heart disease.

f Costs of producing both beer and wine increase dramatically.

€¢ **7** A newspaper reported, "Despite a bumper crop of cherries this year, the price drop for cherries won't be as much as expected because of short supplies of plums and peaches."

a Use a demand and supply graph for the cherry market to explain the effect of the bumper crop alone.

b On the same graph, explain the impact on the cherry market of the short supplies of plums and peaches.

8 Table 3.2 lists the demand and supply schedules for cases of grape jam.

TABLE **3.2** DEMAND AND SUPPLY SCHEDULES FOR GRAPE JAM PER WEEK

Price (per case)	Quantity Demanded (cases)	Quantity Supplied (cases)
$70	20	140
$60	60	120
$50	100	100
$40	140	80
$30	180	60

a On the graph in Figure 3.2, draw the demand and supply curves for grape jam. Be sure to properly label the axes. Label the demand and supply curves D_0 and S_0 respectively.

FIGURE **3.2**

b What are the equilibrium price and quantity in the grape jam market? On your diagram, label the equilibrium point *a*.

c Is there a surplus or shortage at a price of $40? How much?

d The demand and supply schedules can also be represented by the following demand and supply equations:

Demand: $P = 75 - 0.25Q_D$

Supply: $P = 0.5Q_S$

Use these equations to solve for the equilibrium quantity (Q^*); equilibrium price (P^*). (*Hint:* Your answers should be the same as those in **8b**.)

e Suppose the population grows sufficiently that the demand for grape jam increases by 60 cases per week at every price.

   i Construct a table (price, quantity demanded) of the new demand schedule.

   ii Draw the new demand curve on your original graph and label it D_1.

   iii Label the new equilibrium point *b*. What are the new equilibrium price and quantity?

   iv What is the new demand equation? (*Hints:* What is the new slope? What is the new price-axis intercept?)

9 The demand equation for dweedles is

$$P = 8 - 1Q_D$$

The supply equation for dweedles is

$$P = 2 + 1Q_S$$

where P is the price of a dweedle in dollars, Q_D is the quantity of dweedles demanded, and Q_S is the quantity of dweedles supplied. The dweedle market is initially in equilibrium and income is $300.

a What is the equilibrium quantity (Q^*) of dweedles?

b What is the equilibrium price (P^*) of a dweedle?

c As a result of an increase in income to $500, the demand curve for dweedles shifts (the supply curve remains the same). The new demand equation is

$$P = 4 - 1Q_D$$

Use this information to calculate the new equilibrium quantity of dweedles; calculate the new equilibrium price of a dweedle.

d On the graph in Figure 3.3, draw and label: (1) the supply curve, (2) the initial demand curve, (3) the new demand curve.

e   Are dweedles a normal or inferior good? How do you know?

FIGURE **3.3**

10   The demand equation for flubits is

$$P = 80 - 2Q_D$$

The supply equation for flubits is

$$P = 50 + 1Q_S$$

where P is the price of a flubit in dollars, Q_D is the quantity of flubits demanded, and Q_S is the quantity of flubits supplied. Assume that there are no changes in *ceteris paribus* assumptions.

a   If the price of flubits was set at $56, calculate the exact surplus or shortage of flubits.

b   Explain the adjustment process that will bring the situation above to equilibrium.

c   What is the equilibrium quantity (Q^*) of flubits?

d   What is the equilibrium price (P^*) of a flubit?

e   Now assume that as a result of technological advance, the supply curve for flubits shifts (the demand curve remains the same). The new supply equation is

$$P = 20 + 1Q_S$$

Use this information to calculate the new equilibrium quantity of flubits; calculate the new equilibrium price of a flubit.

ANSWERS

True/False and Explain

1   **F**   No single buyer or seller influences price. (58)

2   **T**   Relative price is an opportunity cost. (58)

ⓔ **3**   **T**   If money prices of other goods rise even more, a good's relative price falls. If price of gum rises from $1 to $2, but price of coffee rises from $1 to $4, opportunity cost of pack of gum falls from 1 to 0.5 coffee forgone. (58)

4   **F**   As price rises, *quantity demanded* decreases. (59)

5   **F**   Measures marginal benefit. (60)

6   **T**   Combined meal of hamburger and fries now cheaper. (61)

ⓔ **7**   **F**   Leftward shift for normal good, rightward shift for inferior good. (62)

8   **F**   Supply curve shows minimum price at which last unit supplied. (65)

ⓔ **9**   **F**   True if A and B substitutes in production, but false if substitutes in consumption. (66–67)

ⓔ **10**   **F**   Beef and leather complements in production because produced together of necessity. (65–66)

11   **T**   For complements in production, higher price for one good causes increased quantity supplied and increase in supply other good. (65–66)

12   **F**   At $P >$ equilibrium P, there is surplus (quantity supplied > quantity demanded). (68–69)

ⓔ **13**   **F**   Higher expected future prices cause rightward shift demand and leftward shift supply. Price rises, but Δ quantity depends on relative magnitude shifts. (61–62, 66, 75)

14   **T**   Increased number of firms causes rightward shift supply leading to fall in price and increased quantity. (71)

15   **F**   Quantity will increase but Δ price depends on relative magnitude shifts in demand and supply. (75)

Multiple-Choice

1   **e**   Definitions. (58)

2   **b**   For example, higher-price fries causes decreased demand for hamburgers. (61)

3   **c**   Both income answers could be correct if commodity were normal (**a**) or inferior (**b**). (61–62)

4   **c**   Other answers describe shifts of demand curve. (61–63)

5   **b**   Changes in income shift demand curve rather than causing movement along demand curve. (62)

6   **d**   Decreased quantity demanded is movement up along demand curve. Could also be caused by leftward shift supply. (62–63)

7   **c**   "Other things" shift demand curve. Only price can change along fixed demand curve. (63)

8   **a**   Question describes movement down along supply curve. (64–65)

9   **e**   Answers **a**, **b**, and **c** shift demand, while **d** causes movement along supply curve. (65–67)

10   **a**   Definition of substitute in production. (65–66)

11   **b**   Higher price factor of production shifts supply leftward. (65–66)

12   **d**   Other answers describe shifts of supply curve. (66–67)

13   **d**   Definition of complements in production. Price changes related goods in consumption shift demand. (65–66)

14   **e**   At equilibrium price, plans producers and consumers match; quantity demanded = quantity supplied. (68–69)

15   **d**   All answers describe price above equilibrium price. (68–69)

16   **d**   Other answers make surplus (excess quantity supplied) larger. (68–69)

17   **a**   Shortage is horizontal distance between demand and supply curves at price below equilibrium price. (68–69)

18   **c**   Answers **a** and **b** have indeterminate effect on price, while **d** causes lower price. (75)

19   **d**   Demand shifts leftward. (70–71)

20   **b**   Demand shifts rightward. (70–71)

21   **e**   Supply shifts rightward, demand shifts leftward, price definitely falls. (75)

22   **a**   More working mothers increases preferences for child care, causing increased demand for child-care services. (70–75)

23   **c**   Supply A shifts rightward causing lower-price A. This increases demand for B, causing higher price of B. (70–75)

24   **d**   See Helpful Hint **5**. Set demand equal to supply, solve for $Q^* = 5$. Substitute $Q^* = 5$ into either demand or supply equation to solve for P^*. (78–79)

25   **b**   At $P = \$120$, $Q_D = 30$, and $Q_S = 12.5$. Excess demand so price will rise. (69, 78–79)

Short Answer Problems

1   Wants are our unlimited desires for goods and services without regard to our ability or willingness to make the sacrifices necessary to obtain them. The existence of scarcity means that many of those wants will not be satisfied. On the other hand, if we demand something, then we want it, can afford it, and have made a definite plan to buy it. Demands reflect decisions about which wants to satisfy.

2   Due to the tremendous pace of technological advance, not only has the demand for PCs (personal computers) been increasing, but the supply has been increasing as well. Indeed, supply has been increasing much more rapidly than demand, which has resulted in falling prices. Thus *much* (but not all) of the increase in sales of PCs reflects a movement down along a demand curve rather than a shift in demand.

3   This argument confuses a movement along an unchanging demand curve with a shift in the demand curve. The proper analysis is as follows. The increase in the price of oil (the primary factor of production in the production of gasoline) will shift the supply curve of gasoline leftward. This will cause the equilibrium price of gasoline to increase and thus the quantity demanded of gasoline will decrease. Demand itself will not decrease—that is, the demand curve will not shift. The decrease in supply causes a movement along an unchanged demand curve.

4 The answer to this question requires us to trace through the effects on the two graphs in Figure 3.4: (a) for the brussels sprout market and (b) for the carrot market. The sequence of effects occurs in order of the numbers on the graphs.

Look first at the market for brussels sprouts. The increase in demand shifts the demand curve rightward from D_0 to D_1 (1), and the price of brussels sprouts rises. This price rise has two effects (2) on the carrot market. Since brussels sprouts and carrots are substitutes in consumption, the demand curve for carrots shifts rightward from D_0 to D_1. And, since brussels sprouts and carrots are substitutes in production, the supply curve of carrots shifts leftward from S_0 to S_1. Both of these shifts in the carrot market raise the price of carrots, causing feedback effects on the brussels sprout market. But remember the rule (Helpful Hint **4**) that each curve (demand and supply) for a given market can shift a maximum of *once*. Since the demand curve for brussels sprouts has already shifted, we can only shift the supply curve from S_0 to S_1 (3) because of the substitutes in production relationship. Each curve in each market has now shifted once and the analysis must stop. We can predict that the net effects are increases in the equilibrium prices of both brussels sprouts and carrots, and indeterminate changes in the equilibrium quantities in both markets.

FIGURE **3.4**

(a) Brussel Sprout Market

(b) Carrot Market

5 a The demand and supply curves are shown in Figure 3.5. The equilibrium price is $1.50 per fish.

FIGURE **3.5**

b Prices of related goods; expected future prices; income; expected future income and credit; population; preferences.

c Prices of productive resources; prices of related goods produced; expected future prices; number of suppliers; technology; state of nature.

d At a price of $3, quantity supplied (310) exceeds quantity demanded (60). Fish sellers find themselves with surplus fish. Rather than be stuck with unsold fish (which yields no revenue), some sellers cut their price in an attempt to increase the quantity of fish demanded. Competition forces other sellers to follow suit, and the price falls until it reaches the equilibrium price of $1.50, while quantity demanded increases until it reaches the equilibrium quantity of 225 units.

e At a price of $1, the quantity demanded (260) exceeds the quantity supplied (135)—there is a shortage. Unrequited fish buyers bid up the price in an attempt to get the "scarce" fish. As prices continue to be bid up as long as there is excess demand, quantity supplied increases in response to higher prices. Price and quantity supplied both rise until they reach the equilibrium price ($1.50) and quantity (225 units).

f At a price of $1.50, the quantity supplied exactly equals the quantity demanded (225). There is no excess demand (shortage) or excess supply (surplus), and therefore no tendency for the price or quantity to change.

6 The demand and supply diagrams for parts **a** to **e** are shown in Figure 3.6.

FIGURE **3.6**

(a)

(b)

(c)

(d)

(e)

f Questions like this require the examination of two separate but related markets—the beer and wine markets. Since this kind of question often causes confusion for students, Figure 3.7 gives a more detailed explanation of the answer.

Look first at the beer market. The increase in the cost of beer production shifts the supply curve of beer leftward from S_0 to S_1. The resulting rise in the price of beer affects the wine market since beer and wine are substitutes (in consumption).

Turning to the wine market, there are two shifts to examine. The increase in beer prices causes the demand for wine to shift rightward from D_0 to D_1. The increase in the cost of wine production shifts the supply curve of wine leftward from S_0 to S_1. This is the end of the analysis, since the question only asks about the wine market. The final result is a rise in the equilibrium price of wine and an ambiguous change in the quantity of wine. Although the diagram shows $Q_1 = Q_0$, Q_1 may be $\geq$ or $\leq Q_0$.

FIGURE **3.7**

(a) Beer Market

(b) Wine Market

Many students rightfully ask, "But doesn't the rise in wine prices then shift the demand curve for beer rightward, causing a rise in beer prices and an additional increase in the demand for wine?" This question, which is correct in principle, is about the dynamics of adjustment, and these graphs are only capable of analysing once-over shifts of demand or supply. We could shift the demand for beer rightward, but the resulting rise in beer prices would lead us to shift the demand for wine a *second time*. In practice, stick to the rule that each curve (demand and supply) for a given market can shift a maximum of *once*.

7 a The demand and supply curves for the cherry market are shown in Figure 3.8.

FIGURE **3.8**

Cherry Market

Suppose D_0 and S_0 represent the demand and supply curves for cherries last year. This year's bumper crop increases supply to S_1. Other things being equal, the price of cherries would fall from P_0 to P_1.

b But other things are not equal. Short supplies of plums and peaches (their supply curves have shifted leftward) drive up their prices. The increase in the prices of plums and peaches, which are substitutes in consumption for cherries, increases the demand for cherries to D_1. The net result is that the price of cherries only falls to P_2 instead of all the way to P_1.

8 a The demand and supply curves for grape jam are shown in Figure 3.2 Solution.

FIGURE **3.2** SOLUTION

b The equilibrium is given at the intersection of the demand and supply curves (labelled point *a*). The equilibrium price is $50 per case and the equilibrium quantity is 100 cases per week.

c At a price of $40 there is a shortage of 60 cases per week.

d In equilibrium, the equations become:

Demand: $P^* = 75 - 0.25Q^*$

Supply: $P^* = 0.5Q^*$

To solve for Q^*, set demand equal to supply:

$$75 - 0.25Q^* = 0.5Q^*$$

$$75 = 0.75Q^*$$

$$100 = Q^*.$$

To solve for P^*, we can substitute Q^* into either the demand or supply equations. Look at demand first:

$$P^* = 75 - 0.25Q^*$$

$$P^* = 75 - 0.25(100)$$

$$P^* = 75 - 25$$

$$P^* = 50$$

Alternatively, substituting Q^* into the supply equation yields the same result:

$$P^* = 0.5Q^*$$

$$P^* = 0.5(100)$$

$$P^* = 50$$

e i Table 3.3 also contains the (unchanged) quantity supplied, for reference purposes.

TABLE **3.3** NEW DEMAND AND UNCHANGED SUPPLY SCHEDULES FOR GRAPE JAM PER WEEK

Price (per case)	Quantity Demanded (cases)	Quantity Supplied (cases)
$70	80	140
$60	120	120
$50	160	100
$40	200	80
$30	240	60

ii The graph of the new demand curve, D_1, is shown in Figure 3.2 Solution.

iii The new equilibrium price is $60 per case and the quantity is 120 cases of grape jam per week.

iv The new demand equation is $P = 90 - 0.25Q_D$. Notice that the slope of the new demand equation is the same as the slope of the original demand equation. An increase in demand of 60 cases at every price results in a rightward *parallel* shift of the demand curve. Since the two curves are parallel, they have the same slope. The figure of 90 is the price-axis intercept of the new demand curve, which you can see on your graph. *Remember:* The demand equation is the equation of a straight line ($y = a + bx$)—in this case, $a = 90$.

If you want additional practice in the use of demand and supply equations for calculating equilibrium values of price and quantity, you can use the new demand curve equation together with the supply curve equation to calculate the answers you found in **e iii**.

9 In equilibrium, the equations become

Demand: $P^* = 8 - 1Q^*$
Supply: $P^* = 2 + 1Q^*$

a To solve for Q^*, set demand equal to supply:

$$8 - 1Q^* = 2 + 1Q^*$$

$$6 = 2Q^*$$

$$3 = Q^*$$

b To solve for P^*, we can substitute Q^* into either the demand or supply equations. Look first at demand:

$$P^* = 8 - 1Q^*$$

$$P^* = 8 - 1(3)$$

$$P^* = 8 - 3$$

$$P^* = 5$$

Alternatively, substituting Q^* into the supply equation yields the same result:

$$P^* = 2 + 1Q^*$$

$$P^* = 2 + 1(3)$$

$$P^* = 2 + 3$$

$$P^* = 5$$

c In equilibrium, the equations are

Demand: $P^* = 4 - 1Q^*$
Supply: $P^* = 2 + 1Q^*$

To solve for Q^*, set demand equal to supply:

$$4 - 1Q^* = 2 + 1Q^*$$

$$2 = 2Q^*$$

$$1 = Q^*$$

To solve for P^*, we can substitute Q^* into either the demand or supply equations. Look first at demand:

$$P^* = 4 - 1Q^*$$

$$P^* = 4 - 1(1)$$

$$P^* = 4 - 1$$

$$P^* = 3$$

Alternatively, substituting Q^* into the supply equation yields the same result:

$$P^* = 2 + 1Q^*$$

$$P^* = 2 + 1(1)$$

$$P^* = 2 + 1$$

$$P^* = 3$$

d The supply curve, initial demand curve, and new demand curve for dweedles are shown in Figure 3.3 Solution.

FIGURE **3.3** SOLUTION

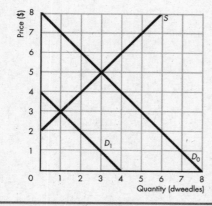

e Dweedles are an inferior good. An increase in income (from $300 to $500) caused a decrease in demand—the demand curve for dweedles shifted leftward.

10 a Substitute the price of $56 into the demand and supply equations to calculate the quantities demanded and supplied at that price. This is the mathematical equivalent of what you do on a graph when you identify a price on the vertical axis, move your eye across to the demand (or supply) curve, and then move your eye down to read the quantity on the horizontal axis.

Substituting into the demand equation, we find

$$P = 80 - 2Q_D$$

$$56 = 80 - 2Q_D$$

$$2Q_D = 24$$

$$Q_D = 12.$$

Substituting into the supply equation,

$$P = 50 + 1Q_S$$

$$56 = 50 + 1 Q_S$$

$$6 = Q_S$$

Quantity demanded exceeds quantity supplied by 6 (12 − 6), so there is a shortage of 6 flubits.

b A shortage means the price was set below the equilibrium price. Competition between consumers for the limited number of flubits will bid up the price and increase the quantity supplied until we reach the equilibrium price and quantity.

c In equilibrium, the equations are

Demand: $P^* = 80 - 2Q^*$

Supply: $P^* = 50 + 1Q^*$

To solve for Q^*, set demand equal to supply:

$$80 - 2Q^* = 50 + 1Q^*$$

$$30 = 3Q^*$$

$$10 = Q^*$$

d To solve for P^*, substitute Q^* into the demand equation:

$$P^* = 80 - 2Q^*$$

$$P^* = 80 - 2(10)$$

$$P^* = 80 - 20$$

$$P^* = 60$$

You can check this answer yourself by substituting Q^* into the supply equation.

e The new equilibrium equations are

Demand: $P^* = 80 - 2Q^*$

Supply: $P^* = 20 + 1Q^*$

To solve for Q^*, set demand equal to supply:

$$80 - 2Q^* = 20 + 1Q^*$$

$$60 = 3Q^*$$

$$20 = Q^*$$

To solve for P^*, substitute Q^* into the supply equations:

$$P^* = 20 + 1Q^*$$

$$P^* = 20 + 1(20)$$

$$P^* = 20 + 20$$

$$P^* = 40$$

You can check this answer yourself by substituting Q^* into the demand equation.

Part 2 Wrap Up
Understanding How Markets Work

PROBLEM

The finance minister has asked your boss at the finance department, Dr. Ina Lastic, to estimate the effects of levying a $24-per-carton tax on cigarettes. Dr. Lastic predicts that the tax will raise significant tax revenues (at least $30 million) because cigarette demand is inelastic.

Unfortunately, Dr. Lastic is unaware of a recent study you read in *The Globe and Mail* about past tax increases that found "Ottawa has not received the entire tax windfall it expected from increased cigarette levies because of growing tobacco smuggling."

She has asked you to perform the following detailed analysis for her predictions. The demand and supply curves (without taxes) for cigarettes are given in Figure P2.1. The before-tax price is $28 per carton, and the before-tax quantity is 2.25 million cartons per year.

a Draw the new "S + tax" curve on Figure P2.1.

b According to Dr. Lastic's predictions, what is the after-tax equilibrium price? equilibrium quantity?

c Calculate her predicted tax revenues.

d Check to see if Dr. Lastic's claim that the demand for cigarettes is inelastic is correct by calculating η between the before-tax equilibrium and the after-tax equilibrium. Was she right?

FIGURE **P2.1** CANADIAN CIGARETTE MARKET

e Dr. Lastic gets high marks for economics so far. Nonetheless, you respectfully point out that her revenue prediction is wrong because she hasn't taken into account the effects of smuggling. Showing an uncharacteristic willingness to stretch herself, she replies, "I'm listening. What's *your* prediction of tax revenue?"

Here's your chance to impress the boss. You know that the supply curve of cigarettes in the United States is the same as the before-tax supply curve in Canada. You have estimated the cost of breaking the law (*CBL*) to suppliers at $16 per carton and risk to consumers of buying smuggled cigarettes is so small that their *CBL* is effectively zero. Use this information to answer the following questions.

i Draw and label any appropriate new curve(s) on Figure P2.1.

ii What is *your* prediction of the after-tax price of a carton of cigarettes? the quantity of cigarettes sold legally? the quantity of smuggled cigarettes sold illegally? (*Hint:* The price of legal and illegal cigarettes will be equal because they are perfect substitutes.)

iii What is your prediction of tax revenue?

MIDTERM EXAMINATION

You should allocate 40 minutes for this examination (20 questions, 2 minutes per question). For each question, choose the one *best* answer.

1 Acadia and Breton have free trade. Acadia imports cheese from Breton and exports sheep to Breton. If Acadia imposes a tariff on cheese, Acadia's cheese-producing industry will
a expand, and its sheep industry will contract.
b expand, and its sheep industry will expand.
c contract, and its sheep industry will contract.
d contract, and its sheep industry will expand.
e expand, and its sheep industry will be unchanged.

2 The magnitude of *both* the elasticity of demand and the elasticity of supply depends on
a the resource substitution possibilities.
b the proportion of income spent on a good.
c the time elapsed since the price change.
d the technological conditions of production.
e none of the above factors.

3 If an increase in price causes a decrease in total revenue, price elasticity of demand is
a negative.
b zero.
c greater than zero but less than one.
d equal to one.
e greater than one.

4 The marginal benefit of a good is
a the maximum amount a person is willing to pay for an additional unit.
b the minimum amount a person is willing to pay for an additional unit.
c equal to marginal cost.
c greater than marginal cost.
e less than marginal cost.

5 The proportion of a sales tax paid by consumers will be greater the more
  1 elastic is demand.
  2 inelastic is demand.
  3 elastic is supply.
  4 inelastic is supply.
a 2 only
b 1 and 3
c 1 and 4
d 2 and 3
e 2 and 4

6 The "big tradeoff" is between
a efficiency and fairness.
b fair results and fair rules.
c equality of income and equality of opportunity.
d the symmetry principle and utilitarianism.
e consumer surplus and producer surplus.

7 If both demand and supply increase, equilibrium price
a will rise and quantity will increase.
b will fall and quantity will increase.
c could rise or fall and quantity will increase.
d will rise and quantity could either increase or decrease.
e will fall and quantity could either increase or decrease.

8 If turnips are an inferior good, then, *ceteris paribus*, a rise in the price of turnips will cause
a a decrease in the demand for turnips.
b an increase in the demand for turnips.
c a decrease in the supply of turnips.
d an increase in the supply of turnips.
e none of the above.

9 In Figure P2.2, if the minimum wage is set at $6 per hour, what is the level of unemployment in millions of hours?
a 50
b 40
c 20
d 10
e 0

FIGURE **P2.2**

10 A demand curve is
  a a consumer surplus curve.
  b a marginal benefit curve.
  c a minimum-willingness-to-pay curve.
  d all of the above.
  e none of the above.

11 If a 10 percent increase in income causes a 10 percent decrease in the consumption of widgets (at a constant price),
  a the price elasticity of demand for widgets equals 1.
  b the income elasticity of demand for widgets is negative.
  c the income elasticity of demand for widgets equals 1.
  d widgets are a normal good.
  e none of the above is true.

12 A price floor set below the equilibrium price results in
  a excess supply.
  b excess demand.
  c the equilibrium price.
  d an increase in supply.
  e a decrease in demand.

13 When there is underproduction of a good,
  a the sum of consumer surplus and producer surplus is greater than the sum for an efficient allocation.
  b the sum of consumer surplus and producer surplus is less than the sum for an efficient allocation.
  c deadweight loss is less than for an efficient allocation.
  d consumer surplus only is lost.
  e producer surplus only is lost.

14 A decrease in the price of X from \$6 to \$4 causes an increase in the quantity of Y demanded (at the current price of Y) from 900 to 1,100 units. What is the cross elasticity of demand between X and Y?
  a 0.5
  b −0.5
  c 2
  d −2
  e **a** or **b**, depending on whether X and Y are substitutes or complements

15 A decrease in quantity supplied is represented by a
  a movement down the supply curve.
  b movement up the supply curve.
  c leftward shift of the supply curve.
  d rightward shift of the supply curve.
  e rightward shift of the demand curve.

16 At current output, the marginal benefit of shoehorns is less than marginal cost. To achieve an efficient allocation,
  1 shoehorn output must increase.
  2 shoehorn output must decrease.
  3 the marginal benefit of shoehorns will rise.
  4 the marginal cost of shoehorns will rise.
  a 1 and 3
  b 1 and 4
  c 2 and 3
  d 2 and 4
  e 1 only

17 Farmland can be used to produce either cattle or corn. If the demand for cattle increases,
  a demand for corn will increase.
  b supply of corn will increase.
  c demand for corn will decrease.
  d supply of corn will decrease.
  e **b** and **c**.

18 Refer to Figure P2.3. The opportunity cost of 1 beer in Partyland is _____, and the opportunity cost of 1 beer in Cowabunga is _____.
  a dependent on where on the *PPF* we measure it; dependent on where on the *PPF* we measure it
  b 100 pizzas; 25 pizzas
  c 3 pizzas; 1 pizza
  d 1 pizza; 1 pizza
  e 1 pizza; 1/3 pizza

FIGURE **P2.3** PARTYLAND AND
COWABUNGA—*PPF* FOR BEER
AND PIZZA

19 Refer to Figure P2.3. The opportunity cost of 1
pizza in Partyland is _____, and the
opportunity cost of 1 pizza in Cowabunga is
_____.

    a dependent on where on the *PPF* we measure
it; dependent on where on the *PPF* we
measure it

    b 100 beers; 25 beers

    c 3 beers; 1 beer

    d 1 beer; 1 beer

    e 1 beer; 3 beers

20 Refer to Figure P2.3. If trade occurs between
Partyland and Cowabunga,

    a there will be a lot of drunk turtles.

    b Partyland will export both pizza and beer,
because it has a comparative advantage in
both.

    c Cowabunga will export both pizza and beer,
because it has a comparative advantage in
both.

    d Partyland will export pizza, and Cowabunga
will export beer.

    e Partyland will export beer, and Cowabunga
will export pizza.

ANSWERS

Problem

    a See Figure P2.1 Solution. Ignore the curve
S + *CBL* for now.

FIGURE **P2.1** SOLUTION
CANADIAN CIGARETTE MARKET

    b The after-tax equilibrium price is $46 per carton.
The after-tax equilibrium quantity is 1.5 million
cartons per year.

    c Tax revenue is 1.5 million cartons × $24 per
carton = $36 million per year.

    d

$$\eta = \left| \frac{\dfrac{\Delta Q}{Q_{ave}}}{\dfrac{\Delta P}{P_{ave}}} \right|$$

$$\eta = \left| \frac{\dfrac{-.75}{1.875}}{\dfrac{18}{37}} \right| = \frac{.4}{.486} = .82$$

The demand curve is inelastic ($\eta < 1$) between
the two equilibrium points. Dr. Lastic's
predictions about tax revenue (without
smuggling) and elasticity were correct.

    e **i** See Figure P2.1 Solution. Since the *CBL* to
consumers is zero, the demand curve does not
shift. The smugglers' supply curve is
S + *CBL*.

        ii Since consumers can buy cigarettes from
smugglers at a price of $40 per carton, no one is
willing to buy at the higher legal price of $46.
The legal price is bid down to $40. At that price,
legal suppliers will supply 0.75 million cartons
(read off of the *S* + *tax* curve), and total market

demand is 1.75 million cartons. Smugglers supply the difference, 1 million cartons.

iii Tax revenue is 0.75 million cartons × $24 per carton = only $18 million per year.

Dr. Lastic is impressed. She says, "When I studied economics, we were taught that illegal activities were the business of law enforcement officials, not economists. What you have shown is that almost any activity can be analysed from an economic perspective. Well done. Let's draft our reply to the minister."

Midterm Examination

1 a Tariff increases domestic price of cheese, decreasing imports, increasing domestic production. Decreased imports = decreased exports in Breton, decreasing its income, decreasing its imports = decrease in Acadia's exports, decreasing Acadia's sheep production. (159–161)

㊉ **2 c** **a**, **d** affect η_s only. **b** affects η only. (91, 97–98)

3 e Total revenue test. (90)

4 a Definition. Relation to *MC* depends if allocation is efficient or not. (110–111)

5 d Definition. (135–138)

6 a Definition. (119)

7 c Rightward shifts demand and supply must increase equilibrium quantity, but effect on price indeterminate. (74–75)

㊉ **8 e** Rise in *P* causes movement along demand curve. (59–63)

9 b Quantity supplied (50) > quantity demanded (10). (133–134)

10 b Also a *maximum* willingness to pay curve. (110–111)

11 b $\eta_y = (\% \Delta Q_D)/(\% \Delta \text{ income}) = -10/10 = -1$; widgets inferior good. (94)

㊉ **12 c** Draw graph. Floor doesn't prevent *P* rising from excess demand. (133–134)

13 b Deadweight loss reduces both consumer and producer surplus relative to an efficient allocation. (115–116)

14 b $\eta_x = (\% \Delta Q_D^Y)/(\% \Delta P^X) = (200/1{,}000)/(-2/5) = -0.5$. (93–94)

15 a Illustration of law of supply. (64–67)

16 c With decreasing *Q*, *MB* must rise and *MC* fall. (114)

17 d Cattle and corn substitutes in production. Increased demand for cattle raises price of cattle, causing decreased supply of corn. (64–66)

18 e Opportunity cost of 1 more beer = lost pizza. For Partyland, going from 0 beer to 25 beers costs 25 pizzas (one for one). Do same calculation for Cowabunga. (154–156)

19 e Same type of calculation as in **3**. (154–156)

20 d Each exports where have comparative advantage (lowest opportunity cost). (154–156)

Chapter 20
Measuring GDP and Economic Growth

Gross Domestic Product

Gross domestic product (GDP)—market value of all final goods and services produced within a country in given time period.

- ♦ Total production measured by market value of each good.

- ♦ Only new **final goods** (bought by final users) measured, not **intermediate goods** (bought by firms from firms, used as inputs in production).

- ♦ GDP measures total production *and* total income *and* total expenditure.

Circular flow of expenditure and income shows four economic sectors (firms, households, governments, rest of world) operating in factor markets and goods (and services) markets.

- ♦ Households sell factor services to firms in return for income—total household income = aggregate income (Y).

- ♦ Firms produce goods and services, and sell **consumption expenditure** (C) to households.

- ♦ Firms' expenditures on **investment** (I = purchase of *new* capital + additions to inventory).

- ♦ Governments buy goods and services from firms (**government expenditures** (G)). Governments also collect taxes and make financial transfers to households and firms, but these not part of circular flow.

- ♦ Rest of world buys our **exports** (X) and sells us **imports** (M): **net exports** = (exports—imports).

Circular flow shows that aggregate income = aggregate production = aggregate expenditure:

$$Y = C + I + G + X - M$$

Capital stock is plant, equipment, buildings, and inventories used to produce goods and services.

- ♦ Investment (I) = purchase of *new* capital.

- ♦ **Depreciation** = decrease in value of firm's capital because of wear and tear.

- ♦ **Gross investment** = net investment + replacing depreciated capital.

- ♦ Δ capital stock = **net investment** = gross investment – depreciation.

Measuring Canada's GDP

Statistics Canada measures GDP two ways on basis of equality:

income = production = expenditure

- ♦ Expenditure approach measures $C + I + G + X - M$.

- ♦ *Income approach* adds up all incomes paid from firms to households (with some adjustments).

  - • Net domestic income at factor cost = wages, etc. + profits + interest/investment income + farmers' income + nonfarm unincorporated business income.

  - • Net domestic product at market prices = net domestic income + indirect taxes – subsidies.

  - • GDP = net domestic product + depreciation.

- ♦ Gap between expenditure and income approaches is **statistical discrepancy**, which arises due to measurement problems.

GDP increases from production of more goods and services, or from higher prices for goods and services.

- ♦ **Nominal GDP**—value of final goods and services produced in a given year valued at that year's prices = sum of expenditures on goods and services.

◆ **Real GDP**—value of final goods and services produced in given year when valued at prices of reference base year. Real GDP measures changes in production only.

◆ Real GDP calculated using quantities produced in each year, but valued with prices from reference base year.

  • In reference base year,
    real GDP = nominal GDP.

  • To calculate real GDP in current year, multiply current year quantity by base year price for each good, and sum resulting values.

The Uses and Limitations of Real GDP

Real GDP used to compare standards of living over time and across countries.

  ◆ One method of comparison is **real GDP per person** (real GDP/population)—value of goods and services enjoyed by average person.

  ◆ Canada's real GDP per person over time shows growth of potential GDP per person (with slowdown after 1960s) as well as fluctuations of real GDP around potential GDP.

    • **Potential GDP**—real GDP when labour, capital, land, and entrepreneurial ability fully employed.

  ◆ Lower growth rates of real GDP per person after 1970s lead to accumulated gap in real GDP (**Lucas wedge**).

  ◆ **Business cycles**—fluctuations of pace of expansion of real GDP.

    • Each cycle has two turning points (a peak and a trough), and two phases (**recession** when real GDP decreases for two or more quarters, and **expansion** when real GDP increases).

International comparisons of real GDP per capita are further flawed by currency conversion problems.

  ◆ Using market exchange rates, U.S. real GDP per person is 19 times that of China.

  ◆ Using **purchasing power parity** or **PPP** prices (prices prevailing in one country such as U.S.), U.S. real GDP per person only 8 times China's.

Real GDP as measure of economic well-being flawed because:

  ◆ Real GDP does not include factors increasing economic well-being (household production,

underground economic activity, health, life expectancy, leisure, political freedom, social justice).

  ◆ Real GDP does not include factors that lower economic well-being (pollution).

  ◆ The Human Development Index is broader measure of economic well-being that includes health and education measures, as well as real GDP per person.

HELPFUL HINTS

1 Studying the circular flow and national accounts can be boring, but it is useful for several reasons. First, they provide crucial equalities that are the starting point for our economic model—studying this material will help you pass the course! Second, many current debates involve tradeoffs between economic growth and environmental damage. Understanding what GDP does and does not measure is crucial to this debate. Third, in macroeconomics we study how several markets operate simultaneously in a joint, interrelated equilibrium—the circular flow gives us our first taste of this interrelation.

2 One of the key equations in this and future chapters is the identity:

$$Y = C + I + G + X - M$$

which underlies Chapters 26 and 27.

Macroeconomics tries to understand what affects GDP, and we start by measuring production (GDP). However, we cannot directly measure production easily. The circular flow helps us measure it indirectly. In the circular flow, production is purchased by the four economic decision makers (measured by expenditure), and money earned from these sales is used to pay incomes. Therefore, production can be measured in three equivalent ways:

income = expenditure = value of production (GDP)

Therefore:

Y (income) $= C + I + G + X - M$ (expenditure)

3 Be sure to distinguish carefully between intermediate goods and investment goods. Both are goods sold by one firm to another, but they differ in terms of their use. Intermediate goods are processed and then resold, while investment goods are final goods. Also note that national income accounts include purchases of residential housing as investment because housing, like business capital stock, provides a continuous stream of value over time.

4 Note the difference between government expenditures on goods and services (*G*) and government transfer payments. Both involve payments by government, but transfer payments are not payments for currently produced goods and services. Instead, they are simply a flow of money, just like (negative) taxes.

5 It is important to understand the difference between real and nominal GDP. Nominal GDP is the value, *in current prices*, of the output of final goods and services in the economy in a year. Real GDP evaluates those final goods and services *at the prices prevailing in a base year (constant prices)*.

Nominal GDP can rise from one year to the next, either because prices rise or because output of goods and services rises. A rise in real GDP, however, means that output of goods and services has risen.

If we had a simple economy that produced only pizzas, this rise in real GDP would be easy to measure—are there more pizzas to eat? In a multiple-good economy, we have a more complex task, and must turn to a weighted average of goods and services we produce.

6 Some instructors will cover the Mathematical Note on the chain-weighted output index method. It is a difficult concept, making it worth summarizing the steps:

a Calculate the value of the current year's quantities and the previous year's quantities using the *previous* year's prices, and calculate the percentage change in the value of the quantities from last year to this year (define %Δ as percentage change):

% Δ in value of production at previous prices =

$$\frac{\text{Sum of current quantities at previous prices} - \text{Sum of previous quantities at previous prices}}{\text{Sum of previous quantities at previous prices}} \times 100$$

b Calculate the value of the current year's quantities and the previous year's quantities using the *current* year's prices, and calculate the percentage change in the value of the quantities from last year to this year:

% Δ in value of production at current prices =

$$\frac{\text{Sum of current quantities at current prices} - \text{Sum of previous quantities at current prices}}{\text{Sum of previous quantities at current prices}} \times 100$$

c The average of these two percentage changes is the percentage change in real GDP:

% Δ in real GDP =

$$\frac{\text{\% Δ in value of production at previous prices} + \text{\% Δ in value of production at current prices}}{2}$$

d Apply this percentage change to last year's real GDP to get this year's real GDP:

This year's real GDP = last year's real GDP × [1 + (%Δ in real GDP)/100]

e By applying this method to each year's quantities, we can link each year's real GDP back to the base year. For example, next year's real GDP would be calculated from the change in real GDP between this year and next year, using this year and next year's prices.

SELF-TEST

True/False and Explain

Gross Domestic Product

1 GDP measures intermediate goods, not final goods.

2 Net investment gives the net addition to the capital stock.

3 In the aggregate economy, income is equal to expenditure and to GDP.

4 If exports currently equal imports, then GDP must equal consumption plus investment plus government expenditures.

5 Net exports are positive if expenditures by foreigners on goods and services produced in Canada are greater than expenditures by Canadian citizens on goods and services produced in other countries.

Measuring Canada's GDP

6 Real GDP is calculated by using the current year quantity and the base year price for each good.

7 If there were only households and firms and no government, market price and factor cost would be equal for any good.

8 Net exports are used in the income approach to measuring GDP.

9 Profits are part of the income approach to measuring GDP.

10 If you are interested in knowing whether the economy is producing more output, you would look at real GDP rather than nominal GDP.

The Uses and Limitations of Real GDP

11 Potential GDP is the level of real GDP when labour, capital, land, and entrepreneurial ability are fully employed.

12 The Lucas wedge shows that business cycles lower economic well-being.

13 The Human Development Index shows the same ranking of countries as does real GDP per person.

14 If underground economic activity was included in GDP calculations, measured GDP levels would be higher.

15 If two economies have the same real GDP per person, the standard of living must be the same in each economy.

Multiple-Choice

Gross Domestic Product

1 The capital stock in the year 2010 equals the capital stock in the year 2009
 a minus depreciation.
 b plus net investment plus depreciation.
 c plus gross investment.
 d plus net investment.
 e plus net investment minus depreciation.

2 For the aggregate economy, income equals
 a expenditure, but these are not generally equal to GDP.
 b GDP, but expenditure is generally less than these.
 c expenditure equals GDP.
 d expenditure equals GDP only if there are no government or foreign sectors.
 e expenditure equals GDP only if there is no depreciation.

3 Which of the following is a consumption expenditure?
  a Spending by the CBC on children's programs
  b Welfare payments to single mothers
  c The purchase of a new car by the IPSCO steel company
  d The purchase of a new car by the Singh household
  e The purchase of a computer by the IPSCO steel company

4 Danielle's Deliveries had $200,000 worth of delivery vans in 2009. During 2010, Danielle scrapped $20,000 worth of worn-out vans and bought $45,000 worth of new vans. What was Danielle's net investment in 2010?
  a $20,000
  b $25,000
  c $45,000
  d $65,000
  e $225,000

5 Which of the following would be counted as investment expenditure in GDP calculations?
  a The government builds a new building.
  b The Hong household buys a computer.
  c IPSCO Steel adds 1 million sheets to inventory.
  d IPSCO Steel sells pipe to Alaska.
  e Fred's Pizza Joint sells an old oven to Velma's Pizza Haven.

6 Which of the following adds to Canadian GDP?
  a I shovel my own driveway
  b I sell my used Honda
  c The production and sale of flour to a bakery
  d The purchase of a CD made in China
  e The ice cream I buy from my grocery store

Measuring Canada's GDP

7 To obtain the factor cost of a good from its market price
  a add indirect taxes and subtract subsidies.
  b subtract indirect taxes and add subsidies.
  c subtract both indirect taxes and subsidies.
  d add both indirect taxes and subsidies.
  e subtract depreciation.

8 Interest plus miscellaneous investment income is a component of which approach to measuring GDP?
  a income approach
  b expenditure approach
  c injections approach
  d output approach
  e opportunity cost approach

9 From the data in Table 20.1, what is net investment in Eastland?
  a −$160
  b $160
  c $240
  d $400
  e $500

TABLE **20.1** DATA FROM EASTLAND

Item	Amount ($)
Wages, salaries, and supplementary labour income	800
Farm income	80
Government expenditures on goods and services	240
Depreciation	240
Gross private domestic investment	400
Personal income taxes net of transfer payments	140
Corporate profits	80
Indirect taxes	120
Net exports	80
Consumption expenditures	640
Interest and miscellaneous investment income	100

10 From Table 20.1, what additional data are needed to compute net domestic income at factor cost?
  a income of nonfarm unincorporated businesses
  b transfer payments
  c subsidies
  d depreciation
  e net taxes

11 From the data in Table 20.1, what is GDP in Eastland?
  a $1,120
  b $1,180
  c $1,360
  d $1,420
  e not calculable with the given information

12 From the data in Table 20.2, compute Southton's nominal GDP in the current year.
  a $197
  b $198
  c $208
  d $209
  e cannot be calculated given the data

TABLE **20.2** DATA FROM SOUTHTON

Item	Price ($) Base	Current	Quantity Base	Current
Rubber ducks	1.00	1.25	100	100
Beach towels	7.00	6.00	12	14

13 From the data in Table 20.2, compute Southton's nominal GDP in the base year.
  a $184
  b $197
  c $198
  d $209
  e cannot be calculated given the data

14 From the data in Table 20.2, compute Southton's real GDP in the base year.
  a $184
  b $197
  c $198
  d $209
  e cannot be calculated given the data

15 From the data in Table 20.2, compute Southton's real GDP in the current year.
  a $184
  b $197
  c $198
  d $209
  e cannot be calculated given the data

The Uses and Limitations of Real GDP

16 The underground economy is all economic activity that
  a produces intermediate goods or services.
  b is not taxed.
  c is legal but unreported or is illegal.
  d has negative social value.
  e is conducted underground.

17 Given that pollution is a byproduct of some production processes,
  a GDP accountants adjust GDP downward.
  b GDP accountants adjust GDP upward.
  c GDP accountants do not adjust GDP unless pollution is a serious problem.
  d GDP tends to overstate economic well-being.
  e GDP tends to understate economic well-being.

18 Which of the following is *not* a reason for GDP incorrectly measuring the value of total output?
  a leisure time
  b household production
  c underground economic activity
  d depreciation
  e environmental quality

19 Which of the following is the major reason China's measured GDP might be underestimated?
  a It includes replacement of depreciated capital stock.
  b It includes production processes that create pollution as a side-effect.
  c It ignores decreases in health and life expectancy.
  d It does not use purchasing power parity prices.
  e It ignores human rights and political freedoms.

20 Which of the following statements by politicians is talking about the business cycle?
  a "Canadian unemployment is falling due to the upturn in the economy."
  b "Crime rates increase every spring as the school year ends."
  c "An average of 220,000 new jobs are created each year in Canada."
  d "More capital investment will create more jobs."
  e "Business always rises just before Christmas."

21 In New Adanac, the average growth rates of potential GDP per capita were 4 percent in the 1980s, but fell to 1 percent in the 1990s. Which of the following statements about this change is true?
  a A strong recession must have started in the 1990s.
  b 1990 was a peak year for the business cycle.
  c The Lucas wedge equals 3% of GDP per person for each of the 10 years.
  d The Lucas wedge equals 1% of GDP per person for each of the 10 years.
  e The Lucas wedge equals 4% of GDP per person for each of the 10 years.

22 From the data in Table 20.3, in which year did Sudland's business cycle reach a peak?
  a 2009
  b 2010
  c 2011
  d 2012
  e 2013

TABLE **20.3** DATA FROM SUDLAND

Year	Actual Real GDP	Potential Real GDP
2007	100	100
2008	107	105
2009	114	111
2010	113	118
2011	114	126
2012	122	134
2013	140	140

23 From the data in Table 20.3, in which year did Sudland's business cycle hit a trough?
   a 2009
   b 2010
   c 2011
   d 2012
   e 2013

24 From the data in Table 20.3, in which year(s) did Sudland have a recession?
   a Only 2010
   b 2010 and 2011
   c 2009, 2010, 2011
   d 2010, 2011, 2012
   e 2010, 2011, 2012, 2013

25 Why is the Human Development Index thought to be a better measure of economic well-being than real GDP per person?
   a It includes a measure of resource depletion.
   b It ignores health, which is hard to measure.
   c It includes leisure time and household production.
   d It includes health and education measures, as well as real GDP per person.
   e It includes only health and education measures, ignoring real GDP per person.

Short Answer Problems

I How can we measure gross domestic product by using either the expenditure or the income approach, when neither of these approaches actually measures production?

2 Suppose nominal GDP rises by 75 percent between year 1 and year 2.

   a If the average level of prices has also risen by 75 percent between year 1 and year 2, what has happened to real GDP?

   b If the average level of prices has risen by less than 75 percent between year 1 and year 2, has real GDP increased or decreased?

3 What *productive* activities are *not* measured and thus are *not* included in GDP? Is this lack of measurement a serious problem?

4 Use the data for Northland given in Table 20.4 to compute the following:

TABLE **20.4** DATA FOR NORTHLAND

Item	Amount (billions of $)
Consumption expenditure (C)	600
Taxes (Tax)	400
Transfer payments (TR)	250
Exports (X)	240
Imports (M)	220
Government expenditure on goods and services (G)	200
Gross investment (I)	150
Depreciation (Depr)	60

   a GDP

   b net investment

   c net exports

5 Use the data for the same economy given in Table 20.5 to compute:

TABLE **20.5** DATA FOR NORTHLAND

Item	Amount (billions of $)
Wages, salaries, and supplementary labour income	550
Indirect taxes	120
Subsidies	20
Farmers' income	20
Corporate profits	80
Interest and miscellaneous investment income	90
Depreciation	60
Income of nonfarm unincorporated businesses	70

   a net domestic income at factor cost

   b net domestic product at market prices

   c GDP

6 Table 20.6 gives data for Easton, where there are three final goods included in GDP: pizzas, beer, and CDs.

   a Calculate nominal GDP in 2009 and 2010.

   b What is real GDP in 2009?

   c What is real GDP in 2010?

TABLE **20.6** DATA FOR EASTON

Goods	2010 Output	2010 Price ($)	2009 (Base Period) Output	2009 (Base Period) Price ($)
Pizza	110	8	105	6
Beer	50	10	55	8
CDs	50	9	40	10

7 Consider the data in Table 20.7 on potential and real GDP in $ for the country of Dazedland.

   a Identify the peaks and troughs of the business cycle for this economy.

   b In which years is this economy in recession?

   c What happened to productivity in 2011?

   d Calculate the Lucas wedge that resulted after 2011. (Assume the population stays constant, so that the changes in real GDP and potential GDP would be reflected in changes in real GDP per person and potential GDP per person.)

TABLE **20.7** DATA FOR DAZEDLAND

Year	Actual Real GDP	Potential Real GDP
2007	200	200
2008	212	210
2009	211	220
2010	209	230
2011	240	240
2012	240	240
2013	248	248
2014	258	256
2015	254	264
2016	266	272

8 Figure 20.1 shows the circular flow for Northweston.

Figure **20.1**

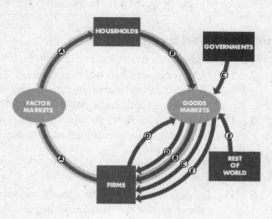

Aggregate income is $450 billion, exports are $40 billion, imports are $30 billion, consumption expenditure is $275 billion, government expenditure is $100 billion.

   a Identify what each label A, B, C, D, E represents as an economic value.

   b What is aggregate expenditure? Explain your steps.

   c What is GDP? Explain your steps.

   d What is investment? Explain your steps.

9 Consider the following economic activities. Identify to which of the markets in the circular flow each activity belongs. Give a one-line reason for each answer.

   a Fred of the Forest buys a new loincloth in preparation for his date with Angela.

   b Fred goes back to school at the University of Sandhurst to get his BA in Vine Swinging.

   c While in school, Fred goes on a Spring Break Week vacation in Florida.

   d Fred has graduated, and is getting paid to knock down trees by Treetop City.

   e Fred buys his first house.

   f Fred and Angela open up Treetop Bed and Breakfast, catering only to Europeans.

10 Consider the list of economic activities in Short Answer Problem **9**. Identify whether the activity involves expenditures, and, if so, to which component of expenditures each activity belongs (*C, I, G, X, M*).

ANSWERS

True/False and Explain

1 **F** Opposite is true. (468)
2 **T** Net investment nets out depreciation (replacement of worn-out capital), leaving only new capital additions. (470)
3 **T** From circular flow, firm production is sold (expenditure) and earnings used to pay out incomes. (469)
4 **T** If $X = M$, then $X - M = 0$, and $Y = C + I + G + 0$. (469)
5 **T** By definition of exports (goods and services sold to rest of the world) and imports (goods bought from the rest of the world), and net exports = exports − imports. (468)
6 **T** Definition. (473)
7 **T** Market price = factor cost + taxes − subsidies. (471–472)
8 **F** They are an expenditure, used in the expenditure approach. (471)
9 **T** Definition. (471–472)
10 **T** Real GDP measures quantity of goods and services, while nominal measures current dollar value and includes price level increases. (473)
11 **T** Definition. (474)
12 **F** Shows impact of productivity slowdown. (474)
13 **F** There is a correlation between real GDP per person and real GDP per person, but rankings are different. (479)
14 **T** Since they are omitted, and they are a productive activity, real GDP would be higher if they were included. (478)
15 **F** Real GDP is imperfect measure of standard of living; answer depends on factors such as exchange rates between each country's currency. (476–477)

Multiple-Choice

1 **d** Definition. (470)
2 **c** Expenditure = money earned by sales of produced goods which is used to pay incomes (including profits). (470)
3 **d** **a** is government expenditure, **b** is transfer payment, **c** and **e** are investment. (468–470)
4 **b** Net investment = gross investment ($45,000) − replacement of depreciated capital ($20,000). (470)

5 **c** **a** is government expenditure, **b** is consumption, **d** is an export and **e** is not current production. (468–470)
6 **e** **a** is household production, **b** is previous production, **c** is an intermediate good, **d** was produced outside Canada. (468)
7 **b** Market price = factor cost + indirect taxes − subsidies, so factor cost = market price − indirect taxes + subsidies. (471–473)
8 **a** Definition. (471–473)
9 **b** Net investment = gross investment − ~~capital consumption~~. (471–473) *depreciation*
10 **a** Table lists the other four components of factor incomes. (471–473)
11 **c** $Y = C + I + G + X - M = 640 + 400 + 240 + 80 = 1{,}360$. (471–473)
12 **d** Nominal GDP = sum of dollar value (= current price × current quantity) of all goods = ($1.25 × 100) + ($6 × 14) = 209. (473)
13 **a** Nominal GDP = sum of current price × current quantity of all goods = ($1 × 100) + ($7 × 12) = 184. (473)
14 **a** In base year, real GDP = nominal GDP. (473)
15 **c** Real GDP = sum of base price × current quantity of all goods = ($1 × 100) + ($7 × 14) = 198. (473)
16 **c** Definition. (477)
17 **d** No such adjustment occurs, so GDP overstates economic well-being. (478)
18 **d** Depreciation is part of GDP. (477–479)
19 **d** See text discussion. (476–477)
20 **a** Upturn implies expansion implies unemployment falls. **b** and **e** are irrelevant and seasonal, **c** is the average over the cycle, **d** is growth in potential GDP. (475–476)
21 **c** We cannot tell when year was, and low growth is not a recession. Lucas wedge = accumulated loss of output from slowdown in real GDP growth = 4% − 1% = 3%. (474–476)
22 **a** Growth turns from positive to negative. (475–476)
23 **b** Real GDP hits its lowest point. (475–476)
24 **a** Negative real GDP growth. (475–476)
25 **d** See text discussion. (479)

Short Answer Problems

1 The analysis of the circular flow showed that firms produce goods and services (what we wish to measure), sell them (what the expenditure

approach measures), and then use the proceeds to pay for factor incomes, rents, profits, etc. (what the income approach measures). Therefore expenditure = production = income.

2 a   Real GDP is unchanged. The increased value of goods and services is only because of increased prices.

   b   The fact that prices have risen less in proportion to the increase in nominal GDP means that real GDP has increased.

3   Activities that produce goods and services not included in GDP are underground economic activity and household production. Underground activities are not reported, because they are illegal or are legal but are not reported to circumvent taxes or government regulations. Household production includes productive activities that households perform for themselves. Because they do not hire someone else to mow the lawn or wash the car, they are not included in GDP. The seriousness of the problem depends on the actual size of activity. The underground economy is estimated as about 5 to 15 percent of the Canadian economy.

4 a   GDP $= C + I + G + (X - M) =$ \$970 billion.
   b   Net $I = I - Depreciation =$ \$90 billion.
   c   Net exports $= X - M =$ \$20 billion.

5 a   Net domestic income at factor cost = wages, salaries, and supplementary labour income + interest and miscellaneous investment income + corporate profits + farmers' income + income of nonfarm unincorporated business = \$810 billion.

   b   Net domestic product at market prices = net domestic product at factor cost + indirect taxes – subsidies = \$910 billion.

   c   GDP = net domestic product at market prices + depreciation = \$970 billion.

6 a   Nominal GDP is the sum of expenditures on all goods in year in question.
For 2009, Nominal GDP $= (\$6 \times 105) + (\$8 \times 55) + (\$10 \times 40) = \$1,470$.
For 2010, Nominal GDP $= (\$8 \times 110) + (\$10 \times 50) + (\$9 \times 50) = \$1,830$.

   b   Since 2009 is the base period, Nominal GDP = Real GDP = \$1,470.

   c   Real GDP in 2010 is calculated by using 2009 prices and 2010 quantities:
$(\$6 \times 110) + (\$8 \times 50) + (\$10 \times 50) = \$1,560$.

7 a   Peaks occur the year before percentage change in real GDP turns from positive to negative, 2008 and 2014. Troughs occur when percentage change in real GDP turns from negative to positive, 2010 and 2015.

   b   The economy is in recession when the growth rate of real GDP is negative, 2009, 2010 and 2015.

   c   Since growth in potential GDP slowed initially to zero and then continued at a slow rate, there is a productivity slowdown.

   d   The Lucas wedge calculates amount of difference between actual real GDP and what it would have been if real GDP had grown at rate of potential GDP after the productivity slowdown. Since potential GDP was initially growing at \$10 per year, that means the potential GDP would have been:
\$250 in 2012,
\$260 in 2013,
\$270 in 2014,
\$280 in 2015,
\$290 in 2016.
The shortfalls compared to actual real GDP are:
\$10 in 2012,
\$12 in 2013,
\$12 in 2014,
\$26 in 2015,
\$24 in 2016
for a total Lucas wedge of \$84.

8 a   A is aggregate income. B is consumption expenditure. C is government expenditure. D is investment. E is net exports.

   b   Aggregate income = aggregate expenditure = \$450 billion.

   c   Aggregate income = aggregate expenditure = GDP = \$450 billion.

   d   Investment is the only missing component of aggregate expenditure, and can be deduced from the equation $Y = C + I + G + X - M$ or $\$450 = \$275 + I + \$100 + \$40 - \$30$, implying $I = \$65$ billion. (Note that components of aggregate expenditure must all flow through the goods market.)

9 a   Goods and service market—purchase of a good.

   b   Goods and service market—purchase of an educational service.

---

c This is an expenditure, but money flows to the United States. Therefore, part of domestic market.

d Factor market—Fred is working for wage income.

e Goods and service market—purchase of a good.

f Goods and services market—purchase of a service.

10 a Expenditure (C).

b Expenditure (C).

c Not a domestic expenditure (M).

d Not an expenditure, a factor service purchase.

e Expenditure (I – house purchases count as investment).

f Expenditure (X).

Chapter 21
Monitoring Jobs and Inflation

KEY CONCEPTS

Employment and Unemployment

Unemployment rises in recessions and falls in expansions.

♦ Unemployment creates problems from lost production/incomes of unemployed and damaged job prospects from lost human capital.

Statistics Canada surveys households on their job status.

♦ **Working-age population** = Number of people 15 years and over.

♦ **Labour force** = employed + unemployed

  • Employed = those with full-time and part-time jobs.

  • Unemployed = without work, actively seeking within last four weeks, waiting to be called back after layoff, or waiting to start new job within four weeks.

♦ **Unemployment rate** = percentage of labour force unemployed. Increases in recessions, but no trend recently.

♦ **Labour force participation rate** = percentage of working-age population in labour force. Strong upward trend until 1990; decreases in recessions, increases in expansions.

♦ **Employment-to-population ratio** = percentage of working-age population with jobs. Increased from 1960s to 1990 (many new jobs created); decreases in recessions, increases in expansions.

Unemployment and Full Employment

Measured unemployment rate excludes some underutilized labour and does not account for unavoidable natural unemployment.

♦ **Marginally attached workers**—neither working nor looking for work, but available and want work.

♦ **Discouraged workers**—stopped looking for jobs due to repeated job search failures.

Every year in Canada, new workers enter labour force and others retire. Many jobs created and destroyed by expansion and contraction of businesses.

♦ The average net effect is new jobs, but some unemployment is created as part of the process.

♦ People become unemployed when they are laid off (job losers), voluntarily quit (job leavers), enter (entrants) or re-enter (re-entrants) labour force to search for jobs.

♦ People end unemployment when they are hired, recalled, or withdraw from labour force.

♦ Primary source of unemployment is job loss, which fluctuates strongly with business cycle.

Types of unemployment are frictional, structural, cyclical.

♦ **Frictional unemployment**—normal turnover. Depends on the number of entrants/re-entrants and job creation/destruction.

♦ **Structural unemployment**—job losses in industries/regions declining due to technological change or international competition.

  • Lasts longer than frictional unemployment, and higher in slow-growing eastern provinces.

  • Structural unemployment also caused by minimum wages and by firms paying **efficiency wages**—wages above going market wage designed to maximize profits by attracting more and more productive applicants, increasing work effort, and decreasing labour turnover rate (lowering recruiting costs).

♦ **Cyclical unemployment**—fluctuations in unemployment over business cycle. Increases in recession, decreases in expansion.

Natural employment—only frictional and structural unemployment (no cyclical unemployment).

♦ **Natural unemployment rate** = natural unemployment as percentage of labour force.

♦ **Full employment**—unemployment rate equals **natural unemployment rate**.

♦ Economists disagree about size of natural rate and amount it fluctuates.

Actual unemployment rate fluctuates around natural rate, as real GDP fluctuates around potential GDP over the business cycle.

♦ **Output gap**—gap between real GDP and potential GDP.

• When the output gap positive, unemployment rate < the natural rate.

• When output gap negative, unemployment rate > the natural rate.

The Price Level and Inflation

Changes in **price level** (average level of prices) determines value of future payments (loans, savings).

♦ **Inflation rate**—percentage change in price level.

♦ Unpredictable inflation

• creates winners/losers by creating unpredictable changes in value of money.

• leads to resources diverted from productive activities to predicting inflation.

♦ **Hyperinflation** is rapid inflation where money loses its value very quickly.

Consumer Price Index (CPI) measures average of prices paid for fixed basket of consumer goods and services.

♦ CPI = 100 for **reference base period** (2002).

♦ CPI basket constructed from monthly surveys of consumers' spending habits.

$$\text{CPI} = \frac{\text{Cost of CPI basket at current prices}}{\text{Cost of CPI basket at base-period prices}} \times 100.$$

Inflation rate = percentage change in CPI.

♦ CPI overstates inflation rate (biased upward) because

• new goods replace old goods.

• quality improvements create some of price rises.

• consumers change consumption towards cheaper goods not reflected in fixed-basket price index.

• consumers substitute toward discount outlets not covered in CPI surveys.

♦ Magnitude of CPI bias probably low in Canada, but leads to distorted contracts, more government outlays, and incorrect wage bargaining.

Alternative price indexes include

♦ **GDP deflator** ((nominal GDP/real GDP) × 100) which measures all goods and controls for biases.

♦ **chained price index for consumption** ((nominal consumption/real consumption) ×100) which does not use fixed quantities.

Core inflation rate excludes volatile elements of CPI to reveal underlying trends.

Real variables (nominal variables divided by GDP deflator) used to see what is "really" happening to key macroeconomic variables.

HELPFUL HINTS

I In a dynamic economy, some unemployment is efficient. There are economic benefits of frictional unemployment to individuals and to society. Younger workers typically experience periods of unemployment trying to find jobs that match their skills and interests. The benefit of the resulting frictional unemployment is a more satisfying and productive work life. Society benefits because the frictional unemployment that accompanies such a job-search allows workers to find jobs in which they are more productive. As a result, total production of goods and services increases. (Compare this case with the case for graduates in the Republic of China up until the 1990s. They were assigned jobs upon graduation, with very little personal input about type of job or location.)

On the other hand, structurally unemployed workers will not get a new job without retraining or relocation. There is a greater cost to the worker and society—structurally unemployed workers are typically unemployed for longer time periods. These workers bear much of the cost of restructuring industries in our economy, although society gains in the long run from shifts of labour and other resources to new industries.

2 The term "full employment," or its equivalent "natural rate of unemployment," does not mean that everyone has a job. Rather, it means that the only unemployment is frictional and structural—there is no cyclical unemployment.

It is possible for the actual rate of unemployment to be less than the natural rate of unemployment, because it is possible for employment to exceed full employment levels. In these situations, people are spending too little time searching for jobs, and therefore less-productive job matches are being made.

3 There are three different types of unemployment, but defining these types does not explain them. Explanations of how unemployment occurs are a goal of the remaining chapters in the textbook!

S E L F - T E S T

True/False and Explain

Employment and Unemployment

I The employment-to-population ratio is the percentage of working-age population in the labour force.

2 If the employment-to-population ratio increases, unemployment always decreases.

3 George was laid off last month, and is waiting to be recalled to his old job, so he is not actively seeking work. George is *not* counted as unemployed.

4 If the working-age population is 600,000, employment is 400,000 and unemployment is 30,000, then the unemployment rate is 7.0%.

5 A university student seeking a job is counted as unemployed.

Unemployment and Full Employment

6 If the number of discouraged workers decreases, the employment-to-population ratio decreases as they begin to look for jobs.

7 Discouraged workers are counted as unemployed but probably should not be.

8 Being unemployed for a few months after graduating from university always hurts the graduate.

9 A decline in the number of jobs in the automobile sector matched by an equal increase in the number of jobs offered in the banking sector will not alter the unemployment rate.

10 At full employment, there is no unemployment.

11 Bill has just graduated from high school and is looking for his first job. Bill is frictionally unemployed.

12 Fluctuations in unemployment over the business cycle create frictional unemployment.

The Price Level and Inflation

13 The CPI overstates the inflation rate because it ignores substitution toward higher-quality goods by households.

14 The market basket used in calculating the CPI changes each year.

15 The magnitude of the CPI bias in Canada is high.

Multiple-Choice

Employment and Unemployment

1 In a country with a working-age population of 20 million, 13 million are employed, 1.5 million are unemployed, and 1 million of the employed are working part time, half of whom wish to work full time. The size of the labour force is
 a   20 million.
 b   15.5 million.
 c   14.5 million.
 d   13 million.
 e   11.5 million.

2 In a country with a working-age population of 20 million, 13 million are employed, 1.5 million are unemployed, and 1 million of the employed are working part-time, half of whom wish to work full-time. The labour force participation rate is
 a   75.5%.
 b   72.5%.
 c   65%.
 d   57.5%.
 e   none of the above.

3 In a country with a working-age population of 20 million, 13 million are employed, 1.5 million are unemployed, and 1 million of the employed are working part time, half of whom wish to work full time. The unemployment rate is
 a   10%.
 b   10.3%.
 c   11.5%.
 d   15.4%.

 e   none of the above.

4 Who of the following would be counted as unemployed in Canada?
 a   Doris only works five hours a week, but is looking for a full-time job.
 b   Kanhaya has stopped looking for work, since he was unable to find a suitable job during a two-month search.
 c   Sharon is a college student with no job.
 d   Maurice has been laid off from his job for 20 weeks, but expects a call back soon.
 e   Bogdan has been laid off from his job, but does not expect a call back and is not looking.

5 If the employment-to-population ratio increases,
 a   the unemployment rate *must* decrease.
 b   the labour force participation rate *must* increase.
 c   the labour force participation rate will be unaffected.
 d   aggregate hours worked *must* increase.
 e   none of the above.

6 The economic costs of unemployment include
 a   workers quitting and going to university.
 b   political problems for government.
 c   lost human capital of the unemployed.
 d   the creation of winners and losers due to job creation/destruction.
 e   the diversion of resources from productive activities to predicting unemployment.

Unemployment and Full Employment

7 Including discouraged workers in the measured unemployment rate would
 a   not change the measured unemployment rate.
 b   lower the measured unemployment rate.
 c   raise the natural rate of unemployment.
 d   raise the full employment rate.
 e   raise the measured unemployment rate.

8 If the number of discouraged workers increases, all else unchanged, the
 a   unemployment rate will increase.
 b   employment-to-population ratio will decrease.
 c   labour force participation rate will increase.
 d   labour force participation rate will decrease.
 e   employment-to-population ratio will increase.

9 Which of the following events would raise cyclical unemployment?
 a Real GDP growth slows down or turns negative.
 b Unemployment benefits increase.
 c The pace of technological change increases.
 d Both job destruction and job creation increase.
 e All of the above.

10 Unemployment will increase if there is an increase in the number of people
 a retiring.
 b withdrawing from the labour force.
 c recalled from layoffs.
 d leaving jobs to go to school.
 e leaving school to find jobs.

11 Who of the following would be considered structurally unemployed?
 a a Saskatchewan farmer who has lost her farm and is unemployed until retrained
 b a Nova Scotia fishery worker who is searching for a better job closer to home
 c a steelworker who is laid off but who expects to be called back soon
 d an office worker who has lost her job because of a general economic slowdown
 e none of the above

12 Who of the following would be considered cyclically unemployed?
 a a Saskatchewan farmer who has lost her farm and is unemployed until retrained
 b a Nova Scotia fishery worker who is searching for a better job closer to home
 c a steelworker who is laid off but who expects to be called back soon
 d an office worker who has lost her job because of a general economic slowdown
 e none of the above

13 Who of the following would be considered frictionally unemployed? A steelworker who
 a loses her job because of technological change.
 b is laid off but expects to be called back within a week.
 c gives up her job because she retires.
 d decides to leave the labour force and become a full-time ballet student.
 e becomes discouraged and stops looking for jobs.

14 In a recession, what is the largest source of the increase in unemployment?
 a job leavers
 b job losers
 c new entrants to the labour force
 d re-entrants to the labour force
 e involuntary part-time workers

15 At full employment, there is no
 a natural unemployment.
 b unemployment.
 c cyclical unemployment.
 d structural unemployment.
 e frictional unemployment.

16 Unemployment caused by permanently decreased demand for horse-drawn carriages is an example of
 a cyclical unemployment.
 b marginal unemployment.
 c frictional unemployment.
 d structural unemployment.
 e discouraged unemployment.

17 The natural rate of unemployment is
 a the rate at which unemployment equals 0%.
 b the same as cyclical unemployment.
 c the rate at which cyclical unemployment equals 6%.
 d the rate at which cyclical unemployment equals 0%.
 e none of the above.

The Price Level and Inflation

18 Comparing the core inflation rate to the Consumer Price Index, the core inflation rate
 a controls for the biases of the CPI.
 b measures all goods produced, not just consumer goods.
 c uses current period quantities, not base period quantities.
 d excludes the volatile elements of the CPI.
 e includes volatile elements not in the CPI.

19 If the inflation rate is positive, the price level in an economy is
 a falling rapidly.
 b rising.
 c constant.
 d falling slowly.
 e zero.

20 How does an unpredictable inflation cause
    problems?
    a Business cycles become more variable.
    b The stock market falls in value.
    c The value of money rises.
    d Resources are diverted from productive
       activities to tax evasion.
    e Resources are diverted from productive
       activities to forecasting inflation.

21 In 2009 the Consumer Price Index measured
    114.3. In 2010 it measured 118.0. What was
    inflation in 2010?
    a 1.18%
    b 3.1%
    c 3.2%
    d 3.7%
    e 18%

22 From the data in Table 21.1, what is Southton's
    consumer price index for the current year?
    a 112
    b 105.6
    c 100.5
    d 100
    e 94.7

TABLE **21.1** DATA FROM SOUTHTON

Item	Price ($) Base	Current	Quantity Base	Current
Rubber ducks	1.00	1.25	100	100
Beach towels	9.00	6.00	12	14

23 Refer to the data in Table 21.1. Between the base
    year and the current year, the relative price of
    rubber ducks
    a remained unchanged.
    b fell.
    c rose.
    d cannot be determined with given
       information.
    e depends on if overall inflation was positive.

24 Which of the following is *not* a reason the
    Consumer Price Index overstates inflation?
    a New goods of higher quality and prices
       replace old goods.
    b Quality improvements create some part of
       price rises in existing goods and services.
    c Consumers change their consumption basket
       toward cheaper goods not reflected in the
       fixed-basket price index.
    d Consumers substitute toward using discount
       outlets not covered in CPI surveys.
    e It does not measure the underground
       economy.

25 The technique used to calculate the CPI
    implicitly assume that consumers buy
    a relatively more of goods with relative prices
       that are increasing.
    b relatively less of goods with relative prices
       that are decreasing.
    c the same relative quantities of goods as in a
       base year.
    d goods and services whose quality improves
       at the rate of growth of real GDP.
    e more computers and CD players and fewer
       black-and-white TVs.

Short Answer Problems

Ⓒ 1 Explain why an economy does not have 0
       percent unemployment when it has full
       employment.

Ⓒ 2 Should the government try to force the
       unemployment rate down as close to zero as
       possible? Discuss some problems such a policy
       might create.

3 Consider the following information about an
   economy: working-age population—20 million;
   full-time employment—8 million; part-time
   employment—2 million (1 million of whom
   wish they had full-time jobs); unemployment—
   1 million.

   a What is the labour force in this economy?
      What is the labour force participation rate?

   b What is the unemployment rate?

   c What is the involuntary part-time rate?

   d What is the employment-to-population
      ratio?

   e If 0.6 million of those unemployed are
      frictionally and structurally unemployed,
      what is the natural rate of unemployment?

f What is the amount of cyclical unemployment?

g Can you tell if this economy is in recession or expansion? Is the output gap positive or negative?

4 Consider the economy described in Short Answer Problem **3**. Over the next year, there is no change in the working-age population, but the number of unemployed rises to 1.5 million, while the number of full-time employed rises to 8.5 million. There are no changes in part-time employment.

a Calculate the new labour force participation rate, the new employment-to-population ratio, and the new unemployment rate.

b How is it possible that all three of these rates rose at the same time? Explain briefly. (*Hint:* What do you think has happened to the number of discouraged workers over this time period?)

5 Are the costs of unemployment more severe for frictional or structural unemployment?

6 Explain the difference between cyclical and structural unemployment. How would you tell a cyclically unemployed person from a structurally unemployed person?

7 Table 21.2 gives data for Southland, where there are three consumption goods: bananas, coconuts, and grapes.

TABLE **21.2** DATA FOR SOUTHLAND

Goods	Quantity in Base-Period Basket	Base Period Price ($)	Base Period Expenditure ($)	Current Period Price ($)	Current Period Expenditure ($)
Bananas	120	6		8	
Coconuts	60	8		10	
Grapes	40	10		9	

a Complete the table by computing expenditures for the base period and expenditures for the same quantity of each good in the current period.

b What is the value of the basket of consumption goods in the base period? in the current period?

c What is the Consumer Price Index for the current period?

d On the basis of the data in this table, would you predict consumers would make any

substitutions between goods between the base period and the current period? If so, what kind of problems would this create for your measurement of the CPI?

8 Examine each of the following changes in John Carter's labour market activity, and explain whether they constitute unemployment, employment, or being out of the labour force. If unemployment, which of the three types of unemployment is represented?

a John graduates from Barsoom High and starts looking for a job.

b John has no luck finding the full-time job he wants and takes a part-time job cleaning out the canals.

c Canal-cleaning doesn't work out for John because of unforeseen allergies, so he quits.

d Discouraged by the lack of work, John stops looking and stays home watching his favourite soap opera, *As Mars Turns*.

e John sees an advertisement on TV for the Barsoom Swordfighter School, and enrols to get his BSF.

f John graduates at the top of his class and joins up with Princess Dejah Thoris' guard.

g Barsoom University invents a new laser personal defence system, and the Princess disbands her guard—John spends a long time looking for work.

h John sees an advertisement seeking someone to help explore the ruins of the lost city of Rhiannon and signs up as security—the six-armed tribes are particularly ferocious there.

9 Consider the data from 1995 in Table 21.3 on Canada as a whole and Newfoundland specifically.

TABLE **21.3**

Economy	Labour Force Participation Rate	Unemployment Rate	Employment-to-Population Ratio
Canada	64.8	9.5	58.6
Newfoundland	53.1	18.3	43.3

Source: Statistics Canada, *Labour Force Review.*

Newfoundland has twice the unemployment of Canada, as well as a radically lower employment-to-population ratio and labour force participation rate. By examining these, can you get any insight into the impact of a high unemployment rate on the labour market in Newfoundland? Why is the gap in the employment-to-population ratio (15.3 points) so much bigger than the unemployment gap (8.8 points)?

⊖ 10 The federal government gives full-time students a tax credit per month of studies. In 1990, Tracy received this credit, which was worth $50 per month, whereas in 2008 Jennifer received a credit worth $200 per month. In 1990, the price level was 78.4, and in 2008 it was 114.2. Was the value of the tax credit money worth more to Jennifer or Tracy? (Ignore any changes in taxes, tuition, etc.)

ANSWERS

True/False and Explain

1 **F** Percentage of working-age population with jobs. (491–493)

2 **F** True if participation decreases or doesn't increase much, otherwise false. (491–493)

3 **F** Since waiting for recall, he is counted. (491)

4 **T** Unemployment rate = (unemployment/ (unemployment +employed)) × 100 = (30,000/430,000) × 100 = 7.0%. (491–493)

5 **F** Counted as out of labour force (not actively seeking work). (494)

6 **F** This change will only change labour force participation. (491–496)

7 **F** Not counted as unemployed, but probably should be. (494)

8 **F** Depends on whether time unemployed leads to better job. (494–496)

9 **F** Workers retrain/relocate leading to more structural unemployment. (494–496)

10 **F** Full employment still has frictional and structural unemployment. (494–496)

11 **T** Searching for jobs = frictionally unemployed. (494–496)

12 **F** Create *cyclical* unemployment. (496–497)

13 **T** See text discussion. (501–502)

14 **F** Changed every 10 years. (499–500)

15 **F** Low due to Statistics Canada's corrections. (502)

Multiple-Choice

1 **c** Employed + unemployed. (491–493)

2 **b** Labour force/working-age population = 14.5/20 = 72.5%. (491–493)

3 **b** Unemployed/labour force = 1.5/14.5 = 10.3%. (491–493)

4 **d** Doris is employed, Kanhaya isn't looking for work, Sharon is out of labour force, Bogdan does not expect to be called back. (491)

5 **e** Any of **a** to **d** *might* occur, but they do not *have* to occur. (491–493)

6 **c** **a** is a gain, **b** is real but not economic cost, **d** normal activity, **e** is nonsense. (490–491)

7 **e** It would add extra unemployed workers to the measured rate. (494)

8 **d** Discouraged workers were unemployed, but stop looking and exit labour force, so unemployment rate decreases, labour force participation decreases, employment-to-population ratio unchanged. (491–494)

9 **a** **b** to **d** raise frictional or structural unemployment, but if real GDP growth slows down, cyclical unemployment increases. (494–497)

10 **e** Others all lower unemployment. (494–496)

11 **a** Structural unemployment includes having wrong skills. Others are frictional or cyclical unemployment. (494–496)

12 **d** Cyclical unemployment is due to economy-wide slowdowns. (494–496)

13 **b** **a** is structural, rest are not officially unemployed. (494–496)

14 **b** See text discussion. (496–497)

15 **c** Definition. (494–496)

16 **d** Definition—unemployment caused by structural change. (494–496)

17 **d** Definition. (494–496)

18 **d** By construction. (502)

19 **b** Positive inflation implies current price level − past price level > 0 by definition. (501)

20 e Forecasting inflation becomes important because unpredictable inflation leads to unpredictable winners and losers because the value of money *falls*. (498)

21 c Inflation = (Δ price level/past price level) × 100 = ((118 – 114.3)/114.3) × 100 = 3.2%. (500)

22 e CPI = [(sum of current prices × base quantities)/(sum of base prices × base quantities)] × 100. (499–500)

23 c Ratio *P*(ducks)/*P*(towels) has risen. (499–502)

24 e This problem is for real GDP. (501–502)

25 c Because assumes a fixed basket. (501–502)

Short Answer Problems

1 An economy always has some unemployment, of people searching for jobs—frictional and structural unemployment. We define full employment as when there is zero cyclical unemployment, but still some frictional and structural unemployment.

2 Pushing down the unemployment rate would eliminate frictional unemployment (which would reduce the number of good job matches) and structural unemployment (which would prevent structural readjustment the economy needs). Therefore it does not seem like a good idea to get unemployment as close to zero as possible!

3 a The labour force is 11 million, the sum of employment and unemployment. Labour force participation rate = percentage of working-age population who are in the labour force = 11/20 or 55 percent.

b The unemployment rate is 9.1 percent, the number of unemployed as a percentage of the labour force.

c It is 9.1 percent, the percentage of the labour force who are part time and want full time.

d It is 50 percent, percentage of working-age population with a job.

e Natural unemployment is frictional plus structural unemployment = 0.6 million. Natural rate of unemployment is 5.45% = (0.6 million/11 million) × 100.

f Cyclical unemployment is actual unemployment minus natural unemployment, or 0.4 million.

g Since there is positive cyclical unemployment, real GDP is below potential GDP and the output gap is negative. It is possible we have a recession (negative real GDP growth), but economy could be expanding out of the recession.

4 a Labour force participation rate = percentage of working-age population who are employed + unemployed = (1.5 + 8.5 + 2)/20 = 60 percent. The employment-to-population ratio is the percentage of the population with a job = 52.5 percent. The unemployment rate is the percentage of the labour force without a job = 12.5 percent.

b One million more people entered the labour force (participation rate increases), half of whom found a job (employment-to-population ratio increases) and half of whom did not (unemployment rate increases). It seems likely this change is due to discouraged workers now retrying to find jobs because overall economy is improving.

5 The costs of unemployment include lost output of the unemployed, and deterioration of skills and abilities; in other words, human capital erodes. These costs are higher for structural unemployment because it lasts longer, and often workers' human capital becomes worthless in the marketplace.

6 Cyclical unemployment is caused by a downturn in the economy, when there is a decrease in demand for all products. Structural unemployment is caused by structural changes in a specific industry or region, and there is a decrease in demand for a certain type of labour whose skills are no longer desired.

Cyclical unemployment will end when the economy turns up. Structural unemployment will end when the workers retrain or move.

7 a Table 21.2 is completed here as Table 21.2 Solution. Note that the base-period quantities are evaluated at current prices to find the value of quantities in the current period.

TABLE **21.2** SOLUTION

Goods	Quantity in Base-Period Basket	Base Period Price ($)	Base Period Expenditure ($)	Current Period Price ($)	Current Period Expenditure ($)
Bananas	120	6	720	8	960
Coconuts	60	8	480	10	600
Grapes	40	10	400	9	360

b The value of the basket of consumption goods in the base period is the sum of expenditures in that period: $1,600. The value of the basket of consumption goods in the current period is obtained as the sum of values of quantities in that period: $1,920.

c The Consumer Price Index is the ratio of the value of quantities in the current period to the base period expenditure, times 100:

$$CPI = (1,920/1,600) \times 100 = 120.$$

ⓒ **d** Since the price of grapes has fallen relative to the prices of bananas and coconuts, we expect consumers to substitute toward the cheaper grapes and away from bananas and coconuts. This substitution means our CPI measure will be biased upward.

8 a He is an entrant, and is frictionally unemployed.

b He is now employed, although he is also involuntarily part time.

c He is a job leaver, and is frictionally unemployed.

d He is a discouraged worker, but technically out of the labour force.

e He is still out of the labour force.

f He is employed.

g He is structurally unemployed.

h He is employed again.

ⓒ **9** The higher unemployment rate in Newfoundland has pushed many workers out of the labour force—they have become discouraged workers and are not even attempting to find work. (We can see this in the lower participation rate.) The bigger gap in the employment-to-population ratio reflects this exiting, because it includes measured unemployed and discouraged workers.

ⓒ **10** There are two ways to answer this question. First, between 1990 and 2008 the tax credit has risen in value by 300 percent (= 150/50 × 100), while the price level has risen by 45.4 percent (= (114.2 − 78.4)/78.4 × 100). Clearly prices have risen less than the dollar value of the credit, raising the value of this money, so Jennifer gains more from it. Second, you could calculate the purchasing power of the tax credit in terms of how many goods it can purchase (remember, the price index measures the cost of a typical family's purchases). For Tracy the credit purchased 0.64 of a typical family's purchases (= 50/78.4), whereas for Jennifer it purchased 1.75 (= 200/114.2). Clearly Jennifer gained more from the credit.

Part 7 Wrap Up
Monitoring Macroeconomic Trends and Fluctuations

PROBLEM

a Consider the following data for the economy of Autoland for 2008 and 2009. Calculate the value of nominal GDP for each year.

TABLE **P7.1** 2008

Item	Amount (billions of $)
Government expenditures on goods and services	60
Government transfer payments	30
Income taxes	80
Wages, etc., paid to labour	200
Export earnings	30
Consumption expenditure	180
Import payments	25
Net investment expenditure	15
Depreciation	5

TABLE **P7.2** 2009

Item	Amount (billions of $)
Wages, etc., paid to labour	200
Indirect taxes	20
Profits	20
Subsidies	5
Interest and miscellaneous investment income	5
Depreciation	10
Farmers' income	10
Income of nonfarm unincorporated business	10

b Using your data from **a**, complete the following table:

TABLE **P7.3**

Year	Nominal GDP (billions of $)	Price Level	Real GDP (billions of 2002 $)
2008		132.5	
2009		140.0	

c What is the inflation rate in 2009?

d If real GDP = potential GDP in 2008, and potential GDP is unchanged in 2009, what has happened to the output gap and cyclical unemployment between 2008 and 2009?

<table>
<tr><td>

MIDTERM EXAMINATION

You should allocate 16 minutes for this examination (8 questions, 2 minutes per question). For each question, choose the one *best* answer.

1 Which of the following people would be counted as unemployed in Canada?
   a   Doris only works 20 hours a week and is not looking for a full-time job.
   b   Kanhaya has stopped looking for work since he has had no luck finding a job.
   c   Sharon is a college student with no job.
   d   Maurice is working in his garden while looking for work.
   e   Taylor is on disability leave.

2 Which of the following is *not* an example of investment in the expenditure approach to measuring GDP? General Motors
   a   buys a new auto stamping machine.
   b   adds 500 new cars to inventories.
   c   buys Canadian government bonds.
   d   builds another assembly plant.
   e   replaces worn-out stamping machines.

3 Which of the following is *not* part of the incomes approach to GDP?
   a   net exports
   b   wages, salaries, and supplementary labour income
   c   corporate profits
   d   farmers' income
   e   income of nonfarm unincorporated businesses

4 In a country with a working-age population of 20 million, 13 million are employed, 1.5 million are unemployed, and 1 million of the employed are working part-time, half of whom wish to work full-time. The employment-to-population ratio is
   a   57.5%.
   b   65%.
   c   72.5%.
   d   75.5%.
   e   none of the above.

</td><td>

5 A business cycle is the
   a   increase in real GDP for more than two periods.
   b   decrease in real GDP for more than two periods.
   c   increase in the economic potential to produce goods and services.
   d   irregular fluctuation of potential GDP around real GDP.
   e   irregular fluctuation of real GDP around potential GDP.

6 Which of the following is a reason why normal measurement of real GDP is too high as an estimate of economic well-being?
   a   It excludes expenditures on health.
   b   It excludes the impact of pollution.
   c   It excludes leisure time.
   d   It excludes household production.
   e   It uses purchasing power parity prices.

7 Unpredictable inflation creates problems for society because
   a   it makes it difficult for consumers to switch to cheaper goods when relative prices are rising.
   b   it creates a negative output gap.
   c   consumers are unable to tell quality changes in goods from price changes.
   d   it leads to society diverting resources from productive activities to predicting inflation.
   e   discount outlets become too important in the overall consumptions decisions of households.

8 If a price index was 150 at the end of 2000 and 165 at the end of 2001, what was the rate of inflation for 2001?
   a   9.1%
   b   10%
   c   15%
   d   50%
   e   65%

</td></tr>
</table>

A N S W E R S

Problem

a For 2008, calculate nominal GDP as the sum of $C + I + G + X - M$. For G, you must use only expenditures on goods and services, and you need to calculate gross investment (= net investment + depreciation, or $20 billion). Thus nominal GDP = 180 + 20 + 60 + 30 − 25 = $265 billion for 2008.

For 2009, you need to use the incomes approach. First, calculate Net domestic income at factor cost = wages, etc. + profits + interest and miscellaneous investment income + farmers' income + income of nonfarm unincorporated business = 200 + 20 + 5 + 10 + 10 = $245 billion. Next, to get net domestic product add indirect taxes and subtract subsidies from net domestic income, or 245 + 20 − 5 = $260 billion. Finally, to get gross domestic product, add depreciation to net domestic product, or 260 + 10 = $270 billion for 2009.

b Table P7.3 is completed here as Table P7.3 Solution, using the formula real GDP = (nominal GDP/price level) × 100.

TABLE **P7.3** SOLUTION

Year	Nominal GDP (billions of $)	Price Level	Real GDP (billions of 2002 $)
2008	265	132.5	200.0
2009	270	140.0	192.9

c The inflation rate is equal to

$$5.7\% = \frac{140.0 - 132.5}{132.5} \times 100$$

d If potential GDP = $200 billion in 2008 and 2009, then in 2009 real GDP was less than potential GDP by $7.1 billion and the output gap has gone from $0 in 2008 to −$7.1 billion in 2009. The decrease in real GDP to below potential GDP means the unemployment rate must be above the natural rate in 2009, so that cyclical unemployment is positive in 2009.

Midterm Examination

1 d Doris is employed part time, Kanhaya not looking for work (discouraged worker), Sharon and Taylor out of labour force. (491–493)

2 c This is purchase of financial assets, not capital stock. (470)

3 a Part of expenditure approach. (471–472)

4 b Employed/working-age population × 100 = 13/20 × 100 = 65%. (491–493)

5 e Definition. (474–476)

6 b Pollution would lower economic well-being. (477–479)

7 d See text discussion. (498)

8 b 10% = [(165 − 150)/150] × 100. (500)

Chapter 22
Economic Growth

The Basics of Economic Growth

Economic growth is sustained expansion of production possibilities, measured as the increase in real GDP.

- ◆ **Economic growth rate** = annual percentage change in real GDP =
  $$\frac{\text{Real GDP this year} - \text{Real GDP last year}}{\text{Real GDP last year}} \times 100$$

- ◆ Standard of living depends on **real GDP per capita** (real GDP/population).

- ◆ Compounding leads to rapid growth—**rule of 70** states that the number of years it take a variable to double in value = 70/(percentage growth rate).

Economic Growth Trends

Canada's growth rate was low in 1950s, higher in 1960s, average in 1970s, slower in 1980s, and average after 1996.

- ◆ Internationally, between 1960 and now, Canada's real GDP per person similar to the United States, but Japan and other Asian countries have been catching up to both countries.

How Potential GDP Grows

Economic growth requires a sustained increase in potential GDP.

- ◆ More real GDP produced requires less leisure and more time spent working.

- ◆ Potential GDP is level of real GDP at full-employment quantity of labour (with fixed amounts of land, entrepreneurial ability, capital).

- ◆ **Aggregate production function** (*PF*) shows relationship between real GDP and quantity of labour employed, all other influences constant.

  - • Increase in quantity of labour employed creates movement up along *PF*.

Aggregate labour market determines quantity of labour hours employed and real GDP supplied.

- ◆ Demand for labour (*LD*)—quantity of labour demanded at each **real wage rate** = (money or nominal wage rate)/price level.

  - • Firms hire labour as long as marginal product of labour > real wage rate.

  - • Law of diminishing returns says firms will hire more labour only if real wage rate falls.

- ◆ Supply of labour (*LS*)—quantity of labour supplied at each real wage rate.

  - • Increase in real wage rate increases quantity of labour supplied because more people work and more people choose to work longer hours.

- ◆ Real wage rate adjusts to create full-employment labour market equilibrium where *LD* = *LS*, with real GDP = potential GDP.

Potential GDP increases if labour supply increases or **labour productivity** (real GDP per hour of labour) increases.

- ◆ Labour supply increases if hours per worker increase, or employment-to-population ratio increases, or working-age population increases.

  - • Labour supply curve shifts right, real wage rate decreases, increasing hiring, causing movement along the *PF*, increasing potential GDP.

- ◆ Increase in labour productivity increases demand for labour—therefore, real wage rate increases, quantity labour supplied increases, *PF* shifts upward, and potential GDP increases.

♦ Increases in population lower real GDP per person, but increases in labour productivity increase it.

Why Labour Productivity Grows

Fundamental precondition for labour productivity growth is appropriate *incentive* system created by firms, markets, property rights, and money.

Given these preconditions, pace of growth is affected by three things that increase labour productivity:

♦ Physical capital growth increases capital per worker.

♦ Human capital growth from education and training (including learning by repetitively doing tasks).

♦ Discovery of new technologies (often embodied in new capital).

Growth accounting calculates how much labour productivity growth is due to each of its sources.

♦ 1 percent increase in capital per hour of labour (with no change in technology) leads to 0.49 percent increase in labour productivity in Canada.

♦ This rule can explain Canadian real GDP growth:

 • 1960–73—high productivity growth due to high technological change and strong capital accumulation.

 • 1973–85—lower productivity growth due to slowdown in technological change and lower capital accumulation.

 • 1985–1991—low capital growth and almost no technological change.

 • 1992–2002—roughly zero capital growth and high technological change.

 • 2002–2007—moderate capital growth and technological change.

♦ Growth accounting shows that Asian countries are growing fast because they are adapting new technologies and investing larger percentage of GDP than Canada.

Growth Theories and Policies

Classical growth theory argues real GDP growth is temporary, because it leads to population explosions.

♦ Advances in technology increase real GDP per hour of labour.

♦ Since real GDP per hour > **subsistence real GDP per hour** (minimum needed to maintain life), population grows, lowering capital per hour of labour, so output per hour of labour falls back to subsistence.

Neoclassical growth theory says real GDP per person grows due to technological change inducing growth in capital per person.

♦ Assumes population growth rate is independent of economic growth.

♦ Driving force of economic growth is technological change, and its interaction with capital accumulation.

♦ Ongoing *exogenous* technological advances increase rate of return on capital, increasing saving and investment, increasing capital per person, creating real GDP growth.

♦ As capital per hour of labour increases, rate of return on capital decreases due to diminishing returns, so capital accumulation and growth end unless new technological advances occur.

♦ Predicts growth rates and income levels per person in different countries should converge, but this convergence doesn't happen empirically.

New growth theory attempts to overcome this shortcoming by explaining technological changes as a profit-maximizing choice.

♦ New discoveries sought for (temporary) profits, but once made, discoveries are copied and benefits are dispersed through economy, *without* diminishing returns.

♦ Knowledge is special kind of capital not subject to diminishing returns or decreasing rate of return.

♦ Inventions increase rate of return to knowledge capital, resulting in increased capital per person and real GDP growth with *no automatic slowdown* because rate of return to capital does not diminish.

Different growth theories lead to four main suggestions for increasing economic growth rates:

♦ Stimulate saving (and investment in capital) by tax incentives.

♦ Subsidize research and development and new technology.

♦ Encourage international trade.

♦ Improve education quality.

HELPFUL HINTS

I Economic growth is a powerful force raising living standards. Countries become rich by achieving high rates of growth in per person GDP and maintaining them over long periods of time. Compounding income can create startling effects. Consider the post-1973 productivity growth slowdown. Growth between 1960 and 1973 averaged 3.3 percent per year, but after 1973 was less than 2.1 percent per year. Between 1973 and 2007, real GDP per person rose by about 103 percent (= $[(1.021)^{34} - 1] \times 100$). However, if growth had continued at the pre-1973 rate of 3.3 percent, real GDP per person would have increased by about 202 percent (= $[(1.033)^{34} - 1] \times 100$). Even the worst recession over this period lowered real GDP per person by about 5 percent (see Robert Lucas's discussion of the Lucas Wedge in Chapter 20). Avoiding the productivity growth slowdown would clearly have had a big payoff!

2 The key to understanding different theories of growth is the role of "the law of diminishing returns" in each theory. This law states that adding more of one input, other inputs held constant, eventually leads to a diminishing returns to adding extra inputs.

In neoclassical theory, the discovery of a new technology increases the rate of return on capital, increasing saving and investment, and increasing the amount of capital used. However, the increase in capital eventually leads to diminishing returns. Think of the introduction of new, more powerful computers. As the number of computers increases, holding constant the number of workers, the extra output of the nth computer will not be as high as the productivity of the first computer. Eventually, productivity of extra capital must decrease (decreasing the rate of return), and economic growth automatically slows down.

New growth theory has a different idea of technology and capital, with no diminishing returns, and no slowdown in economic growth. New growth theory examines "knowledge capital," a concept of technology that not embodied in capital, but in ideas. These ideas might include new management techniques, or new production processes (such as assembly lines) that can be copied from business to business without diminishing returns. Consider

the introduction of new and better software (such as word processing software). As more copies of the software are introduced into different businesses around the country, we do not run into diminishing returns until the entire country has access to the new knowledge. Even then, improved software will be continually developed and introduced without diminishing returns (so that the rate of return does *not* decrease), and economic growth need not automatically slow down.

SELF-TEST

True/False and Explain

The Basics of Economic Growth

I The standard of living depends on the level of real GDP.

Economic Growth Trends

2 Canada's growth speedup in the 1990s was unusual in Canadian history.

3 Asian countries are catching up with Canada's real GDP per person.

How Potential GDP Grows

4 The aggregate production function shows the relationship between real GDP and labour inputs.

5 As the real wage rate increases, the quantity of labour demanded decreases, other things remaining constant.

6 Increasing population decreases the real wage rate and potential GDP.

7 An increase in labour productivity decreases real wages and increases potential GDP.

Why Labour Productivity Grows

8 Higher levels of human capital, with the same physical capital per person, will not raise per person income.

9 Rapid changes in technology create growth without need for new capital.

10 The slowdown in productivity growth after 1973 was due to a slowdown in the growth of capital per hour of labour, with a constant rate of technological change.

11 The only way labour productivity can increase is if there is more physical capital.

Growth Theories

12 Neoclassical growth theory argues economic growth eventually slows down because the rate of return on capital diminishes as the amount of capital increases.

13 Classical growth theory argues economic growth leads to a smaller population growth rate.

14 High economic growth has typically been accompanied by high saving rates.

15 In new growth theory, there are no diminishing returns for knowledge capital.

Multiple-Choice

The Basics of Economic Growth

1 Growthland's real GDP per capita was $112 billion in 2009 and $117 billion in 2010. What is the growth rate of Growthland's real GDP per capita?
a 4.3%
b 4.5%
c 5%
d 12%
e 17%

2 If Amazonia's growth rate of real GDP per capita is 7%, how many years before real GDP per capita doubles?
a Impossible to calculate without more data
b 3.5
c 7
d 10
e 14.3

Economic Growth Trends

3 Canada's economic growth rates were highest in which of the following decades?
a 1930s
b 1960s
c 1970s
d 1980s
e 1990s

4 Compared to growth in other countries, between 1960 and 2007 Canada
a fell behind most other countries.
b dramatically caught up to and passed other countries.
c worsened dramatically versus the United States, but did better versus other countries.
d did as well or better than most countries except certain Asian countries.
e did none of the above.

5 Which of the following statements about Canada's long-term growth trends is *false*?
   a Economic growth rates have been steady, except for the business cycle.
   b Economic growth rates shows periods of slow and high growth.
   c Economic growth rates were faster in the 1990s than in the 1980s.
   d Economic growth rates have generally been faster in Japan than in Canada.
   e African countries have fallen further behind Canada in recent years.

How Potential GDP Grows

6 The aggregate production function shows
   a how much real GDP changes as capital stock changes, all else remaining the same.
   b how much real GDP changes as price level changes, all else remaining the same.
   c how much labour demand changes as real wage rate changes, all else remaining the same.
   d how much labour demand changes as money wage rate changes, all else remaining the same.
   e none of the above.

7 The labour demand curve is
   a positively sloped and shifts with changes in the capital stock.
   b positively sloped and shifts with changes in the quantity of labour employed.
   c negatively sloped and shifts with changes in the capital stock.
   d negatively sloped and shifts with changes in the quantity of labour employed.
   e negatively sloped and shifts with changes in the real wage rate.

8 If the money wage rate is $12 per hour and the GDP deflator is 150, what is the real wage rate per hour?
   a $18
   b $15
   c $12
   d $8
   e $6

9 Which of the following quotations describes the upward-sloping labour supply curve?
   a "Recent higher wage rates have led to more leisure."
   b "The recent lower price level has induced people to work fewer hours."
   c "The recent higher real wage rate has induced people to work more hours."
   d "The recent high investment in capital equipment has raised hiring by firms."
   e "Adding extra workers leads to lower productivity of each additional worker."

10 *Ceteris paribus*, an increase in labour productivity results in a
   a higher real wage rate and higher potential GDP per hour of work.
   b lower real wage rate and higher potential GDP per hour of work.
   c higher real wage rate and lower potential GDP per hour of work.
   d lower real wage rate and lower potential GDP per hour of work.
   e constant real wage rate in the long run.

11 *Ceteris paribus*, an increase in population results in a
   a higher level of labour employed and higher potential GDP per hour of work.
   b lower level of labour employed and higher potential GDP per hour of work.
   c higher level of labour employed and lower potential GDP per hour of work.
   d lower level of labour employed and lower potential GDP per hour of work.
   e constant level of labour employed and constant potential GDP per hour of work.

Why Labour Productivity Grows

12 Which of the following is *not* a source of economic growth?
   a increasing stock market prices
   b better educated workers
   c growing stock of capital equipment
   d appropriate incentive system
   e advances in technology

13 Suppose productivity increased 20 percent last year. Capital per hour of labour increased by 12 percent as well. The increase in capital was responsible for
   a all of the productivity increase.
   b 70% of the productivity increase.
   c 60% of the productivity increase.
   d 40% of the productivity increase.
   e 30% of the productivity increase.

14 Suppose productivity increased 20 percent last year. Capital per hour of labour increased by 12 percent as well. An increase in technology was responsible for
  a all of the productivity increase.
  b 70% of the productivity increase.
  c 60% of the productivity increase.
  d 40% of the productivity increase.
  e 30% of the productivity increase.

15 Which of the following was a cause of Canada's post-1973 growth slowdown?
  a higher population pressures
  b lower saving
  c diminishing returns
  d slowdowns in technological change
  e too-rapid increases in technological change

16 Which of the following is an example of learning-by-doing?
  a The use of a laptop instead of pen and paper to take class notes.
  b A student being better at note-taking at the end of the fourth year than in the first year of university.
  c A student with five economics classes doing better in a third-year business class than a student with only one economics class.
  d A student installing a software upgrade on their computer.
  e Falling asleep on your economics text while studying.

17 Which of the following would shift the aggregate production function upward?
  a a decrease in the stock of capital
  b a decrease in the real wage rate
  c an increase in labour employed
  d an increase in the price level
  e a technological discovery

Growth Theory and Policies

18 Which of the following is a suggestion for increasing Canadian economic growth rates?
  a Stimulate saving by taxing consumption.
  b Reduce the time period for patent protection to increase replication.
  c Put less public research funds into universities.
  d Protect our industries from foreign competition.
  e Tax education.

19 Government subsidies for research and development are justified
  a because there is too little private saving.
  b because it is too expensive for small firms.
  c there are external benefits to research and development that firms ignore.
  d in order to take advantage of gains from specialization and exchange.
  e in order to overcome diminishing returns.

20 In neoclassical growth theory, if the rate of return on capital increases due to a technological advance, then
  a the rate of return on capital will eventually decline.
  b capital per hour of labour will decrease.
  c real GDP per hour of labour will decrease.
  d the rate of return on capital will never decline.
  e population growth will explode.

21 In new growth theory, if the rate of return on capital increases due to a technological advance, then
  a the rate of return on capital will eventually decline.
  b capital per hour of labour will decrease.
  c real GDP per hour of labour will decrease.
  d the rate of return on capital will never decline.
  e population growth will explode.

22 Incentives are important in the new growth theory because they
  a imply there are no diminishing returns.
  b lead to higher rates of saving.
  c imply that economic growth does not lead to population growth.
  d create specialization and exchange.
  e lead to profit-seeking searches for new discoveries.

23 In classical growth theory, economic growth eventually stops after a technological advance because
  a of diminishing returns.
  b knowledge capital is easily replicated.
  c the rate of return on capital decreases back down to the target rate of savers.
  d real GDP per person becomes too high.
  e of high population growth resulting from increasing real GDP per person.

24 Compared to physical capital, knowledge capital
  a can be replicated without diminishing returns.
  b can be held in your hand.
  c leads to an automatic slowdown in growth.
  d cannot be replicated without diminishing returns.
  e is none of the above.

25 The key difference between neoclassical growth theory and new growth theory is that
  a capital is not subject to diminishing returns under new growth theory.
  b capital is subject to diminishing returns under new growth theory.
  c increases in technology increase population which drives workers' incomes back down to subsistence levels in neoclassical theory.
  d technological advances are exogenous in new growth theory.
  e the one-third rule only holds in new growth theory.

Short Answer Problems

I Pinkland has a population of 500 in 2009 and 525 in 2010. Its real GDP is $5,500,000 in 2009 and $6,050,000 in 2010.

  a Calculate Pinkland's real GDP per capita in each year.

  b Calculate the growth rates of real GDP and real GDP per capita between 2009 and 2010.

  c If Pinkland's economic growth rate of real GDP per capita continues at this level, how many years will it take to double real GDP per capita?

2 Blueland's real GDP per capita is $100 and growing at 7% per year. Redland's real GDP per capita is $1,000 and is growing at 3.5% per year. Use the rule of 70 to construct a table showing how many years it will take Blueland's real GDP per capita to catch up to Redland's, if these growth rates remain constant.

3 Explain what happens in classical growth theory when advances in technology increase real GDP per person.

4 Some economists speculate that the Asian miracle economies have achieved such fast growth at least partially due to their adeptness at replicating new technology from other countries. Explain how and why replicating is a good source of growth.

5 Paul Krugman and others argue that in fact the Asian miracle economies' extra-high economic growth is mostly due to the mobilization of capital and labour resources that were previously underutilized, and that North American worries that these countries will surpass Canada and the United States are unfounded. Assuming it is true, explain why this argument implies these worries are unfounded.

6 Use an aggregate production function to explain why an increase in the amount of capital per hour of labour leads to economic growth.

7 You are given the data in Table 22.1 on the economy of Erehwon where the growth accounting rule is that a 1% increase in capital per hour of labour leads to a 0.5% increase in labour productivity. Labour supply and population are unchanged over these three years. Calculate the contributions to productivity growth of changes in capital per hour of labour (as a fraction of the total change) and technological change, and fill in the table.

TABLE 22.1

Year	2008	2009	2010
Capital per hour of labour ($)	125	150	200
Productivity ($)	35	40	46.7
Contribution of capital	—	?	?
Contribution of technological change	—	?	?

8 **An economy starts with the 2009 aggregate production function in Table 22.2, with 120 hours of labour hired in 2009.**

  a Graph this economy's 2009 aggregate production function.

  b A technological innovation in 2010 increases labour productivity by 10%. Show the impact of this change in the remaining columns of Table 22.2, and on your graph from part **a**.

  c Where is the likely new 2010 production point for this economy? Explain briefly.

TABLE **22.2**

Labour (hrs/yr)	Real GDP (2009)	Real GDP per hour of labour (2009)	Real GDP (2010)	Real GDP per hour of labour (2010)
100	500	5.00		
110	540	4.91		
120	570	4.75		
130	590	4.54		
140	600	4.29		
150	605	4.03		

9 Consider the economy from Short Answer Problem **8**. The 2009 labour market equilibrium was at a real wage rate of $15, with 120 hours of labour hired. After the technological innovation, assuming no population increase, explain using a graph of the labour market for this country what has happened to labour demand, labour supply, amount of labour hired and the real wage rate in 2010. Exact numbers are not needed, just an indication of the types of changes.

10 Some commentators argue that, until recently, Japan had a higher growth rate than Canada or the United States because the Japanese people care more about the future and less about present consumption, leading to a higher Japanese saving rate. Explain within the context of growth theory whether this argument seems correct.

ANSWERS

True/False and Explain

1 F **Depends on real GDP *per capita*. (516)**

2 F Growth was higher in the 1960s. (518)

3 T See text discussion. (519–520)

4 T Definition. (521)

5 T Definition of labour demand curve. (522)

6 F Increasing population increases labour supply, decreases real wage, but more labour hired so potential GDP increases. (523–524)

7 F Shifts *LD* curve rightward, and increase real wage rate. (525)

8 F Human capital growth is part of advances in technology. (527)

9 F Rapid technological change is embodied in new human and physical capital. (527)

10 F Due to slowdown in both—see text discussion. (528–530)

11 F Technological advances or increases in human capital also raise labour productivity (521)

12 T Due to law of diminishing returns. (532)

13 F Economic growth increases real GDP per hour, which increases population growth. (531)

14 T See discussion of East Asian economies. (535)

15 T Because knowledge capital can be duplicated at zero marginal cost. (533–534)

Multiple-Choice

1 b Growth rate = ((∆ real GDP per capita)/original level) × 100 = (5/112) × 100 = 4.5%. (516)

2 d By rule of 70: 70/7 = 10. (517)

3 b See text discussion. (518)

4 d See text discussion. (519–520)

5 a Growth rates have fluctuated. (519–520)

6 e Definition: how much real GDP changes as labour hired changes. (521–523)

7 c Negatively sloped due to diminishing marginal product. **d** and **e** imply movements along demand curve. (519–523)

8 d Real wage = (money wage/price level) × 100. (519–523)

9 c Higher wages, higher quantity of labour supplied. **a**, **b** are opposite relationships, **d** and **e** refer to labour demand. (519–523)

10 a Productivity increase increases labour demand, raising real wage rate. Potential GDP per hour of work = productivity, so must have increased. (523–526)

11 c Labour supply shifts rightward, real wage falls, more people hired, but potential GDP per hour of work falls due to diminishing marginal productivity. (523–526)

12 a Prices have no impact on productivity, others increase it. (526–527)

13 e Capital increase of 12 percent leads to real GDP per hour of labour increase of 6 percent (0.49×12), or 30 percent of productivity increase. (528–530)

14 b From **13**, 70 percent is left over for technology to explain. (528–530)

15 d See text discussion. (528–530)

16 b The student has learned by repetition. (527)

17 e Technological discovery increases productivity of labour. (526–527)

18 a **b** would lower return to and number of inventions, **c** would lower research and number of inventions, and trade and education should be encouraged. (535)

19 c See text discussion. (535)

20 a If rate of return on capital is high, saving increases supply of capital, increasing capital per hour of labour (and more real GDP per hour of labour). Eventually rate of return on capital decreases due to law of diminishing returns. (531–534)

21 d If rate of return on capital is high, saving increases supply of capital, increasing capital per hour of labour (and more real GDP per hour of labour), but no change in rate of return on capital since law of diminishing returns doesn't apply to knowledge capital. (531–534)

22 e This assumption makes technological change endogenous, and continuous. (531–534)

23 e This growth leads to decrease in real GDP per hour of labour. (531–534)

24 a Due to its nature—see text discussion. (531–534)

25 a Due to different nature of knowledge capital. (531–534)

Short Answer Problems

1 a Real GDP per capita = real GDP/population. In 2009, equals $5,500,000/500 = $11,000. In 2010, equals $6,050,000/525 = $11,524.

b Growth rate of real GDP =
$$\frac{6,050,000 - 5,500,000}{5,500,000} \times 100\% = 10\%.$$
Growth rate of real GDP per capita =
$$\frac{11,524 - 11,000}{11,000} \times 100\% = 4.8\%.$$

c From the rule of 70, $70/4.8 = 17.5$ years.

2 The rule of 70 means Blueland's real GDP per capita doubles every 10 years (= 70/7) while Redland's doubles every 20 years (= 70/3.5). Table 22.3 below shows the progress of each country's real GDP over several decades, and shows that Blueland will catch up to Redland in about 70 years.

TABLE 22.3

Year	Blueland Real GDP per capita	Redland Real GDP per capita
0	100	1,000
10	200	
20	400	2,000
30	800	
40	1,600	4,000
50	3,200	
60	6,400	8,000
70	12,800	
80	25,600	16,000

3 Technology advances increase the demand for labour, and real GDP per hour of labour. As real GDP per hour goes up, population growth increases, increasing the supply of labour, decreasing real GDP per hour back down to the subsistence wage rate, so workers are no better off than at the beginning.

4 Knowledge capital can be replicated without diminishing returns, so that the rate of return on capital increases after replication, which in turn brings more saving and investment. Capital per hour of labour can increase without limit, implying growth can increase without limit.

5 If Asian growth is due to increasing amounts of capital and labour, eventually these countries will run into diminishing returns to each of these inputs, so increases in productivity will slow down, meaning economic growth will also slow.

6 The aggregate production function illustrates how output increases as the amount of labour hired increases, holding constant labour productivity. Labour productivity increases with more physical capital, more human capital or technological advances. If capital per hour of labour increases, the productivity of workers is increasing, so output per hour of labour is increasing—there is faster economic growth. This is illustrated graphically by an upward shift in the aggregate production function, reflecting more output for each amount of labour used.

⊕ 7 Table 22.1 is reproduced below as Table 22.1 Solution, with the calculations in place.

TABLE **22.1** SOLUTION

Year	2008	2009	2010
Capital per hour of labour ($)	125	150	200
Productivity ($)	35	40	46.7
Contribution of capital	—	70%	100%
Contribution of technological change	—	30%	0

The percentage change in capital from 2008 to 2009 was 20 percent ((25/125) × 100), implying a resulting percentage change in productivity of 10 percent. The total change in productivity was 14.3 percent ((5/35) × 100), leaving 4.3 percent due to technological change. Capital's contribution was (10/14.3) × 100 = 70 percent, and technology's contribution was 30 percent.

The percentage change in capital from 2009 to 2010 was 33.3 percent ((50/150) × 100), implying a resulting percentage change in productivity of 16.7 percent. The total change in productivity was 16.7 percent ((6.7/40) × 100), leaving no contribution due to technological change. Capital's contribution was 100 percent.

8 a Figure 22.1 below shows the graph of the 2009 production function, labelled PF_{2009}.

Figure 22.1

b Table 22.2 Solution below shows the impact of the 10% increase in productivity as 10% higher real GDP at each level of labour, which translates into 10% higher real GDP per hour of labour hired.

The new 2010 production function in Figure 22.1 is labelled PF_{2010}.

TABLE **22.2** Solution

Labour (hrs/yr)	Real GDP (2009)	Real GDP per hour of labour (2009)	Real GDP (2010)	Real GDP per hour of labour (2010)
100	500	5.00	550	5.5
110	540	4.91	594	5.4
120	570	4.75	627	5.23
130	590	4.54	649	4.99
140	600	4.29	660	4.71
150	605	4.03	665.5	4.44

c If the original labour hired was 120, we know that the higher productivity (5.23 > 4.75) means firms want to hire more labour, not less. Therefore, we can assume labour hired is at least 120, if not higher. Reading off the PF_{2010} curve, production will at least be at real GDP of 627, if not higher.

9 Figure 22.2 shows the original labour demand curve (LD0), labour supply curve (LS0) and the original wage and quantity labour hired. As in the answer to Short Answer Problem 8 c, labour demand will rise due to higher productivity. Labour supply is initially unchanged due to unchanged population, so the higher labour demand leads to a higher real wage rate, inducing a higher quantity of labour supplied, shown as a movement along the labour supply curve to a new, higher level of labour hired in the market equilibrium. Figure 22.2 shows this change. We cannot tell exactly how much the real wage rate increases, or how much more labour is hired, but it will be higher than the original levels for both.

Figure **22.2**

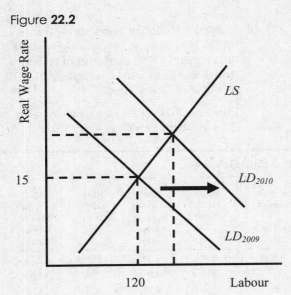

10   If the Japanese people had a higher saving rate, this meant the increase in the supply of capital in Japan is higher in any situation. In general, Japan would have a higher capital stock per person than Canada, and it would be increasing each year at a higher rate, in turn leading to a higher growth rate of real GDP per person in Japan than in Canada. Thus this argument seems to hold true.

Chapter 23

Finance, Saving, and Investment

Financial Markets and Financial Institutions

Financial markets channel saving from households to firms, who invest in new capital.

♦ *Finance*—activity of providing funds for capital expenditures. *Money*—used to pay for items and make financial expenditures.

♦ Physical capital is tools, instruments, machines, buildings used to produce goods and services. **Financial capital** is funds firms use to buy physical capital which produces real GDP.

♦ **Gross investment** = amount spent on new capital. **Net investment** = Δ value of capital stock = gross investment – depreciation.

♦ **Wealth** = value of things people own. Δ wealth = **saving** (= income – net taxes – consumption) + capital gains/losses.

Three types of financial markets:

♦ Loan markets involve businesses or households borrowing from banks, including household **mortgages**—legal lending contracts giving lender ownership of house if borrower defaults.

♦ **Bond markets** involve firms, governments issuing/selling **bonds** (promise to make specified payments on specified dates).

  • Bond terms can be months up to decades.

  • **Mortgage-backed securities** are bonds paying income from package of mortgages.

♦ Firms' **stock** shares (certificate of ownership and claim to profits) traded in **stock markets**.

Financial markets highly competitive from simultaneous borrowing and lending by **financial institutions** (firms operating on both sides of financial markets), including banks, trust and loan companies, credit unions, caisse populaires, pension funds, insurance companies.

♦ During 2008 financial crisis, pension funds and financial institutions were hurt as investments in mortgage-backed securities collapsed in value when U.S. housing market collapsed.

♦ Companies become insolvent when **net worth** (total market value of lending – total market value of borrowing) is negative.

♦ Companies become illiquid if they are solvent but have insufficient cash to meet debt payments.

♦ Insolvent companies forced to merge or taken over by government.

♦ Interest rate on asset = $\dfrac{\text{interest received}}{\text{price of asset}} \times 100$

♦ Price of asset and interest rate inversely related.

The Market for Loanable Funds

Market for loanable funds—aggregate of all financial markets.

♦ Adding financial flows from loanable funds to circular flow shows how investment is financed.

♦ Households' income spent on consumption or saving or **net taxes** (T = taxes – transfer payments received from governments): $Y = C + S + T$.

♦ Circular flow from Chapter 20 shows: $Y = C + I + G + X - M$.

♦ Combining above, I financed by private saving (S) + government saving ($T - G$) + borrowing from rest of world ($M - X$):

$I = S + (T - G) + (M - X)$

♦ If $T > G$, government can lend some of its surplus.

♦ If foreigners sell Canadians more goods than they buy from us ($M > X$), we must borrow from them to finance difference, so foreign savings flows to Canada for investment purposes.

♦ I financed by **national saving** ($= S + (T - G)$) + foreign borrowing.

Nominal interest rate = dollars paid yearly in interest by borrower to lender as percent of dollars borrowed.

♦ **Real interest rate**—nominal rate adjusted for inflation ($\approx$ nominal interest rate – inflation rate).

♦ Real interest rate is opportunity cost of loanable funds—determined in market for loanable funds.

Quantity of loanable funds *demanded* to finance investment, government budget deficit, international lending.

♦ Higher real interest rate, lower is quantity of loanable funds demanded—**demand for loanable funds** (*DLF* curve) has negative relationship between real interest rate and quantity demanded.

♦ *DLF* shifts rightward if expected profit increases.

Quantity of loanable funds *supplied* from saving, government budget surplus, international borrowing.

♦ Higher real interest rate, higher is quantity of loanable funds supplied—**supply of loanable funds** (*SLF* curve) has positive relationship between real interest rate and quantity supplied.

♦ *SLF* curve shifts rightward if disposable income increases, expected future income falls, wealth falls, or default risk falls.

Real interest rate adjustments achieve equilibrium where quantity loanable funds demanded = quantity supplied.

♦ Factors shifting *DLF* rightward lead to new equilibrium with higher real interest rate, more loanable funds supplied.

♦ Factors shifting *SLF* rightward lead to new equilibrium with lower real interest rate, more loanable funds demanded.

♦ Real interest rate has no trend over time.

Starting in 2001, U.S. Federal Reserve (the Fed) provided loanable funds (increasing *SLF*), leading to lower interest rates and large increase in house prices.

♦ In 2006, Fed slowed *SLF* growth, interest rates rose, and many mortgage-holders defaulted, pushing financial institutions into insolvency.

Government in the Market for Loanable Funds

Government budget surplus increases supply of loanable funds, lowering real interest rate—investment increases more than private saving decreases.

♦ Budget deficit increases demand for loanable funds, raising real interest rate—investment decreases (**crowding-out**) more than private saving increases.

♦ Ricardo-Barro effect states rational taxpayers know increases in budget deficit (surplus) imply higher (lower) future taxes, so they adjust saving by equivalent amount—no change in real interest rate.

The Global Loanable Funds Market

Loanable funds market is global—suppliers move to national markets with highest real interest rates, demanders to markets with lowest real interest rate.

♦ Flows in funds mean there will be one real interest rate globally (for assets with equal risk).

♦ Riskier assets will pay interest rate = rate on safe loan + risk premium.

♦ Country with higher interest rate than global rate will be a net borrower globally and have negative net exports as a result.

♦ Country with lower interest rate than global rate will be a net lender globally and have positive net exports as a result.

♦ Changes in demand and supply for small countries like Canada have no effect on global interest rate. Changes for larger country shift world *DLF* or *SLF* and affect global interest rate.

HELPFUL HINTS

I   Financial markets and financial institutions are at the centre of many economic activities. In Chapter 22 on economic growth, investment in physical capital plays a key role in creating economic growth. This chapter explains how household saving, government saving, and investment from foreigners is channelled via financial markets and institutions to firms that purchase capital goods to carry out investment.

These concepts will reappear in Chapter 24 ("Money, the Price Level, and Inflation") and Chapter 30 ("Monetary Policy"), where we will see the role of the central bank in setting interest rates in financial markets (affecting investment and overall economic activity). Chapter 25 will highlight key relationships between interest rates, exchange rates, and the overall economy. Chapter 28 illustrates the impact of financial market problems on the business cycle, and Chapter 29 explains how government fiscal policy interacts with the financial markets to affect interest rates and investment.

Financial markets and institutions are the key to understanding many other economic activities and policies. In the 2007–2009 financial crisis, a combination of external forces and loose monetary policy created a housing bubble. When the bubble started collapsing in 2007, this led to difficulties with financial institutions, difficulties that have spread to the goods and services markets, and to the labour market. At the time of writing this Study Guide, governments of the western economies are carrying out massive monetary expansions and planning the largest fiscal stimuli in history in an attempt to avert a long recession. We will explore how these policies generally work in Chapters 29 and 30.

2 Although Canada is a strong developed country with a high standard of living, it is still a relatively small player on world financial markets. This means that the (risk-adjusted) real interest rate in Canada is set in the world market. Consequently, even though Canada has a strong financial sector without a housing crisis, we can still be affected by a U.S.-born financial crisis. The U.S. crisis has led to higher U.S. real interest rates (and higher aversion to risk), and these higher interest rates have spread to Canadian financial markets, creating negative effects for the Canadian economy.

SELF-TEST

True/False and Explain

Financial Markets and Financial Institutions

1 When a household buys stock in a company, this is an example of gross investment.

2 A company is illiquid when it has negative net worth.

3 A mortgage is a bond paying income based on a package of house loans.

4 If a household has saving of $2,000 and a capital loss of $3,000, its net wealth will decrease.

5 If the interest rate on an asset increases, the price of the asset increases.

The Market for Loanable Funds

6 The higher a household's expected future income, the more loanable funds they will supply.

7 If the nominal interest rate is 6% and the inflation rate is 4%, the real interest rate is 10%.

8 With no government and no international sector, if the demand for loanable funds is greater than the supply of loanable funds at the current real interest rate, the real interest rate will increase.

9 With no government and no international sector, an increase in the profits firms expect to earn will lead to a higher real interest rate in the loanable funds market.

10 $I = S + (G - T) + (M - X)$.

11 If the inflation rate increases and the nominal interest rate has increased, the real interest rate must be constant.

Government in the Market for Loanable Funds

12 If there is no Ricardo-Barro effect, a higher government deficit lowers investment, other things being equal.

13 If there is a Ricardo-Barro effect, a higher government deficit lowers investment, other things being equal.

The Global Loanable Funds Market

14 If Calonia is a net lender to the rest of the world, it will have positive net exports.

15 Calonia is a small part of the global loanable funds market. If Calonia's demand for loanable funds is greater than Calonia's supply of loanable funds at the current real interest rate, the real interest rate will increase.

Multiple-Choice

Financial Markets and Financial Institutions

1 The capital stock does *not* include the
  a inventory of raw cucumbers ready to be made into pickles by the Smith Pickle Company.
  b Smith family holdings of stock in the Smith Pickle Company.
  c pickle factory building owned by the Smith family.
  d pickle-packing machine in the pickle factory building owned by the Smith family.
  e pickle inventories in the pickle factory building owned by the Smith family.

2 Eel Electronics has lent $10 million and borrowed $8 million. It has cash earnings per month of $100,000 and debt payments per month of $120,000. Eel Electronics is
  a solvent and liquid.
  b insolvent and illiquid.
  c solvent and illiquid.
  d insolvent and liquid.
  e solvent if interest rates are low enough.

3 On Jan. 1, 2009, Bobcat Excavations had $50,000 worth of bobcat machines. During 2009, these machines fell in value by 50%. Bobcat also bought $35,000 worth of new machines. What was Bobcat's net investment in 2009?
  a $10,000
  b $25,000
  c $35,000
  d $60,000
  e $85,000

4 In which market would you find mortgage-backed securities?
  a stock market
  b bond market
  c housing market
  d capital market
  e loan market

5 Elena starts the year with $2,500 worth of stock and no other wealth. Her grandmother gives her a $5,000 Canada Saving Bond. Elena earns $15,000 in income, pays $1,000 in taxes, and spends $15,000 on consumption goods. Her stocks rise in value to $3,000. What is Elena's wealth at the end of the year?

a $6,500
b $7,000
c $7,500
d $8,000
e $9,000

6 Elena owns a Canada Saving Bond initially worth $5,000, which pays $500 per year. The value of the bond rises in the bond market to $7,500. What is the new interest rate on the bond?

a 5%
b 6.67%
c 10%
d 20%
e 500%

7 The key characteristic of financial institutions is that they

a are always liquid.
b will lend to anyone.
c buy a diversified portfolio of assets.
d simultaneously borrow and lend.
e provide risk-sharing services.

The Market for Loanable Funds

8 Which of the following shifts the supply curve of loanable funds leftward?

a increase in current disposable income
b decrease in current disposable income
c decrease in expected future income
d increase in the real interest rate
e decrease in the real interest rate

9 Which of the following is *false*?

a $Y = C + I + G + M - X$
b $I = S + (T - G) + (M - X)$
c $Y = C + S + T$
d $Y + M = C + I + G + X$
e $Y = C + I + G + X - M$

10 Saving can be measured as income minus

a taxes.
b transfer payments.
c net taxes minus consumption expenditure.
d consumption expenditure.
e net taxes plus subsidies.

11 In Canada's economy, investment is financed by

a $C + I + G + X - M$.
b $C + S + T$.
c $S + T + M$.
d $S + (T - G) + (X - M)$.
e $S + (T - G) + (M - X)$.

12 Which of the following causes a household to increase the amount it saves?

a decrease in current disposable income
b increase in expected future income
c increase in net taxes
d decrease in expected future income
e none of the above

13 Investment will be higher if

a the government deficit is higher.
b national saving is higher.
c net exports are higher.
d the real interest rate is higher.
e government spending is higher.

14 Southton has investment of $100, household saving of $90, net taxes of $25, government spending of $30, exports of $25 and imports of $10. What is national saving?

a $85
b $90
c $95
d $100
e $105

15 If the inflation rate increases by 3 percent and the nominal interest rate increases by 2 percent, the

a real interest rate increases.
b opportunity cost of borrowing increases.
c opportunity cost of borrowing decreases.
d opportunity cost of spending increases.
e level of spending decreases.

16 Table 23.1 shows the initial market for loanable funds in Northland. The prime minister of Northland gives a brilliant speech, convincing firms in Northland of future strong economic growth in the country. The likely new equilibrium has a real interest rate of ___ with a quantity of loanable funds of ____.

a 6%; $100 billion.
b 7%; $100 billion.
c 7%; $120 billion.
d 5%; $120 billion.
e 5%; $80 billion.

TABLE **23.1** DATA FROM NORTHLAND

Real Interest Rate	Demand for Loanable Funds ($ billions)	Supply of Loanable Fund ($ billions)
3%	160	40
4%	140	60
5%	120	80
6%	100	100
7%	80	120
8%	60	140

17 Table 23.1 shows the initial market for loanable funds in Northland. Disposable income then increases. The likely new equilibrium has a real interest rate of ____ with a quantity of loanable funds of ____.
a 6%; $100 billion.
b 7%; $100 billion.
c 7%; $120 billion.
d 5%; $120 billion.
e 5%; $80 billion.

Government in the Market for Loanable Funds

18 Table 23.1 shows the initial market for loanable funds in Northland. There is no Ricardo-Barro effect. If the government moves from a balanced budget to a surplus of $20 billion, the new equilibrium has a real interest rate of ____ and quantity of loanable funds traded equal to ____.
a 6.5%; $110 billion
b 6.5%; $90 billion
c 5.5%; $90 billion
d 5.5%; $110 billion
e 6%; $120 billion

19 In the market for loanable funds, if the Ricardo-Barro effect does not hold, a higher government surplus leads to
a increased real interest rate, and increased investment.
b increased real interest rate, and decreased investment.
c decreased real interest rate, and increased investment.
d decreased real interest rate, and decreased investment.
e no effect on real interest rate or investment.

20 Figure 23.1 shows the loanable funds market for a country that is not part of the global market. Currently the country has a government budget balance = 0. There is no Ricardo-Barro effect. If the government introduces a deficit of $20 billion, the new real interest rate = ____ and the new level of investment = ____.
a 7%; $40 billion
b 5%; $60 billion
c 7%; $50 billion
d 5%; $50 billion
e 6%; $50 billion

The Global Loanable Funds Market

21 Figure 23.1 shows the loanable funds market for a country that is part of the global market, with no government budget deficit or surplus. If the world interest rate is 4%, we have net ____ and investment of ____.
a lending of $40 billion; $40 billion.
b borrowing of $40 billion; $30 billion.
c borrowing of $0 billion; $50 billion.
d borrowing of $40 billion; $70 billion.
e lending of $40 billion; $70 billion.

22 Which of the following newspaper quotations describes a situation where Canada would end up with lower investment?
a "A rise in the U.S. government budget deficit is forcing up world interest rates."
b "World lenders are worried about Canada's government budget deficit."
c "The booming Chinese economy is dramatically raising its spending on new investment projects."
d All of the above.
e None of the above.

23 In the global economy, investment is financed by
a $S + (T - G)$.
b $S + (T - G) - (X - M)$.
c $S + (G - T)$.
d $S + (T - G) + (X - M)$.
e $S + (T - G) + (M - X)$.

24 In Canada's economy, the real interest rate is determined by
   a national investment.
   b national saving.
   c the government budget deficit/surplus.
   d all of the above.
   e none of the above.

25 Calonia is a small country in the global loanable funds market, and is currently an international borrower. If there is no Ricardo-Barro effect, what will happen in Calonia's loanable funds market if the government deficit increases?

   a Less borrowing from the rest of the world.
   b Investment will increase.
   c In the circular flow, consumption expenditure will fall.
   d Investment will not change.
   e Investment will decrease.

Short Answer Problems

1 The Athabasca Oil Exploration Company starts the year with $1 million worth of equipment. It has debts of $500,000, for a beginning net worth of $500,000. During the year, the following events occur:

   - Athabasca borrows $2.5 million to buy $2 million worth of new equipment plus $500,000 worth of stock in another company.
   - The stock in the other company increases in value to $600,000.
   - Athabasca's old equipment depreciates in value to a worth of $250,000.

   a Calculate Athabasca's gross and net investment for the year, and the end of year value of its physical capital stock.

   b At the end of the year, what is Athabasca's net worth? Is it solvent?

2 In an interview in the late 1990s, the Governor of the Bank of Canada argued that Canada's interest rates had fallen drastically in the late 1990s because the federal and provincial governments had drastically reduced the size of their budget deficits, and that this would increase investment spending. Assume initially that Canada does not participate in the global loanable funds market. With the help of a graph, explain if his explanation makes sense.

3 Return to the statements made by the Governor in question **2**. In reality, Canada does participate in the global loanable funds market, and was a net borrower in the late 1990s. In this case, would Canada's lower budget deficits lead to lower interest rates? Once again, draw a (new) graph of the loanable funds market as part of your answer.

4 Consider the following data on Calonia:

TABLE **23.2** DATA FOR CALONIA

Item	Amount (billions of $)
Consumption expenditure (C)	600
Net taxes (T)	300
Exports (X)	240
Imports (M)	220
Government expenditure on goods and services (G)	200
Net investment (I)	150
Depreciation	60
Household income (Y)	1030

Use this data to calculate Calonia's:

   a Gross investment
   b Net exports and foreign borrowing or lending
   c Government deficit or surplus
   d Household saving
   e National saving
   f Total funds available for investment

5 Marie started the year with $100,000 of stock. During the year, the following events occurred:
   - Marie's stocks rose in value to $128,000. She sold $20,000 of stock at the end of the year to use as a down payment on her new house.
   - Marie borrowed $172,000 from the bank, and with her stock sale proceeds as the difference, bought a house for $192,000.
   - Marie earned $35,000, and paid $12,000 in taxes.
   - Marie consumed $22,000.

   Showing all steps, calculate Marie's wealth at the end of the year.

6 Opar is an isolated economy that does not trade with the world. It has constant real GDP of 100 million opals, government expenditure is constant at $12 million opals, and the government deficit is constant at 2 million opals. Consider the values of consumption and investment shown in Table 23.3.

TABLE 23.3 DATA FROM OPAR

Real Interest Rate	C	Supply of loanable funds (Saving)	I	Demand for loanable funds
3%	75		22	
4%	70		18	
5%	65		14	
6%	60		10	
7%	55		6	
8%	50		2	

a   Calculate and fill in the two blank columns of the table. What is the real interest rate and quantity of loanable funds in Opar in equilibrium?

Pellucidar is another isolated economy that does not trade with the world. It has constant real GDP of 120 million opals, government expenditure is constant at $15 million opals, and the government deficit is constant at 4 million opals. Consider the values of consumption and investment shown in Table 23.4.

b   Calculate and fill in the two blank columns of the table. What is the real interest rate and quantity of loanable funds in Pellucidar in equilibrium?

TABLE 23.4 DATA FROM PELLUCIDAR

Real Interest Rate	C	Supply of loanables funds (Saving)	I	Demand for loanable funds
3%	100		32	
4%	95		28	
5%	90		24	
6%	85		20	
7%	80		16	
8%	75		12	

7   An enterprising entrepreneur builds a machine that drills through the earth and connects Opar to Pellucidar. International trade opens up, and so does a loanable funds market between the two countries.

Table 23.5 below shows the total *world* loanable funds market.

TABLE 23.5 WORLD DATA

Real Interest Rate	C	Supply of loanable funds (Saving)	I	Demand for loanable funds
3%	175		54	
4%				
5%				
6%				
7%				
8%				

a   Using your data from Tables 23.3 and 23.4, fill in the remaining information and find the world equilibrium real interest rate and quantity of loanable funds traded.

b   For Opar after world trade, what is the level of domestic saving, domestic investment, net exports and international lending or borrowing?

c   For Pellucidar after world trade, what is the level of domestic saving, domestic investment, net exports and international lending or borrowing?

8   Suppose that a technological innovation dramatically raises expected profits in Canada. Assuming that Canada is initially neither a net lender nor a net borrower on the global loanable funds market. Draw a graph of Canada's loanable funds market and show the impact (if any) of the innovation on the demand for loanable funds, the supply of loanable funds, the real interest rate, investment, net exports, and foreign borrowing or lending.

9   Suppose that a new government is elected in Canada, and unexpectedly cuts all taxes in half. Assume that the Ricardo-Barro effect does not hold and that Canada is initially neither a net lender nor a net borrower on the global loanable funds market. Draw a graph of Canada's loanable funds market, show the impact (if any) of the innovation on the demand for loanable funds, the supply of loanable funds, the real

interest rate, investment, net exports, and foreign borrowing or lending.
Explain in words how your answer would change if the Ricardo-Barro effect does hold.

ⓒ 10   Explain the role of financial markets (especially U.S. and global loanable funds markets) and financial institutions in the evolution of the 2008 financial crisis.

ANSWERS

True/False and Explain

1   F   Example of financial capital, not physical capital. (544)

2   F   Insolvent = negative net worth. Illiquid = solvent (positive net worth) but insufficient cash to meet debt payments. (547)

3   F   Mortgage is contract giving lender house ownership if borrower defaults. (545–546)

4   T   Δ Net wealth = saving – capital loss = $2,000 – $3,000 = –$1,000. (544–545)

5   F   With constant interest payment, interest rate and asset price are inversely related. (548)

6   F   Higher future income, less saving, less loanable funds supplied. (551–552)

7   F   Real ≈ nominal – inflation = 6% – 4% = 2%. (549–550)

8   T   Excess demand pushes up real interest rate, decreasing quantity demanded, increasing quantity supplied until equal at new equilibrium real interest rate. (552)

9   T   Higher expected profits lead to higher demand for loanable funds, creating a shortage, raising real interest rates. (552–553)

10   F $I = S + (T - G) + (M - X)$. (548–549)

11   F   Real = nominal – inflation. Depends on how much nominal rate and inflation rate have increased. (549–550)

12   T   Higher deficit means more government borrowing, shifting *DLF* rightward, increasing real interest rate, lowering investment. (556)

13   F   Effect from **12** is countered by rational taxpayers saving for higher future tax payments—*SLF* shifts rightward. (556)

14   T   When Calonia lends, rest of the world is using the funds to pay for Calonia's positive net exports = rest of world's negative net exports. (557)

15   F   Real interest rate determined by global rate. If Calonia's demand greater than supply, Calonia borrows from rest of world. (557–558)

Multiple-Choice

1   b   Definition. (544)

2   c   Net worth = $10 million – $8 million > 0 (solvent), and cash payments < debt payments (illiquid). (547)

3   a   Net investment = gross investment – depreciation = $35,000 – $25,000 (0.50 × $50,000) = $10,000. (544)

4   b   Bonds paying income from package of mortgages. (545)

5   b   New wealth = original wealth + Δ wealth = original wealth + saving + capital gain/loss + stock gift = original wealth + after-tax income – consumption + capital gain/loss + stock gift = $2,500 + $15,000 – $1,000 – $15,000 + $500 + $5,000 = $7,000. (544)

6   b   Interest rate = (interest payment)/value × 100 = $500/$7,500 × 100 = 6.67%. (548)

7   d   Definition. (546)

8   b   Less income available for saving. (551–552)

9   a   Should be $X - M$ and not $M - X$. (548–549)

10   c   From $S = (Y - T) - C$. (548–549)

11   e   Definition. (548–549)

12   d   Higher future income means for saving for future. (551–552)

13   b $I = S + (T - G) + (M - X)$ tells us **a, c, e** are false and **b** is true. Higher real interest rate discourages investment. (548–551)

14   a   National saving = $S + (T - G)$ = $90 + $25 – $30 = $85. (548–549)

15   c   Real interest rate decreases since increase in inflation rate > increase in nominal interest rate. Opportunity cost of spending decreases and spending increases. Real interest rate decreases, opportunity cost of borrowing decreases. (549–550)

16 c Expected future profits increase shifts *DLF* rightward, raising real interest rate and quantity of loanable funds. (552–553)

17 d Higher disposable income shifts *SLF* rightward, real interest rate falls, quantity of loanable funds increases. (552–553)

18 a Deficit shifts *DLF* rightward by $20 billion at every level. New equilibrium where new *DLF* and old *SLF* intersect. (556)

19 c *SLF* shifts rightward— real interest rate decreases, increasing investment. (556)

20 a *DLF* shifts rightward by $20 billion— real interest rate increases to 7%, decreasing investment along old *DLF*. (556)

21 d Imagine flat *SLF* at 4%, borrow difference between domestic *DLF* and *SLF*. (557–559)

22 d **a** shifts world *SLF* leftward, **b** raises the risk premium (adds a risk premium to the world interest rate when Canada borrows), **c** shifts world *DLF* rightward. (557–559)

23 a In global economy $X = M$. (557–559)

(ct) **24 e** It is determined by the world real interest rate. (557–558)

(ct) **25 d** *SLF* horizontal at global real interest rate. More funds will flow in to finance the deficit. With no change in real interest rate, there is no change in investment. (557–558)

Short Answer Problems

1 a Gross investment = total spending on (physical) capital equipment = $2 million. Net investment = gross investment – depreciation = $2 million – $750,000 = $1.25 million. Capital stock = old capital stock + net investment = $1 million + $1.25 million = $2.25 million.

b Net worth = total market value of (physical and financial) assets – total market value of borrowing = $2.25 million + $600,000 – $3 million = –$150,000. It has negative net worth, it is insolvent.

2 Figure 23.2 shows the effects the governor is talking about in action. DLF_0 is the original demand for loanable funds, with r_0 the original real interest rate.

Figure **23.2**

Deficit reduction causes a decline in the demand for loanable funds– shift to DLF_1. With no global markets, this leads to a lower real interest rate r_1. The lower real interest rate increases the quantity of investment demand, shown as the movement along the *DLF* curve. Assuming deficits are now zero, the quantity of investment demand goes from I_0 to I_1. (Assuming no Ricardo-Barro effect.)

3 Figure 23.3 on the next page shows the situation with a global market. Since Canada was initially a net borrower, we know the world interest rate (r_{WORLD}) is initially lower than a Canadian-only equilibrium, and at this interest rate the demand for loanable funds is greater than the supply.

Figure **23.3**

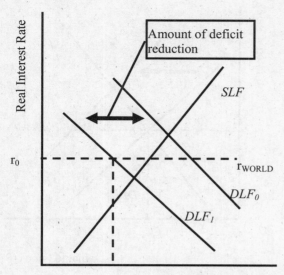

With the deficit reduction comes a decline in the demand for loanable funds, the leftward shift to DLF_1. With global markets, this does not change the real interest rate, and there is also no change in the level of investment (still measured on DLF_1).

In reality, another change occurred. The lower Canadian deficit reduced the perception of the riskiness of Canadian assets. The risk premium fell, and the r_{WORLD} that Canada pays did fall a bit, and the quantity of investment demanded did increase a bit.

4 a   Gross investment = net investment + depreciation = $150 + $60 = $210 billion.

b   Net exports = $X - M$ = $240 - $220 = $20 billion. Since net exports positive, we are lending to foreigners; foreign lending= $20 billion.

c $G - T$ = $200 - $300 = -$100 billion, a government surplus.

d   Household saving = $Y - C - T$ = $1030 - $600 - $300 = $130 billion.

e   National saving = $S + (T - G)$ = $130 + $100 = $230 billion.

f I = national saving – foreign lending = $230 -$20 = $210 billion.

5   First, we must calculate Marie's saving, which is income – consumption – net taxes = $35,000 –

$12,000 - $22,000 = $1,000. This will be added to her wealth.

Second, value of the stocks = $128,000 – $20,000 in sales = $108,000.

Third, she has a house worth $192,000.

So, assets = $1,000 + $108,000 + $192,000 = $301,000. However, we must deduct her debts of $172,000 for net wealth of $129,000.

6 a   Table 23.3 Solution is filled in below. Saving is calculated as $S = Y - C - T$, where income is constant at 100 million opals, and taxes are 10 million opals given the deficit of 2 million opals and government expenditure of 12 million opals. The demand for loanable funds = I + the deficit of 2 million opals.

TABLE **23.3** SOLUTION

Real Interest Rate	C	Supply of loanable funds (Saving)	I	Demand for loanable funds
3%	75	15	22	24
4%	70	20	18	20
5%	65	25	14	16
6%	60	30	10	12
7%	55	35	6	8
8%	50	40	2	4

Equilibrium occurs when quantity demanded equals quantity supplied of 20 million opals at 4%.

b   Table 23.4 Solution is filled in below, using the same method as in **a**. Equilibrium occurs at an interest rate of 6% with 24 million opals traded.

TABLE **23.4** SOLUTION

Real Interest Rate	C	Supply of loanable funds (Saving)	I	Demand for loanable funds
3%	100	9	32	36
4%	95	14	28	32
5%	90	19	24	28
6%	85	24	20	24
7%	80	29	16	20
8%	75	34	12	16

7 a Table 23.5 Solution is calculated first by
adding the consumption of each country at
each real interest rate, etc. The world real
interest rate occurs when world quantity
supplied equals world quantity demanded at
44 million opals and real interest rate of 5%.

TABLE 23.5 SOLUTION

Real Interest Rate	C	Supply of loanable funds (Saving)	I	Demand for loanable funds
3%	175	24	54	60
4%	165	34	46	52
5%	155	44	38	44
6%	145	54	30	36
7%	135	64	22	28
8%	125	74	14	20

b At a real interest rate of 5%, in Opar the
quantity supplied of loanable funds is 25
million opals, the quantity demanded is
16 million opals. This leaves a surplus of
9 million opals that are lent internationally
(foreigners borrow 9 million opals), so that
net exports equal +9 million opals.

c At a real interest rate of 5%, in Pellucidar
the quantity supplied of loanable funds is
19 million opals, the quantity demanded is
28 million opals. This leaves a shortage of
9 million opals that are borrowed
internationally (foreigners lend 9 million
opals), so that net exports equal –9 million
opals.

8 Figure 23.4 shows the loanable funds
market. Since Canada is neither a net lender
nor a net borrower, the Canadian quantity
demanded and supplied of loanable funds is
initially equal at the world real interest rate.

Figure **23.4**

The initial impact of the increased
profits is increased investment by firms,
leading to a rightward shift in the demand
for loanable funds to DLF_1, with a resulting
increase in the quantity of loanable funds
traded from LF_0 to LF_1 (the difference
equals the additional investment) and no
change in the real interest rate. There is no
change in the Canadian supply, so extra
loanable funds come from the global market
by borrowing internationally the difference
between LF_0 and LF_1. As a net international
borrower, Canada must now have negative
net exports equal to that amount.

9 Figure 23.5 shows the loanable funds
market. Since Canada is neither a net lender
nor a net borrower, the Canadian quantity
demanded and supplied of loanable funds is
initially equal at the world real interest rate.

Figure **23.5**

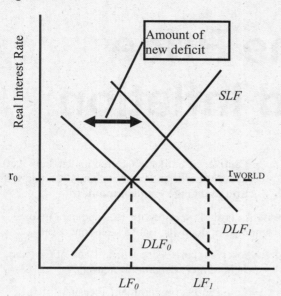

The initial impact of the lower taxes is an increased deficit, leading to a rightward shift in the demand for loanable funds to DLF_1, with a resulting increase in the quantity of loanable funds traded from LF_0 to LF_1 (the difference equals the new deficit) and no change in the real interest rate. There is no change in Canadian supply, so extra loanable funds come from the global market by borrowing internationally the difference between LF_0 and LF_1. As a net international borrower, Canada must now have negative net exports equal to that amount.

A higher deficit might change the risk premium people demand to lend to Canada, raising the r_{WORLD} that Canada pays.

If the Ricardo-Barro effect holds, Canadian taxpayers would realize that the deficit implies higher future taxes, and save more to pay these taxes. The extra saving would shift the SLF curve rightward by the same amount as the DLF shifted rightward, and the net effect would be no need to borrow internationally.

10 Starting in 2001, the U.S. Federal Reserve (the Fed) provided loanable funds to financial markets, shifting the SLF rightward, pushing down real interest rates. In combination with increased competition in mortgage markets, lower real interest rates fuelled borrowing for new homes, pushing up housing prices dramatically. Financial institutions packaged these mortgages into bonds called mortgage-backed securities, and other financial institutions purchased these securities.

By 2006, inflationary fears led the Fed to slow the growth of the supply of loanable funds, leading to higher real interest rates. Higher real interest rates led to the situation where mortgage-holders were unable to make their payments, defaulting on their mortgages. Higher interest rates also led to less borrowing to buy houses, pushing down housing prices and again leading to defaults.

When mortgage-holdings defaulted, many of the mortgage-backed securities did not make their income payments, and fell in value. Financial institutions that had purchased these securities had either a liquidity problem (not enough cash flow to make their debt payments) or they had negative net worth and became insolvent. Since many firms own financial assets from each other, this problem spread. In addition, via the global loanable funds market, the problem spread from the United States (the largest part of the global loanable funds market) to the rest of the world.

Chapter 24
Money, the Price Level, and Inflation

KEY CONCEPTS

What Is Money?

Money is something acceptable as a **means of payment** (method of settling a debt), and has three functions:

♦ Medium of exchange—accepted in exchange for goods and services.

  • Better than **barter** (direct exchange of goods for goods)—guarantees double coincidence of wants.

♦ Unit of account—agreed measure for prices.

♦ Store of value—exchangeable at a later date.

Two official measures of money:

♦ **M1**: currency outside banks + chequable deposits of individuals and firms.

♦ **M2**: M1 + all other deposits.

Money is **currency** (coins + Bank of Canada notes) and deposits (convertible into currency, used to pay debts).

♦ Cheques are only an instruction to bank.

♦ Credit cards are ID cards for loans, not money.

♦ Currency plus some deposits are means of payments; other deposits are not, but have liquidity.

The Banking System

Banking system consists of depository institutions, Bank of Canada, payments system.

♦ **Depository institutions** take deposits from households and firms, and make loans to others.

• **Chartered banks** (chartered under Bank Act), **credit unions** and caisses populaires, and **trust and mortgage loan companies**.

♦ Banks provide services for fees and earn income lending out deposits. Banks have four assets:

  • reserves (cash + deposits at Bank of Canada), held to meet demand for currency.

  • liquid assets (government Treasury bills).

  • securities (longer-term government bonds).

  • loans to corporations and households.

♦ Banks make profits by paying depositors low interest rates and lending at high rates, in return for services of:

  • Creating liquidity.

  • Pooling risks.

  • Lowering cost of borrowing funds.

  • Lowering cost of monitoring borrowers.

Bank of Canada is Canada's **central bank** (supervises financial institutions, markets, payments system, and conducts monetary policy).

♦ Acts as banker to other banks and government, and as **lender of last resort** (makes loans to banking system when there is a reserve shortage).

♦ Bank of Canada is sole issuer of bank notes.

♦ Bank of Canada balance sheet shows assets (government securities and loans to banks, usually zero) and liabilities (bank notes and deposits of banks and government).

♦ **Monetary base** (Bank of Canada notes/coins + depository institutions' deposits at the Bank) can be changed using **open market operation**, when government securities are bought or sold.

MONEY, THE PRICE LEVEL AND INFLATION **335**

Payments system allows banks to settle inter-bank transactions. Two components:

♦ **Large Value Transfer System (LVTS)** is electronic payments system for chartered banks; **Automated Clearing Settlement System (ACSS)** involves smaller payments than LVTS.

How Banks Create Money

Banks create money (deposits) when lend out excess reserves (**reserves** = notes/coins + deposits at Bank of Canada).

♦ Quantity of deposits that can be created limited by monetary base, level of desired reserves, and desired currency holding.

♦ People desire to hold some money as currency— **currency drain ratio** = currency/deposits.

♦ If bank gets new deposit, creates **excess reserves** (actual reserves − desired reserves).

- **Reserve ratio** = reserves/total deposits.

- **Desired reserve ratio** = ratio of reserves to total deposits banks wish to hold.

♦ Banks loan out excess reserves.

- Borrower spends loan (and keeps some as currency), recipient of spent money deposits it at her bank.

- New bank has more reserves, some desired, but some are excess reserves, leading to further steps in deposit multiplier process.

♦ Total Δ quantity of money = increase in currency + increase in deposits.

♦ **Money multiplier** = (Δ quantity of money)/(Δ monetary base).

The Market for Money

People choose money holdings based on price level, nominal interest rate, real GDP, financial innovation.

♦ People hold money for its buying power.

- Increase in price level (P) causes equal increase in nominal money demanded (M), so no change in real money demanded (M/P).

♦ Interest rate = opportunity cost of holding money.

- Higher interest rate decreases quantity of real money demanded.

♦ **Demand for money** is relationship between quantity of real money demanded and interest rate, holding constant other factors.

♦ Increase in real GDP shifts MD curve rightward.

♦ Financial innovation has ambiguous effect on MD curve—decreases demand for currency and some deposits, increases demand for other deposits.

Money market equilibrium occurs when quantity of money demanded equals quantity of money supplied.

♦ Short-run equilibrium determined by quantity of money supplied (determined by actions of banks and Bank of Canada).

♦ Bank of Canada adjusts quantity of money to hit its target.

- Changes in interest rate create equilibrium in money market.

- If interest rate above equilibrium, people have excess money holdings.

- Therefore, they buy financial assets, increasing price of financial assets, and decreasing interest rates toward equilibrium.

♦ In long-run, supply and demand in loanable funds market determine real interest rate, nominal interest rate = real interest rate + expected inflation rate.

The Quantity Theory of Money

Quantity theory of money predicts increase in quantity of money leads to equal percentage increase in price level.

♦ Quantity theory starts with **velocity of circulation** ($V = PY/M$), which leads to equation of exchange ($MV = PY$).

- Assumes velocity unaffected by Δ M.

- Then, % ΔP = % ΔM − % ΔY.

♦ Historical evidence suggests money growth rate correlated with inflation rate, but greater than inflation rate.

Mathematical Note: The Money Multiplier

Deriving the money multiplier starts with definitions:

♦ Desired currency holding = a × Deposits.

♦ Desired reserves = b × Deposits.

♦ a = currency drain ratio; b = desired reserve ratio.

Next, MB = desired currency holding + desired reserves
$= (a + b) \times$ deposits.

♦ $\Delta MB = (a + b) \times \Delta$deposits.

M = deposits + desired currency holding
$= (1 + a) \times$ deposits.

♦ $\Delta M = (1 + a) \times \Delta$deposits.

Money multiplier = $\Delta M/\Delta MB = (1 + a)/(a + b)$.

♦ Larger desired reserve ratio (b) means smaller money multiplier.

♦ Larger currency drain ratio (a) means smaller money multiplier.

HELPFUL HINTS

I   What is money? Whatever meets the functions of money is money. For example, cigarettes functioned as money in prisoner-of-war camps. However, you should be able to answer this question on several levels. First, as a general definition: money is a medium of exchange. Second, as a classification: chequable deposits are money but savings deposits are not. Third, as more specific definitions: M1 and M2 are official definitions of money.

We refer to our income earnings as the "money we make working." However, in economics, money means the *stock* of money we are holding in currency plus deposits (M1 or M2). Money does *not* mean the *flow* of income earnings—be careful of this distinction.

Distinguish between the act of holding money and the act of consumption spending. Holding money means dealing with money markets, not goods and services markets. The choice for households in this chapter is between holding bonds and holding money. The choice for consumer spending involves saving versus spending.

2   Changes in *nominal* interest rates and the exchange rate play important roles in creating shifts in aggregate demand, and business cycle shocks.

Chapters 24, 25, and 30 explain what affects the values of nominal interest and exchange rates, showing the crucial role of the money market. Chapter 24 explains the demand for money, and part of the determination of the supply of money. Chapter 25 explains exchange rate determination, and the role of the Bank of Canada. Chapter 30

further explains how the supply of money is determined by actions of the Bank of Canada within the deposit creation process.

3   Become thoroughly familiar with the money multiplier process by which banks create money.

Two fundamental facts allow banks to create money. First, banks create money by creating new chequable deposits. Second, banks hold fractional reserves. Fractional reserves mean that when a bank receives a deposit, it only holds part of it as reserves and lends the rest. The bank is not indulging in a scam—it is still maintaining assets (reserves plus loans) to match its liabilities (deposits). When that loan is spent, at least part of the proceeds will likely be deposited in another bank, creating a new deposit (money).

The deposit multiplier process follows from this last fact: banks make loans when they receive new deposits. These loans are spent—some leaves the process as currency drain, and the rest returns to another bank, creating another new deposit. The process repeats itself, adding more deposits (but in progressively smaller amounts) in each round. Practise going through examples until the process becomes second nature. As you go, note the role played by the profit-seeking behaviour of banks. Profit-seeking leads them to turn reserves, which earn no revenues, into loans, which earn revenues.

4   The important equation of exchange says:

$$\text{Quantity of money} \times \text{Velocity of circulation} = \text{Price level} \times \text{Real GDP}$$

The quantity of money times the average number of times each dollar is spent (equalling total expenditure) is equal to the dollar value of the goods and services on which it was spent. The equation is always true by definition—it is an identity. By further assuming that both the velocity of circulation and potential GDP are independent of the quantity of money in the long run, we get the quantity theory of money. The assumptions imply that when the quantity of money increases by 10 percent, in the long run the price level increases by 10 percent to maintain equality between the two sides of the equation.

SELF-TEST

True/False and Explain

What Is Money?

1 Money is anything generally acceptable as a means of payment.

2 A fixed term deposit at a chartered bank is part of M1.

3 If the public shifts deposits from chequing accounts to nonchequing accounts, M1 will decrease and M2 increase.

The Banking System

4 One of the key economic functions of banks is acting as a lender of last resort.

5 Individual households are generally better at pooling risk than are depository institutions.

6 A bank reserves consist of cash in its vault plus its deposits at the Bank of Canada.

How Banks Create Money

7 The size of the monetary base limits the amount of deposit creation in the money creation process.

8 If a depositor uses a debit card to buy something, her bank's actual reserve ratio declines.

The Market for Money

9 If the price level increases, the quantity of real money people want to hold increases.

10 If interest rates increase, the quantity of real money demanded decreases.

11 The development of near-money deposits and growth in the use of credit cards in the 1970s caused the demand for M1 to shift leftward.

12 If households or firms have more money than they want to hold, they will buy financial assets, causing asset prices to increase and the interest rate to decrease.

13 If the price of a bond increases, the interest rate earned on the bond decreases.

The Quantity Theory of Money

14 If the quantity of money is $50 billion and nominal GDP is $200 billion, the velocity of circulation is 1/4.

15 The international data does not support the quantity theory of money.

Multiple-Choice

What Is Money?

1 Which of the following is a function of money?
   a medium of exchange
   b measure of liquidity
   c pooling risk
   d store of exchange
   e reducing transactions costs

2 Which of the following is a component of M2 but *not* of M1?
   a currency in circulation
   b personal chequing deposits
   c personal nonchequing deposits
   d currency in bank vaults
   e Canada Savings Bonds

3 Which of the following is *most* liquid?
   a chequing deposits
   b real estate
   c government bonds
   d savings deposits
   e cheques

4 Which of the following is *not* a store of value?
   a credit cards
   b personal chequing deposits
   c term deposits
   d other chequable deposits
   e nonchequing deposits

The Banking System

5 Which of the following statements about depository institutions is *false*?
   a They maximize their owner's wealth, ignoring all else.
   b They keep reserves to meet cash withdrawals.
   c A credit union is a depository institution.
   d They pool and therefore reduce risk.
   e They borrow at low interest rates and lend at higher interest rates.

6 Which of the following is an economic service provided by a depository institution?
   a borrowing low and lending high
   b keeping cash reserves
   c pooling liquidity
   d lowering the cost of borrowing funds
   e creating liquid liabilities

7 When a bank receives short-term deposits and issues long-term loans, this is an example of
   a being a lender of last resort.
   b lowering the cost of borrowing.
   c creating liquidity.
   d taking unnecessary risks.
   e pooling risk.

8 Which of the following is an asset of the Bank of Canada?
   a Currency in circulation
   b Government securities held in the Bank of Canada
   c Deposits of chartered banks at the Bank of Canada
   d Coins in circulation
   e Deposits of governments at the Bank of Canada

9 Which of the following actions occurs if a bank has net payments owing on inter-bank transactions at the end of the day?
   a It lends money to other banks.
   b It borrows money from other banks.
   c It deposits money at the Bank of Canada.
   d The Bank of Canada acts as a lender of last resort.
   e Nothing, this happens all the time.

How Banks Create Money

10 The Bank of Speedy Creek currently has actual (and desired) reserves of $40, loans of $460 and deposits of $500. What is its desired reserve ratio?
   a 4%
   b 8%
   c 12.5%
   d 25%
   e 40%

11 The Bank of Speedy Creek currently has actual (and desired) reserves of $40, loans of $460 and deposits of $500. Huck Finn comes along and deposits $10. After Huck's deposit, but before any other actions have occurred, the total amount of *monetary base* in the economy
   a is unchanged, with currency $10 higher and deposits $10 lower.
   b has increased by $10.
   c has decreased by $10.
   d is unchanged, with deposits $10 higher and currency $10 lower.
   e depends on if Huck deposited his money in a savings deposit or a demand deposit.

12 The Bank of Speedy Creek currently has actual (and desired) reserves of $40, loans of $460 and deposits of $500. Huck Finn comes along and deposits $10. After Huck's deposit, but before any other actions have occurred, the total amount of *money* in the economy has

   a stayed the same, with currency and deposits unchanged.

   b stayed the same, with currency falling and deposits rising.

   c decreased, with currency falling and deposits staying the same.

   d increased, with currency unchanged and deposits rising.

   e decreased, with currency falling and deposits unchanged.

13 The Bank of Speedy Creek currently has actual (and desired) reserves of $40, loans of $460 and deposits of $500. Huck Finn comes along and deposits $10. After Huck's deposit, but before any other actions have occurred, the Bank of Speedy Creek will have excess reserves of

   a zero.

   b $9.

   c $9.20.

   d $10.

   e $40.

14 The Bank of Speedy Creek currently has actual (and desired) reserves of $40, loans of $460 and deposits of $500. Huck Finn comes along and deposits $10. After Huck's deposit, given that the Bank of Speedy Creek is profit-seeking, what amount of new loans will it make?

   a zero

   b $9

   c $9.20

   d $10

   e $40

15 The Bank of Speedy Creek currently has actual (and desired) reserves of $40, loans of $460 and deposits of $500. Huck Finn comes along and deposits $10. After Huck's deposit, and after the Bank of Speedy Creek has lent the amount it wishes to lend, the total amount of reserves in the bank will be $_____, the total amount of loans will be $_____, and the total amount of deposits will be $_____.

   a 40.80; 469.20; 510

   b 40; 460; 500

   c 50; 470; 520

   d 41; 469; 510

   e 42.50; 467.50; 510

16 If new deposits are made in the banking system, which of the following will limit the amount of the new money created?

   a The desired reserve ratio only.

   b The currency drain ratio only.

   c The monetary base only.

   d The desired reserve ratio and the currency drain ratio, but not the monetary base.

   e The desired reserve ratio, the currency drain ratio and the monetary base.

17 Which of the following steps in the description of the money multiplier process is *wrong*?

   a Banks lend out excess reserves.

   b Bank deposits increase.

   c The deposits are spent.

   d Some new spending returns as deposits, and currency comes in as new deposits.

   e Banks once again have excess reserves, and the process continues.

The Market for Money

18 Consider Figure 24.1. Which of the following best describes the response of this household to an *increase* in their annual income?

   a movement from *a* to *f*

   b movement from *a* to *c*

   c movement from *e* to *a*

   d movement from *b* to *a*

   e movement from *a* to *e*

FIGURE **24.1** THE DEMAND FOR REAL MONEY BALANCES BY AN INDIVIDUAL HOUSEHOLD

19 Which of the following could cause the demand curve for M1 to shift leftward?

   a increase in real GDP

   b decrease in interest rates

   c expanded use of credit cards

   d increase in quantity of money supplied

   e increase in the price level

20 Real money is equal to nominal money
   a   divided by real GDP.
   b   minus real GDP.
   c   divided by the price level.
   d   minus the price level.
   e   divided by velocity.

21 If the interest rate is above the equilibrium rate, how is equilibrium achieved in the money market?
   a   People buy goods to get rid of excess money, lowering the price of goods, and lowering the interest rate.
   b   People sell goods to get rid of excess money, lowering the price of goods, and lowering the interest rate.
   c   People sell bonds to get rid of excess money, lowering the price of bonds, and lowering the interest rate.
   d   People sell bonds to get rid of excess money, raising the price of bonds, and lowering the interest rate.
   e   People buy bonds to get rid of excess money, raising the price of bonds, and lowering the interest rate.

22 Money market equilibrium occurs
   a   when interest rates are constant.
   b   when the level of real GDP is constant.
   c   when quantity of real money supplied equals quantity of real money demanded.
   d   only under a fixed exchange rate.
   e   when bond prices are constant.

The Quantity Theory of Money

23 The quantity theory of money begins with the equation of exchange, $MV = PY$, and then adds the assumptions that
   a   velocity varies inversely with the rate of interest, and the price level is independent of the quantity of money.
   b   velocity and the price level are independent of the quantity of money.
   c   potential GDP and the quantity of money are independent of the price level.
   d   potential GDP and the price level are independent of the quantity of money.
   e   velocity and potential GDP are independent of the quantity of money.

24 According to the quantity theory of money, in the long run
   a V/M is constant.
   b Y/M is constant.
   c Y/P is constant.
   d M/P is constant.
   e M/V is constant.

25 According to the quantity theory of money, an increase in the quantity of money will increase the price level
   a   but have no effect on real GDP or velocity of circulation.
   b   as well as increasing both real GDP and velocity of circulation.
   c   as well as increasing real GDP but decreasing velocity of circulation.
   d   as well as decreasing real GDP but increasing velocity of circulation.
   e   but have no effect on real GDP while decreasing velocity of circulation.

Short Answer Problems

1 Banks can no longer issue their own paper money, but can create deposit money by crediting people's deposits. Since there is no paper money deposited to back up this creation, is this created money real? Is it acceptable in society? Why or why not?

2 Briefly explain how and why banks create new money during the deposit multiplier process (in a multibank system).

3 Why do people care about the quantity of real money they hold rather than the quantity of nominal money?

4 Suppose that Bank 1 has excess reserves equal to $1,000. (In Chapter 30 we will see how such a situation might arise from the actions of the Bank of Canada.) Assume that the desired reserve ratio for all banks in the multibank system is 20 percent (0.2). There is a currency drain ratio of 33 percent (0.33). Table 24.1 gives information for the first round of the money creation process that will be generated by this new deposit.

   a   Follow the next five rounds of the money creation process by completing Table 24.1.

TABLE 24.1 MONEY CREATION PROCESS

Bank Number	Initial Deposit = New Reserves	Desired Reserves	Excess Reserves	New Loans	Withdrawals Leading To:		Total Increase in Money
					New Currency	New Deposit	
1	1,000	0	1,000	1,000	250	750	1,000
2							
3							
4							
5							
6							

   b   What is the total increase in the quantity of money after six rounds?

ⓔ **5 a** For the banking system in Short Answer Problem **4**, what is the money multiplier?

b After all rounds have been completed, what is the total increase in the quantity of money?

ⓒⓣ **c** How much of this increase in money is new currency in circulation, and how much is new deposits?

ⓔ **6** For the entire banking system in Short Answer Problem **4**, compared to the starting point of $1,000 in excess reserves, what are the final total amounts of desired/actual reserves, loans, and deposits?

7 There is only one chartered bank in the country of Adanac, and it has the following assets and liabilities:

Currency reserves	$20 million
Reserves held at the Bank of Adanac	$10 million
Loans	$700 million
Securities	$20 million
Deposits	$750 million

a Assuming that the bank has freely chosen its reserves, what is its desired reserve ratio?

b If the amount of currency in circulation is $50 million, what is the monetary base? What is the money supply?

c What is the currency drain ratio?

d What is the money multiplier?

8 Assume the central bank adjusts the quantity of money to keep the quantity of real money supplied constant.

a Describe what happens to the money supply in this situation..

Show on a graph and briefly explain what each of the following will do (in sequence) to the demand for real money (defined as M1) and therefore the equilibrium interest rate. Assume that the real money supply remains constant.

b The price level rises.

c There is a financial innovation (widespread adoption of electronic funds transfers) that reduces the need to use chequing accounts.

d Real GDP falls during a recession.

9 Briefly explain the role of the Bank of Canada in the banking system.

10 We observe an economy in which the price level is 1.5, real GDP equals potential GDP at $240 billion, and the quantity of money is $60 billion.

a What is the velocity of circulation?

b According to the quantity theory of money, what is the long-run result of an increase in the quantity of money to $80 billion?

ANSWERS

True/False and Explain

1 T Basic function of money. (568)

2 F See definition of M1. (569–570)

ⓒⓣ **3 F** M1 decreases as chequing accounts decrease, but chequing and nonchequing accounts both part of M2, so no change in M2. (569–570)

4 F This is function of central bank. (572–573)

5 F Large size allows banks to pool risk. (571–572)

6 T Definition. (571)

7 T Limits amount available for desired reserves and desired currency holdings. (576)

8 T Withdrawal decreases reserves = decrease in deposits, which leads to decrease in reserve/deposit ratio. (576–577)

9 F Real money demand independent of price level. (578)

10 T Increase in interest rate increase opportunity cost of holding money, decreases quantity money demanded. (578)

11 T Shift toward M2—see text discussion. (580)

12 T Agents substitute toward bonds, increasing bond demand, increasing bond prices, which implies decrease in bond interest rate. (581)

13 T Price of bond and its interest rate are inversely related. (581)

14 F $V = PY/M = 200/50 = 4$. (582)

15 F Correlation between money growth and inflation is not perfect, but it is strong. (583)

Multiple-Choice

1 **a** See text discussion. (568)

2 **c** Definition. (569)

3 **a** Most readily changed into currency. (570)

4 **a** Credit cards not guaranteed for future purchases—credit card company might cancel your card. (569)

5 **a** Must be prudent about risk too. (571)

6 **d** See text discussion. (572)

7 **c** Short-term deposits are more liquid for depositors than lending long-term themselves. (572)

8 **b** Definition. (573)

9 **b** Must borrow to cover its net LTVS position. (575)

10 **b** Desired reserve ratio = chosen reserves/deposits = 40/500 = 0.08. (576)

11 **d** Decrease in currency in circulation = increase in bank reserves. (576–577)

12 **b** Decrease in currency as deposit made = increase in deposits. (576–577)

13 **c** Excess = actual ($50) – desired ($40.80 = 0.08 × $510). (576–577)

14 **c** Banks will lend the amount of excess reserves. (576–577)

⟨ct⟩ 15 **a** The $10 deposit is divided between the new desired reserves (0.08 × $10) and new loans. (576–577)

⟨ct⟩ 16 **e** Monetary base limits possible amount of new reserves and new currency in circulation. The higher the desired reserve ratio, the more money banks hold back at each stage. The higher the currency drain ratio, the more households hold back at each stage. (576)

17 **d** Some of the new spending is kept back as currency and not deposited. (579)

18 **e** *a* to *f*, *e* to *a* are decreases in income, others are Δ interest rates. (579)

19 **c** Financial innovation means people use less money. Other changes create rightward shift or no shift. (579)

20 **c** Definition. (578)

21 **e** If interest rate > equilibrium, this implies too much money, which implies buying bonds,

leading to increase in price of bonds and therefore decrease in interest rates. (581)

22 **c** Definition. (581)

23 **e** See text discussion. (582–583)

⟨ct⟩ 24 **d** Because theory assumes Y/V ($= M/P$) is constant. (582–583)

25 **a** Due to assumption that neither GDP nor velocity affected by Δ quantity of money. (582–583)

Short Answer Problems

1 This created money is real, because it is backed by the assets of the bank, which consist of the bank's reserves, loans, and holdings of securities.

Deposit money is generally accepted in society (you can buy goods, pay debts, etc., with it) because people know that the banks will provide currency upon demand.

2 Banks create money by making new loans. When banks get a new deposit, this leaves them with excess reserves. The desire to make profits leads banks to lend out excess reserves, creating a matching deposit, which is new money. When these loans are spent, the person receiving the money deposits much of it in a bank deposit, creating excess reserves, and the process continues.

3 Nominal money is simply the number of dollars, while real money is a measure of what money will buy. Real money decreases if the price level rises while the number of dollars is constant. What matters to people is the quantity of goods and services that money will buy, not the number of dollars. If the price level rises by 10 percent, people will want to hold 10 percent more dollars (given a constant real income and interest rates) to keep the same purchasing power.

4 **a** Table 24.1 is completed here as Table 24.1 Solution. Note that 80 percent of each new deposit will be lent and 20 percent will be held as reserves. Of the borrowed money, one-quarter is kept as currency and three-quarters is spent and ends up being deposited in the next bank, where it becomes a new deposit.

TABLE

24.1 SOLUTION

Bank Number	Initial Deposit = New Reserves	Desired Reserves	Excess Reserves	New Loans	Withdrawals Leading To:		Total Increase in Money
					New Currency	New Deposits	
1	1,000	0	1,000	1,000	250	750	1,000
2	750	150	600	600	150	450	1,600
3	450	90	360	360	90	270	1,960
4	270	54	216	216	54	162	2,176
5	162	32.40	129.60	129.60	32.40	97.20	2,305.60
6	97.20	19.44	77.76	77.76	19.44	58.32	2,383.36

b After six rounds, the total (cumulative) increase in the quantity of money is $2,383.36, as shown in the table.

5 a The money multiplier is calculated from the formula $(1 + a)/(a + b)$, where a is currency drain ratio (0.33 in this case) and b is desired reserve ratio (0.2 in this case). Substituting these values in the formula yields $(1 + 0.33)/(0.2 + 0.33) = 2.51$.

b The total increase in money is $2.51 \times$ initial amount of new reserves, or $2,510.

c Given that currency drain ratio of 0.33, then amount of currency must be one-quarter (25%) of the amount of new money ($0.33 = 25/75$), or roughly $627.50. Amount of new deposits is therefore 75 percent of the amount of new money, or $1,882.50.

6 The total change in reserves will be 20 percent of the new deposits, or $376.50. We already know the total amount of new deposits is $1,882.50. The amount of new loans is the difference between these two numbers, or $1,500.06. *Note:* This value follows from the requirement that total amounts of new assets held by the chartered banks (loans and reserves) equals total amount of new liabilities (deposits).

7 a Desired reserve ratio = desired reserves/deposits = 30/750 = 0.04.

b Monetary base = reserves + currency in circulation = $80 million. Money supply = currency in circulation + deposits = $800 million.

c Currency drain ratio = (currency in circulation)/(deposits) = 50/750 = 1/15 = 0.0667.

d Money multiplier can be calculated in two ways. First, as the ratio of the money supply to the monetary base = 800/80 = 10. Second,

from formula $(1 + a)/(a + b)$ where a is currency drain ratio and b is desired reserve ratio. This formula gives the answer as $(1 + 0.0667)/(0.04 + 0.0667) = 10$.

8 a If the central bank is targeting the quantity of money, quantity of money supplied is fixed, and money supply curve is vertical (at *MS* in Figure 24.2).

FIGURE **24.2**

b Change in price level has no impact on real money demand, so no impact on equilibrium interest rate (r). In Figure 24.2, demand for real money remains at MD_0, and interest rate remains at r_0.

c This financial innovation reduces the need to use chequing accounts, which are part of M1. Therefore demand for real money falls to MD_1, and equilibrium interest rate falls to r_1 in Figure 24.2.

d Decrease in real GDP lowers demand for real money to MD_2, and equilibrium interest rate falls to r_2 in Figure 24.2.

9 The Bank of Canada supervises financial institutions and markets and the financial system, and conducts monetary policy. It acts as banker to other banks and to the government, and acts as lender of last resort by making loans to the banking system when there is a shortage of reserves. It is also the sole issuer of bank notes.

10 a The velocity of circulation is

$$\text{Velocity of circulation} = \frac{\text{Price level} \times \text{Real GDP}}{\text{Quantity of money}}$$

With the given values for the price level, real GDP, and quantity of money, we have

$$\text{Velocity of circulation} = \frac{1.5 \times 240}{60} = 6$$

b Quantity theory of money predicts that in the long run an increase in quantity of money causes an equal percentage increase in the price level. An increase in money from $60 billion to $80 billion is a one-third (33%) increase. Thus quantity theory of money predicts the price level will increase by a third (33%). Since the initial price level is 1.5, the predicted price level will be 2.0. (Can also be calculated using the equation of exchange.)

Chapter 25
The Exchange Rate and the Balance of Payments

Currencies and Exchange Rates

To buy foreign goods/assets, Canadians need **foreign currency** (foreign notes, coins, bank deposits); to buy Canadian goods/assets, foreigners need Canadian dollars.

- Foreigners and Canadians exchange dollars for foreign currency in the **foreign exchange market**.

- **Exchange rate** = price at which one currency exchanges for another—**nominal exchange rate** (E) = foreign currency per Canadian dollar.

- Currency depreciation (appreciation) is decrease (increase) in value of Canadian dollar in terms of another currency.

- **Real exchange rate** (RER) is relative price of Canadian-produced goods and services versus foreign produced—$RER = E \times (P/P^*)$ where P/P^* = Canadian/foreign price level.

- **Canadian-dollar effective exchange rate index (CERI)** = average exchange rates of Canadian dollar versus 6 currencies, weighted by trade importance.

  - Since 1998, nominal exchange rate fluctuated strongly versus U.S. dollar and yen, steady versus euro.

  - CERI shows appreciation between 2002 and 2007, and depreciation since then.

The Foreign Exchange Market

Exchange rate is determined by supply and demand in foreign exchange market.

- Demand for Canadian dollars = supply of foreign currency; supply of Canadian dollars = demand for foreign currency.

- Quantity of Canadian dollars demanded in foreign exchange market = planned amount to buy at a given price, based on demands for Canadian exports and assets—depends on:

  - Exchange rate.

  - World demand for Canadian exports.

  - Interest rates in Canada and other countries.

  - Expected future exchange rate.

- Increase in exchange rate decreases quantity demanded of Canadian dollars (movement up to left along demand curve), because

  - Exports become more expensive for foreigners, decreasing demand for exports and therefore demand for dollars.

  - Expected profits decrease from buying Canadian dollars to hold until they appreciate.

- Quantity of Canadian dollars supplied in foreign exchange market = planned amount to sell at a given price = planned purchases of foreign currencies to buy imports and foreign assets—depends on:

  - Exchange rate.

  - Canadian demand for imports.

  - Interest rates in Canada and other countries.

  - Expected future exchange rate.

♦ Increase in exchange rate increases quantity supplied of Canadian dollars (movement up to right along supply curve), because

  • Imports become cheaper for Canadians, increasing demand for imports/demand for foreign currency = increase in supply of Canadian dollars.

  • Expected profits increase from buying foreign currency to hold until appreciates, increasing demand for foreign currency = increase in supply of Canadian dollars.

♦ Market equilibrium determined by demand and supply—exchange rates adjust instantly as required to achieve equilibrium for all exchange rates.

Changes in Demand and Supply: Exchange Rate Fluctuations

Demand curve for Canadian dollars shifts *rightward* if

♦ World demand for Canadian exports increases.

♦ **Canadian interest rate differential** (Canadian interest rate – foreign interest rate) increases, increasing demand for Canadian assets.

♦ Expected future exchange rate increases, increasing expected profits from buying Canadian dollars and holding them until they appreciate.

Supply curve of Canadian dollars shifts *leftward* if

♦ Canadian demand for imports decreases.

♦ Canadian interest rate differential increases.

♦ Expected future exchange rate increases.

Expected changes in exchange rates occur due to:

♦ **Purchasing power parity** (two currencies have same value or purchasing power)—if no parity, and Canadian dollar buys more than U.S. dollar, demand for Canadian dollar increases, supply decreases and Canadian dollar appreciates.

♦ **Interest rate parity** (two currencies earn same rate of return, adjusted for expected Δ exchange rate)—if parity does not hold (adjusted for risk), and if returns are higher in Canada, increased demand for Canadian dollar instantly increases exchange rate.

Nominal exchange rate determined by above forces, and in short run this also determines real exchange rate.

♦ In long-run: $E = RER \times (P/P^*)$—price levels in each country determine nominal exchange rate, and via quantity theory of money, quantity of money in each country determines nominal exchange rate.

Financing International Trade

Balance of payments accounts measure Canada's international transactions.

♦ **Current account**—net exports + net interest income + net transfers.

♦ **Capital account**—foreign investment in Canada – Canadian investment abroad.

♦ **Official settlements account**—net changes in Canada's **official reserves** (government's holdings of foreign currency). If official reserves increase, official settlement balance is negative.

♦ Current account balance + capital account balance + official settlements balance = 0.

♦ To pay a current account deficit we must borrow from abroad or decrease official reserves.

Net borrower country borrows more from rest of world than lends in current year (capital account surplus).

♦ **Net lender**—lending more to rest of world than borrowing in current year (capital account deficit).

♦ **Debtor nation**—has borrowed more than lent to rest of world over history, **creditor nation** reverse.

Current account balance primarily determined by **net exports** $(X - M)$. From circular flow, net exports = **private sector balance** $(S - I)$ + **government sector balance** $(T - G)$.

♦ In short run, nominal exchange rate affects net exports, in long run has no effect.

Exchange Rate Policy

Three different exchange rate policies:

♦ Current policy is **flexible exchange rate**—exchange rate determined by supply and demand, changes in interest rates influence exchange rate.

♦ **Fixed exchange rate** policy pegs the exchange rate at a target value—if Δ exchange rate, Bank of Canada must buy/sell Canadian dollars to change demand/supply—works only as long as foreign currency reserves last.

♦ **Crawling peg** policy intervenes to meet selected target *path* (changing target exchange rate).

HELPFUL HINTS

1 There is an important difference between trade within a single country and trade between countries—currency. Individuals trading in the same country use the same currency, and trade is straightforward. International trade (to be examined in detail in Chapter 31) is complicated by the fact that individuals in different countries use different currencies. A Japanese vendor selling goods wants payment in Japanese yen, but a Canadian buyer is likely holding only Canadian dollars. This chapter addresses this complication by examining the foreign exchange market.

2 Think of foreign exchange rates as prices determined by supply and demand. They are prices of currency determined in markets for currency. The demand for Canadian dollars in the foreign exchange market arises from the desire on the part of foreigners to purchase Canadian goods and services (which requires dollars) or Canadian financial or real assets.

The supply of Canadian dollars is a special type of supply, because the offer to sell a Canadian dollar is equivalent to an offer to buy foreign currency. Supply depends on Canadians' desire to buy foreign goods and services (which requires foreign currency), and to buy foreign assets. Remember that the supply of Canadian dollars equals the demand for foreign currency— this will help you understand shifts in the supply of Canadian dollars.

As an example, think about what happens if currency speculators acquire new information making them think the Canadian dollar will appreciate next month (which implies foreign currencies will depreciate next month). Speculators will plan to buy Canadian dollars *this* month, and sell foreign currencies this month, in order to make a profit. Thus, demand for the Canadian dollar shifts rightward this month, and supply of foreign exchange shifts leftward.

3 The exchange rate is volatile because supply and demand often shift in a reinforcing manner, since they are both affected by the same changes in expectations. These changes in expectations are driven by two forces: purchasing power parity and interest rate parity. Each of these is a version of the law of one price, which states that anytime there is a difference in the price of the same good in two markets, natural economic forces (unless restricted) will eliminate that discrepancy and establish a single price. Suppose that the price in market 1 increases relative to the price in market 2. Individuals will now buy in market 2 (lower price) and not in market 1 (higher price). This increase in demand in market 2 and decrease in demand in market 1 will cause the two prices to come together. This principle also applies to international markets: natural market forces result in a single world price for the same good (allowing for effects of tariffs, transport costs, etc.).

Suppose that purchasing power parity does not hold. For example, suppose that the wholesale price of an MP3 player in Canada is $100, and in Japan it is 10,000 yen, and that the exchange rate is currently 125 yen per dollar. The dollar price of the player in Japan is $80 (10,000 yen/125 yen per dollar). People expect the demand for the player in Canada to decrease (= a decrease in demand for Canadian dollars), and the demand for the player in Japan to increase (= supply of dollars rising), which would lead to the exchange rate depreciating toward 100 yen per dollar (purchasing power parity level). Expectations will lead to a decrease in demand for the Canadian dollar and an increase in supply of the Canadian dollar, so that the exchange rate will depreciate even before demand for the player adjusts!

The law of one price also holds for prices of assets like bonds. Recall from Chapter 23 that bond prices are inversely related to interest rates; interest rate parity is a version of the law of one price. Consider a situation where, taking into account the expected depreciation of the Canadian dollar, the Canadian interest rate was higher than the U.S. rate (which implies the price of bonds is lower in Canada). Buyers would demand Canadian bonds, raising their price and lowering Canadian interest rates. In addition, they would be selling U.S. bonds, lowering their price and raising U.S. interest rates. These actions occur until the interest rate differential between the two countries has shrunk to a level where it just reflects the expected depreciation of the Canadian dollar—interest rate parity holds.

| S E L F - T E S T |

True/False and Explain

Currencies and Exchange Rates

1 If the exchange rate between the Canadian dollar and the Japanese yen changes from 130 yen per dollar to 140 yen per dollar, the Canadian dollar has appreciated.

2 If the Canadian dollar can buy $0.75 U.S., the U.S. dollar can buy $1.25 Canadian.

The Foreign Exchange Market

3 The demand for Canadian dollars by foreigners is automatically matched by Canadian demand for foreign currency.

4 A decrease in the exchange rate increases the quantity demanded for Canadian dollars because exports become cheaper for foreigners.

5 The expected profits effect says that an increase in the exchange rate will decrease the quantity supplied of Canadian dollars.

Changes in Demand and Supply: Exchange Rate Fluctuations

6 An increase in Canadian interest rates increases demand for the Canadian dollar.

7 The demand and supply of Canadian dollars tend to move independently of each other.

8 Countries with currencies expected to appreciate will have higher interest rates than countries with currencies expected to depreciate.

9 If the yen price of the dollar is 100 yen per dollar and the price of a traded good is $10 in Canada, purchasing power parity implies that the price in Japan will be 1,000 yen.

10 If the foreign exchange value of the Canadian dollar is expected to increase, the supply of Canadian dollars increases.

Financing International Trade

11 There can be no such thing as a balance of payments surplus/deficit, because by definition a *balance* of payments must always *balance*.

12 If a nation is a net borrower from the rest of the world, it must be a debtor nation.

13 If Canada borrows more from the rest of the world than it lends to the rest of the world, Canada has a capital account surplus.

Exchange Rate Policy

14 If the Bank of Canada sets a target exchange rate, and demand for the Canadian dollar increases, the Bank of Canada will sell Canadian dollars.

15 Under a flexible exchange rate, Bank of Canada policy will not affect the exchange rate.

Multiple-Choice

Currencies and Exchange Rates

1 The exchange rate between the Canadian dollar and the British pound is 0.5 pounds per dollar. If a radio sells for 38 pounds in Britain, what is the dollar price of the radio?
   a $19
   b $25
   c $38
   d $57
   e $76

2 Consider Table 25.1. Between 2009 and 2010, the Canadian dollar _____ versus the euro and _____ versus the yen.
   a   appreciated; depreciated
   b   appreciated; appreciated
   c   depreciated; depreciated
   d   depreciated; appreciated
   e   not changed; not changed

TABLE **25.1**

Currency	2009 Exchange Rate	2010 Exchange Rate
EU euro	2 euros/dollar	3 euros/dollar
Japanese yen	120 yen/dollar	90 yen/dollar

3 Consider Table 25.1. Between 2009 and 2010, the yen
   a   must have depreciated in value versus the euro.
   b   must have appreciated in value versus the euro.
   c   may or may not have appreciated in value versus the euro.
   d   will have appreciated in value versus the euro if the euro has a high weight in CERI.
   e   will have appreciated in value versus the euro if the euro has a lower weight in CERI.

The Foreign Exchange Market

4 If the demand for Canadian dollars increases, this is matched by a(n)
   a   increase in demand for foreign exchange.
   b   increase in supply of foreign exchange.
   c   increase in supply of Canadian dollars.
   d   decrease in demand for foreign exchange.
   e   decrease in supply of foreign exchange.

5 The quantity of Canadian dollars demanded depends on all of the following *except*
   a   the exchange rate.
   b   the interest rate in Canada.
   c   interest rates in the rest of the world.
   d   the Canadian demand for imports.
   e   the expected future exchange rate.

6 A decrease in the exchange rate increases the quantity demanded of Canadian dollars because
   a   exports become more expensive for foreigners.
   b   imports become more expensive for Canadians.
   c   expected profits from buying Canadian dollars increase.
   d   expected profits from buying foreign currency decrease.
   e   cross exchange rates adjust quickly.

7 Which of the following best describes the expected profit effect?
   a   A lower exchange rate leads to importers using the forward market to lower exchange rate risk.
   b   A lower exchange rate leads to buying foreign currency to hold until it appreciates.
   c   A higher exchange rate leads to buying foreign currency to hold until it appreciates.
   d   A higher exchange rate leads to buying Canadian dollars to hold until they appreciate.
   e   A higher exchange rate leads to exporters using the forward market to lower exchange rate risk.

8 An increase in the exchange rate increases the quantity supplied of Canadian dollars because
   a imports become cheaper for Canadians, increasing demand for imports and therefore demand for foreign currency which equals an increase in quantity supplied of Canadian dollars.
   b imports become more expensive for Canadians, increasing demand for imports and therefore demand for foreign currency which equals an increase in quantity supplied of Canadian dollars.
   c our exports become cheaper for foreigners, increasing demand for exports and therefore demand for foreign currency which equals an increase in quantity supplied of Canadian dollars.
   d expected profits increase from buying and holding Canadian dollars until they appreciate in value, which increases quantity supplied of Canadian dollars.
   e expected profits increase from selling and holding foreign currency until it appreciates in value, which increases quantity supplied of Canadian dollars.

9 If the exchange rate is too high in the foreign exchange market,
   a there is a surplus and the exchange rate will increase.
   b there is a surplus and the exchange rate will decrease.
   c exports are cheap, and the demand curve for Canadian dollars will shift rightward.
   d there is a shortage and the exchange rate will decrease.
   e there is a shortage and the exchange rate will increase.

Changes in Demand and Supply: Exchange Rate Fluctuations

10 Which of the following quotations best describes purchasing power parity?
   a "The recent high Canadian interest rate has increased demand for the Canadian dollar."
   b "The market feeling is that the Canadian dollar is overvalued and will likely depreciate."
   c "The price of bananas is the same in Canada and the United States, adjusting for the exchange rate."
   d "The expected depreciation of the Canadian dollar is currently lowering demand for it."
   e None of the above.

11 When would the exchange rate decrease in value the most?
   a Supply and demand of dollars both increase.
   b Supply of dollars increases, and demand decreases.
   c Supply of dollars decreases, and demand increases.
   d Supply and demand of dollars both decrease.
   e When Bank of Canada intervenes.

12 Which of the following shifts the supply curve of Canadian dollars rightward?
   a Increase in demand for foreign goods by Canadian citizens.
   b Decrease in demand for Canadian goods by foreigners.
   c The dollar is expected to appreciate.
   d U.S. interest rates decrease.
   e None of the above.

13 Which of the following shifts the demand curve for Canadian dollars rightward?
   a Increase in demand for foreign goods by Canadian citizens.
   b Decrease in demand for Canadian goods by foreigners.
   c The dollar is expected to appreciate.
   d The dollar is expected to depreciate.
   e U.S. interest rates increase.

14 If interest rates in Canada are greater than interest rates in Japan, interest rate parity implies that
   a the inflation rate is higher in Japan.
   b Japanese financial assets are poor investments.
   c the yen is expected to depreciate against the dollar.
   d the yen is expected to appreciate against the dollar.
   e Canadian financial assets are poor investments.

15 Consider Figure 25.1. Which graph best shows the impact of an increase in demand for Canadian exports?
   a Graph (a)
   b Graph (b)
   c Graph (c)
   d Graph (d)
   e Graph (e)

FIGURE **25.1**

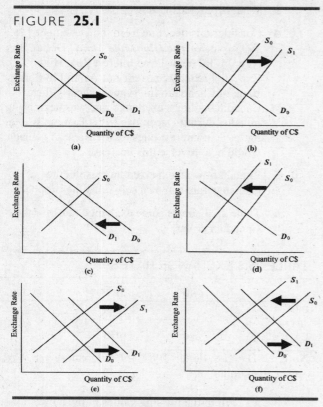

16 Consider Figure 25.1. Which graph best shows the impact of an increase in the Canadian interest rate differential?
  a Graph (a)
  b Graph (c)
  c Graph (d)
  d Graph (e)
  e Graph (f)

17 Consider Figure 25.1. Which graph best shows the impact of a decrease in Canadian demand for imports?
  a Graph (a)
  b Graph (b)
  c Graph (c)
  d Graph (d)
  e Graph (f)

Financing International Trade

18 Suppose Canada initially has all balance of payments accounts in balance (no surplus or deficit). Then Canadian firms increase imports from Japan, financing that increase by borrowing from Japan. There will now be a current account
  a surplus and a capital account surplus.
  b surplus and a capital account deficit.
  c deficit and a capital account surplus.
  d deficit and a capital account deficit.
  e deficit and a capital account balance.

19 The country of Mengia came into existence at the beginning of year 1. Given the information in Table 25.2, in year 4 Mengia is a
  a net lender and a creditor nation.
  b net lender and a debtor nation.
  c net borrower and a creditor nation.
  d net borrower and a debtor nation.
  e net lender and neither a creditor nor a debtor nation.

TABLE **25.2**

Year	Borrowed from Rest of World (billions of dollars)	Lent to Rest of World (billions of dollars)
1	60	20
2	60	40
3	60	60
4	60	80

20 Assuming that Mengia's official settlement account is always in balance, in which year or years in Table 25.2 did Mengia have a current account surplus?
  a year 1
  b year 2
  c years 1, 2, and 3
  d years 1 and 2
  e year 4 only

21 If Mengia's official settlement balance was in deficit every year, for which year or years in Table 25.2 can you say for sure there was a current account surplus?
  a year 1
  b year 2
  c years 2 and 3
  d years 1 and 2
  e years 3 and 4

22 Suppose a country's government expenditures are $400 billion, net taxes are $300 billion, saving is $300 billion, and investment is $250 billion. This country has a government budget
 a   surplus and a private sector surplus.
 b   surplus and a private sector deficit.
 c   deficit and a private sector surplus.
 d   deficit and a private sector deficit.
 e   surplus and a private sector balance.

23 The distinction between a debtor or creditor nation and a net borrower or net lender nation depends on the distinction between
 a   the level of saving and the saving rate.
 b   the level of saving and the rate of borrowing.
 c   the stock of net debt and the flow of net borrowing.
 d   exports and imports.
 e   nothing really; they are the same.

Exchange Rate Policy

24 The Bank of Canada cannot set the exchange rate at any level it desires because
 a   such intervention violates international law.
 b   the foreign exchange market is unregulated.
 c   doing so would make Canada a debtor nation.
 d   doing so would require unlimited foreign currency reserves.
 e   interest rate parity forbids it.

25 If the Bank of Canada wishes to increase the exchange rate to maintain its crawling peg, it should
 a   lower interest rates.
 b   increase the quantity of money.
 c   buy foreign exchange.
 d   sell Canadian dollars.
 e   buy Canadian dollars.

Short Answer Problems

I Suppose there is an increase in demand for Canadian exports. Illustrate and explain with a graph of the foreign exchange market what this change will do when there is a
 a   flexible exchange rate.
 b   fixed exchange rate.

2 What determines the value of the nominal exchange rate in the short run, in a market with no government intervention?

3 What is purchasing power parity?

(ct) 4 Consider this headline from the December 12, 1997 issue of *The Globe and Mail*: "Dollar Hits New 11-1/2 Year Low: Interest Rate Hike Expected After Recurrence of Asian Flu Forces Bank of Canada to Intervene." Clearly the Canadian dollar's exchange rate was decreasing in value during December 1997. Explain why an increase in interest rates by the Bank of Canada would help reverse this decrease.

(ct) 5 Explain how an expected increase in the exchange rate can be a self-fulfilling prophecy.

6 Table 25.3 shows some exchange rates for the Canadian dollar.

TABLE 25.3 EXCHANGE RATES

	USD	JPY*	CAD
USD	—	0.78	?
JPY*	?	—	?
CAD	1.06	0.83	—

Note: USD = U.S. dollar, JPY* = 100 Japanese yen, CAD = Canadian dollar.

 a   Fill in the missing values in the table, showing all calculations.

 b   If you were a trader, could you make money by starting with $100 Canadian, buying some USD, using your USD to buy some Japanese yen, and then use your yen to buy Canadian dollars? (Ignore minor rounding errors of 1% or less.)

7 Suppose that one month later, the Canadian values in the final row now read:

	USD	JPY*	CAD
CAD	1.20	0.69	—

 a   Against which currency or currencies has the Canadian dollar depreciated?

 b   List at least two factors that might have caused this depreciation.

 c   Against which currency or currencies has the Canadian dollar appreciated?

 d   List at least two factors that could have caused this appreciation.

8 Suppose that the nominal exchange rate between the Canadian dollar and the euro is 2 euros per dollar, that the price level in Canada is 122.7, and the price level in Europe is 200.5.

a What is the real exchange rate expressed as units of Eurozone real GDP per unit of Canadian real GDP?

b Does purchasing power hold?

c If purchasing power does not hold, explain what will happen in the foreign exchange market in the long run to create purchasing power parity.

9 You are trying to decide whether to buy some laptops for your business in either Canada or the United States. Looking at identical machines on the Dell Canada and the Dell U.S. websites, you find that they sell for US$750 in the United States and C$1,000 in Canada.

a Where would you buy the laptop if the exchange rate between the Canadian dollar and the U.S. dollar was US$0.80 per C$?

b If there is a profit opportunity, where would you resell it if you wanted to make a profit? (Ignore any taxes, tariffs, transportation costs, and differences in quality.)

c Does purchasing power parity hold?

ct d If many Canadian *and* American businesses acted like you, and if the exchange rate was flexible, what would happen to the value of the exchange rate? What would be the new equilibrium nominal exchange rate that would make purchasing power parity hold for laptops, if the U.S. dollar price and the Canadian dollar price stayed constant?

10 The international transactions of a country for a given year are reported in Table 25.4.

TABLE 25.4

Transaction	Amount (billions of dollars)
Exports of goods and services	100
Imports of goods and services	130
Transfers to the rest of the world	20
Loans to the rest of the world	60
Loans from the rest of the world	?
Increases in official reserves	10
Net interest income	0

a What is the official settlements balance?

b What is the amount of loans from the rest of the world?

c What is the current account balance?

d What is the capital account balance?

ANSWERS

True/False and Explain

1 T Dollar is more valuable—takes more yen to buy one dollar. (594)

2 F Inverting $0.75 USD/CAD yields $1.33 = 1/0.75. (594)

3 F Automatically matched by the *supply* of foreign currency. (597)

4 T If $CAD is cheaper, takes less foreign currency to buy each $CAD, making our exports cheaper, increasing demand for exports which increases quantity demanded $CAD. (597–598)

5 F The expected profits leads to *increased* selling of Canadian dollars. (599)

6 T Increases interest rate differential, making Canadian assets more attractive to foreigners. (601)

7 F Both affected by expected future exchange rate and interest rates, so move together. (601–602)

ct 8 F Expected appreciation implies increased earnings in foreign currency terms, which increases demand for foreign bonds, which decreases interest rates until interest rate parity holds. (604)

9 T Under purchasing power parity, the yen price identical in each country. $10 × 100 yen/$ = 1,000 yen. (604)

10 F Expected increase in foreign exchange value of dollar implies a profit opportunity from holding dollars, which increases demand for dollars. (601–605)

ct 11 F Overall flow of money in/out of country = sum of the 3 balances of payment must balance. Each of 3 balances may be in deficit/surplus/balance. (606–607)

12 F May or may not be true. For net borrower, *current* net borrowing > 0. For debtor nation, sum of *all* net borrowing > 0. (608)

13 T Definition—note which way the money is flowing. Surplus = net $ flow in. (606–607)

14   T   Shifts supply curve C$ rightward, offsetting shift in demand. (611–612)

15   F   Will not affect it intentionally, but might unintentionally, since changes in monetary policy affects interest rates, which affect demand and supply of Canadian dollars. (611–612)

Multiple-Choice

1   e $76 = £38 × ($2 per £). (594)

2   a   Takes more euros to buy C$1 (increase in value), and less yen (decrease in value). (594)

3   b   2009: 1/60 euro/yen = (2 euros/$)/ (120yen/$). 2010: 1/30 euro/yen = (3 euros/$)/(90 yen/$). Takes more euros in 2010 to buy 1 yen, so yen has appreciated. (594)

4   b   Buyers of Canadian $ must supply foreign exchange to buy it. (597)

5   d   Affects supply of Canadian $. (597–598)

6   c   Expected profits effect—low Canadian $ is likely to appreciate. (598)

7   c   High Canadian $ value = low foreign currency value, which is then more likely to appreciate and make a profit. (601)

8   a   Imports effect. (599–600)

9   b   If exchange rate high, there is a surplus (quantity supplied > quantity demanded) and therefore downward pressure on price (exchange rate). (600)

10   c   Two currencies have same purchasing power. (604)

11   b   Draw a graph. (604)

12   a   Increased demand for foreign currency increases supply of Canadian dollars. (602)

13   c   a has no impact on demand, b, d, and e shift demand leftward. (601)

14   d   Therefore Canadian dollar expected to depreciate, offsetting the interest rate differential. (604–605)

15   a   Greater demand for exports = greater demand for Canadian $ to buy exports. (601–604)

16   e   Higher interest rate differential makes Canadian assets more desirable, increasing demand for these assets (and therefore increasing demand for Canadian $) and decreasing demand for foreign assets (and therefore decreasing demand for foreign currency = decrease in supply of Canadian currency). (601–602)

17   d   Lower Canadian demand for imports means lower Canadian demand for foreign currency = decrease supply Canadian $. (601–602)

18   c   Imports > exports implies current account deficit. Borrowing > lending implies capital account surplus. (Think about which direction money is flowing.) (606–607)

19   b   Current lending > borrowing implies net lender. Sum of past borrowing > sum of lending implies debtor nation. (608)

20   e   Official settlements balance = 0 implies current account surplus = capital account deficit, which occurs only when lending > borrowing. (606–607)

21   e   Since current account + capital account + official settlements account = 0, when official settlements is a deficit, to be sure current is a surplus, it must be the case that capital is 0 or a deficit. (606–607)

22   c   Government sector deficit = $T - G$ = 300 – 400 = –100. Private sector surplus = $S - I$ = 300 – 250 = +50. (609–610)

23   c   Debtor/creditor depends on stock of accumulated net debt. Borrower/lender depends on current year flow. (608)

24   d   Such intervention requires buying/selling Canadian dollars, which changes foreign currency reserves, which cannot occur forever. (611–612)

25   e   This increases demand for C$. **a** decreases demand, **b**–**d** increase supply. (612–613)

Short Answer Problems

1   a   Under a flexible exchange rate, the government does not intervene. Therefore, the exchange rate will adjust to find the new equilibrium. An increase in demand for Canadian exports leads to an increase in demand for Canadian dollars in order to buy those exports, shown in Figure 25.2 as a

rightward shift in the demand curve. The result is a new equilibrium with a higher exchange rate (ER_1) and a higher quantity of Canadian dollars exchanged ($C\$_1$) each day in the foreign exchange market.

FIGURE **25.2**

b   Under a fixed exchange rate, the government intervenes to keep the exchange rate fixed at the target (original) value. Therefore, the exchange rate will *not* adjust to find the new equilibrium. As above, an increase in demand for Canadian exports leads to an increase in demand for Canadian dollars in order to buy those exports, shown in Figure 25.3 as a rightward shift in the demand curve. However, now the Bank of Canada supplies Canadian dollars to match this increase (buying foreign currency), so there is also a rightward shift in the supply curve. The result is a new equilibrium with the same exchange rate (ER_0) and an even higher quantity of Canadian dollars exchanged ($C\$_2$) each day in the foreign exchange market.

FIGURE **25.3**

2   The value of the exchange rate is determined by supply and demand. The supply of the Canadian dollar is affected by three things—changes in the Canadian interest rate differential, changes in the expected future exchange rate, and the Canadian demand for imports. The demand for the Canadian dollar is also affected by the first two factors, as well as by the world demand for Canadian exports. Finally, changes in the interest rate differential and in the expected future exchange rate are driven by purchasing power parity and interest rate parity.

3   Purchasing power parity follows from arbitrage and the law of one price. It means that the value of money is the same in all countries. For example, if the exchange rate between the dollar and the yen is 120 yen per dollar, purchasing power parity says that a good that sells for 120 yen in Japan will sell for 1 dollar in Canada. Thus, the exchange rate is such that money (dollars or yen) has the same purchasing power in both countries.

ⓒⓣ **4**   An increase in Canadian interest rates increases the Canadian interest rate differential, which increases the desirability of Canadian assets relative to foreign assets. This increases demand for Canadian dollars by foreigners, and decreases demand for foreign exchange by Canadians, which decreases the supply of the Canadian dollar. These shifts in demand and supply increase the exchange rate.

ⓒⓣ **5**   If the exchange rate is expected to increase, there will be an increase in demand for Canadian dollars to try and make a profit from the increase. In addition, there will be a decrease in supply of Canadian dollars, because the expected increase implies a decrease in the value of foreign currency and therefore a decrease in the demand for foreign currency, which is matched by a decrease in supplied of Canadian dollars. The impact of these two changes is a shift leftward in the supply curve and a shift rightward in the demand curve for Canadian dollars, which both put upward pressure on the Canadian exchange rate!

6 a Table 25.3 Solution here shows the appropriate values. Values are calculated by inverting the existing values: e.g., 1.28 = 1/0.78.

TABLE **25.3** SOLUTION

	USD	JPY*	CAD
USD	—	0.78	0.94
JPY*	1.28	—	1.21
CAD	1.06	0.83	—

b The columns for each currency tell us what they buy. $100 Canadian will buy US$94. Going to the USD column, we can see that US$94 will buy 120 (= 94 × 1.28) hundreds of yen. Going to the JPY* column, we can see that 120 hundreds of yen can buy $100 (= 120 × 0.83) Canadian. Therefore, there is no profit opportunity, the rates are aligned.

7 a One U.S. dollar now buys more Canadian dollars (1.20 > 1.06), so that the U.S. dollar has appreciated against the Canadian dollar, which means the Canadian dollar has depreciated against the U.S. dollar.

b There are five possible reasons for the depreciation:

- Canadian demand for U.S. imports might have increased, shifting the supply curve rightward.

- U.S. demand for Canadian exports might have decreased, shifting the demand curve leftward.

- Canadian interest rate differential (versus the United States) might have decreased, shifting the demand curve leftward and the supply curve rightward.

- Expected future exchange rate might have decreased, shifting the demand curve leftward and the supply curve rightward.

- The Bank of Canada might have intervened in the market, shifting the supply curve rightward by buying U.S. dollars.

c 100 Japanese yen now buy less Canadian dollars (0.69 < 0.83), so the yen has depreciated, or the Canadian dollar has appreciated versus the yen.

d There are five possible reasons for the appreciation:

- Canadian demand for Japanese imports might have decreased, shifting supply curve leftward.

- Japanese demand for Canadian exports might have increased, shifting demand curve rightward.

- Canadian interest rate differential (versus Japan) might have increased, shifting demand curve rightward and supply curve leftward.

- Expected future exchange rate might have increased, shifting demand curve rightward and supply curve leftward.

- The Bank of Canada (or the Bank of Japan) might have intervened in the market, shifting supply curve leftward by selling yen.

8 a The real exchange rate is calculated with the formula:

$$RER = E \times (P_{CAN}/P_{EURO})$$
$$= 2 \times (122.7/200.5) = 1.224$$

The real exchange rate is 1.224 units of Eurozone real GDP per unit of Canadian real GDP.

b No, purchasing power parity does not hold. When it holds, the real exchange rate = 1. If we bought the "average" Eurozone good at 200.5 euros, this converts to 100.25 C$ (= 200.5/2), which is less than the price of the average Canadian good (122.7).

c There is a profit opportunity to be made by moving relatively cheaper Eurozone goods from Europe to Canada. Traders carrying out this arbitrage will be buying up European goods, and demanding euros in order to do this. The extra demand for euros will raise the value of the euro and lower the value of the Canadian dollar (lower the nominal exchange rate) to something less than 2 euros per C$. This in turn will eventually erase the profit opportunity, as the real exchange rate converges on 1.

9 a   The Canadian laptop costs US$800 = C$1,000 × US$0.80 per C$. Therefore, it is cheaper from the U.S. website.

b   It is profitable to buy it in the United States for US$750 and sell it in Canada for US$800.

c   No, the two currencies do not have the same purchasing power—U.S. dollars buy more.

d   The extra demand for U.S. laptops would tend to push up demand for U.S. dollars, leading to an appreciation of the U.S. dollar (and a depreciation of the Canadian dollar). The value of the exchange rate that makes purchasing power parity hold would be the value A that solves US$750 = C$1,000 × US$$A$ per C$, which is a value of 0.75.

10 a   Because official reserves increased, the official settlements balance is −10.

b   Current account balance + Capital account balance + Official settlements balance = 0, or (100 − 130 − 20) + (Loans from rest of world − 60) + (−10) = 0, so Loans from rest of world = 120.

c   Current account balance is a $50 billion deficit: exports minus imports minus transfers to the rest of the world plus net interest income to the rest of the world.

d   Capital account balance is a surplus of $60 billion: loans from the rest of the world minus loans to the rest of the world.

Part 8 Wrap Up
Macroeconomic Trends

PROBLEM

At the time of writing this Study Guide (January 2009), most countries in the world were reacting to the financial crisis of 2008 with a variety of expansionary fiscal and monetary policies. We will not study fiscal and monetary policies and their short-term impacts on the economy until Chapters 29 and 30, but we can examine the impact of these policies on the loanable funds market, interest rates, exchange rates, investment and long-term economic growth.

a Consider the global market for loanable funds. Expansionary fiscal policies will dramatically increase the size of government deficits around the world, while expansionary monetary policies will increase the supply of loanable funds. Using a graph for the global loanable funds market, show the impact of these policies on the loanable funds market.

b Canada is a relatively small country in the world market, currently having net international lending and government deficits both roughly equal to 0. Two things happen next. First we have the changes in part **a** above (assume the deficit effect in part **a** is *stronger* than the monetary policy effect) changing the world real interest rate. Second, the Canadian government is also increasing the size of its government deficit. Show the impact of these two changes on the Canadian loanable funds market. Explain with the aid of your graph what happens to net international lending/borrowing, Canadian investment, Canadian saving, and the government deficit.

c What will be the impact of the changes from part **b** on the Canadian balance of payments? Assume that the official settlements account stays with a balance of 0 throughout your analysis.

d What is the impact of the changes in part **b** on the level of domestic investment in Canada? (Assume no Ricardo-Barro effect.) Under neoclassical growth theory, explain what this change would do to long-term economic growth.

MIDTERM EXAMINATION

You should allocate 32 minutes for this examination (16 questions, 2 minutes per question). For each question, choose the one *best* answer.

1 The key difference between neoclassical growth theory and classical growth theory is that
  a capital is not subject to diminishing returns under classical growth theory.
  b capital is subject to diminishing returns under classical growth theory.
  c increases in technology lead to increases in population that drive workers' incomes back down to the subsistence level in classical theory.
  d technological advances are exogenous in classical growth theory.
  e the one-third rule only holds in the neoclassical growth theory.

2 In the market for loanable funds, if the Ricardo-Barro effect holds, a higher government deficit leads to
  a an increase in interest rates, and an increase in investment.
  b an increase in interest rates, and a decrease in investment.
  c a decrease in interest rates, and an increase in investment.
  d a decrease in interest rates, and a decrease in investment.
  e no effect on interest rates or investment.

3 A bank can create money by
  a selling some of its investment securities.
  b increasing its reserves.
  c lending its excess reserves.
  d printing more cheques.
  e converting reserves into securities.

4 If the current account is in deficit, and the capital account is also in deficit, the change in official reserves is
  a negative.
  b positive.
  c probably close to zero, but might be either negative or positive.
  d zero.
  e not affected.

5 Which of the following shifts the supply curve of loanable funds rightward?
  a increase in current disposable income
  b decrease in current disposable income
  c increase in expected future income
  d increase in the real interest rate
  e decrease in the real interest rate

6 Consider the following data on the economy of Adanac:

Currency reserves of private banks	$ 5 billion
Currency in circulation	15 billion
Personal + nonpersonal chequing deposits	40 billion
Personal nonchequing deposits	25 billion
Nonpersonal nonchequing deposits	25 billion
Fixed term deposits	125 billion
Canada Savings Bonds	200 billion

In this economy, what is the value (in billions of dollars) of M1? of M2?
  a 105; 230
  b 110; 235
  c 55; 430
  d 55; 230
  e 60; 430

7 Which of the following quotations best describes the interest rate parity effect?
  a "The recent high Canadian interest rate has increased the demand for the Canadian dollar."
  b "The market feeling is that the Canadian dollar is overvalued and will likely appreciate."
  c "The price of bananas is the same in Canada and the United States, adjusting for the exchange rate."
  d "The expected appreciation of the Canadian dollar is currently lowering demand for it."
  e None of the above.

8 Suppose productivity has increased by 15 percent over last year. Capital per hour of labour increased by 10 percent as well. The increase in capital was responsible for
  a all of the increase in productivity.
  b 80% of the increase in productivity.
  c 67% of the increase in productivity.
  d 33% of the increase in productivity.
  e 20% of the increase in productivity.

9 Which of the following would cause the dollar to depreciate against the yen?
  a increase in the Canadian money supply
  b increase in interest rates in Canada
  c decrease in interest rates in Japan
  d increase in the expected future exchange rate
  e increase in the current exchange rate

10 Which of the following quotations describes a movement along the labour demand curve?
  a "Recent higher wage rates have led to more leisure being consumed."
  b "The recent lower price level has induced people to work more hours."
  c "The recent higher real wage rate has induced people to work more hours."
  d "The recent high investment in capital equipment has raised hiring by firms."
  e None of the above.

11 The amount of real money people want to hold will increase if either real income increases or the
  a price level increases.
  b price level decreases.
  c interest rate increases.
  d interest rate decreases.
  e price of bonds decreases.

12 Figure PW8.1 shows the loanable funds market for an economy that is part of the global market, with no government budget deficit or surplus. If the world interest rate is 7%, what is net lending or borrowing on the world market, and what is investment?
   a Net lending is $20 billion and investment is $40 billion.
   b Net borrowing is $20 billion and investment is $40 billion.
   c Net borrowing is $0 billion and investment is $50 billion.
   d Net borrowing is $20 billion and investment is $60 billion.
   e Net lending is $20 billion and investment is $60 billion.

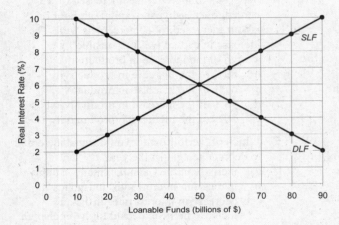

13 The Bank of Canada is following a flexible exchange rate policy. What happens if the demand for Canadian dollars increases?
   a The Bank of Canada will buy Canadian dollars.
   b The Bank of Canada will sell Canadian dollars.
   c The Bank of Canada will buy foreign exchange.
   d The Bank of Canada will sell foreign exchange.
   e The Bank of Canada will do nothing.

14 Which theory of economic growth concludes that in the long run, people do not benefit from growth?
   a classical theory
   b neoclassical theory
   c new growth theory
   d old growth theories
   e none of the theories

15 Anglers' Fishing has lent $12 million and borrowed $18 million. It has cash earnings per month of $140,000 and debt payments per month of $120,000. Anglers' Fishing is
   a solvent and liquid.
   b insolvent and illiquid.
   c solvent and illiquid.
   d insolvent and liquid.
   e solvent as long as interest rates are low enough.

16 If households and firms find that their holdings of real money are less than desired, they will
   a sell financial assets, causing interest rates to increase.
   b sell financial assets, causing interest rates to decrease.
   c buy financial assets, causing interest rates to increase.
   d buy financial assets, causing interest rates to decrease.
   e buy goods, causing the price level to increase.

ANSWERS

Problem

a The deficits mean governments of the world will be borrowing more, increasing the demand for loanable funds, shown as a shift rightward in *DLF*. The monetary policies will shift *SLF* rightward. The net effect is an increase in the amount of loanable funds traded, with an unclear effect on the world real interest rate, depending on whether the shift in demand or supply is stronger. In Figure PW8.2 on the next page, the demand shift is shown as stronger, as assumed in part **b** below, leading to a rise in the world real interest rate.

b As a small player in the world market, Canada faces a given world real interest rate. Figure PW8.3 on the next page shows the Canadian market. At the initial equilibrium with SLF_D, DLF_0, and r_0, Canada has no government deficit or international borrowing/lending, so quantity supplied of loanable funds is equal to quantity demanded here at LF_0.

Figure **PW8.2**

Figure **PW8.3**

When the world rate rises to r_1, this is as if the effective *SLF* shifts upwards to SLF_W^1. In addition, the new Canadian government deficit means a shift rightward in the *DLF* to DLF_1 in Canada. In the new equilibrium, the total amount of loanable funds traded in Canada is now LF_1. Of this amount, only LF_B is

generated from internal savings (the higher interest rate has encouraged some increase in domestic saving), so net international borrowing by Canada is $LF_1 - LF_B$. In addition, the higher interest rate causes a decline in domestic investment to LF_A. Finally, the size of the government deficit is the difference between DLF_1 and DLF_0, the amount $LF_1 - LF_A$.

c If Canada has net international borrowing, there is a net inflow of funds, and a capital account surplus. Since the official settlements balance is zero, then the current account balance must be the exact opposite of the capital account surplus—a current account deficit.

d As illustrated in part **b**, domestic investment in physical capital has fallen. Lower investment means lower economic growth in the neoclassical theory of growth, as lower capital growth slows down growth in capital per worker, and therefore slows down growth in productivity of each worker.

MIDTERM EXAMINATION

1 c In neoclassical theory, population growth not driven by economic growth. In both theories, capital subject to diminishing returns and technology is exogenous. (531–535)

2 e If there is a government deficit, households increase saving in anticipation of higher future taxes. (556)

3 c Lending reserves is done by crediting borrowers' deposits, creating more deposits = more money. (566–577)

4 a Official settlements balance = – (Capital account + Current account) > 0, which implies change in official reserves < 0. (606–607)

5 a Households save some of their disposable income. (551–552)

6 d M1 = currency in circulation + chequing deposits, M2 = M1 + personal nonchequing deposits + nonpersonal nonchequing deposits + fixed term deposits. (569)

7 a If two currencies do not have the same interest rate, market conditions will change demand for assets and the dollar. (604)

8 d Capital increase of 10 percent leads to increase in real GDP per hour of work of 5 percent, or 33 percent of increase in productivity. (518–520)

9 a **a** decreases interest rates, which decrease demand for Canadian dollars. **b–d** are increase in demand, **e** move along, not a shift. (601–605)

10 e **a**, **b**, **c** are *LS* effect, **d** shift in *LD* curve. (521–526)

11 d Real money demand not affected by Δ price level, decrease in price of bonds increases interest rate, lowering quantity of real money demanded. (578–579)

12 a At 7%, quantity supplied is $60 billion and quantity demanded (investment) is $40 billion, for net international lending of $20 billion. (557–558)

13 e Under flexible exchange rate regime, Bank ignores exchange rate market. (611)

14 a In long run, technological advances increase demand for labour and real GDP per capita, but population increases lowering real GDP *per capita* back to original level. (531–535)

15 d Net worth = $12 million – $18 million < 0 (insolvent), and cash payments > debt payments (liquid). (547)

16 a They sell bonds for money, extra sales decreases price of bonds and increases interest rates. (581)

Chapter 26
Aggregate Supply and Aggregate Demand

Aggregate Supply

The *AS–AD* model explains how equilibrium real GDP and the price level are determined and fluctuate.

Quantity of *real GDP supplied* depends on quantities of labour, physical and human capital, state of technology.

♦ At a given time, only quantity of labour can vary.

♦ Labour market can be at full employment, above full employment, or below full employment.

♦ Potential GDP is quantity of real GDP supplied at full employment.

• Over business cycle, employment fluctuates around full employment, as real GDP fluctuates around potential GDP.

Two *AS* concepts: long-run (*LAS*) and short-run (*SAS*).

♦ **Long-run aggregate supply (*LAS*)** is relationship between quantity of real GDP supplied (*Y*) and price level when money wage rate changes in step with price (*P*) level to achieve full employment.

• *LAS* curve is vertical at potential GDP—increase in *P* leads to equivalent percentage increase in factor prices, which means profits and real wages remain constant—no Δ employment, no Δ quantity supplied *Y*.

• *LAS* shifts rightward when potential GDP increases, due to increase in full employment quantity of labour, increase in capital stock, technological advance.

♦ **Short-run aggregate supply (*SAS*)** is relationship between quantity of real GDP supplied and price level when the money wage rates, other factor prices, and potential GDP are held constant.

• *SAS* curve is upward-sloping—increase in *P* leads to an increase in profits and employment and an increase in quantity supplied *Y*.

♦ *SAS* shifts along with *LAS*, but also shifts if Δ factor prices.

♦ Money wage changes due to expected changes in inflation and departures from full employment creating changes in labour market.

Aggregate Demand

Quantity of real GDP demanded is total amount of final goods and services produced in Canada that economic agents plan to buy. It depends on price level, expectations, fiscal/monetary policy, and world economy.

♦ **Aggregate demand (*AD*)** is total quantity real GDP demanded ($Y = C + I + G + X - M$) at given price level (*P*).

♦ Increase in *P* decreases quantity real GDP demanded, represented by movement up along *AD* curve because of *wealth* and *substitution effects*.

♦ Changes in other factors *shift AD* curve.

• If **fiscal policy** cuts taxes (which increases **disposable income**) or increases government expenditure, *AD* increases.

• If **monetary policy** decreases interest rates or increases quantity of money, *AD* increases.

- If exchange rate decreases or foreign income increases, *AD* increases.

- Increase in expectations of future disposable income or future inflation or future profits increases *AD*.

Explaining Macroeconomic Fluctuations

There are two different types of macroeconomic equilibrium. Long-run equilibrium is state toward which the economy is heading. Short-run equilibrium is the normal state of the economy, and occurs at each point in time along path to long-run equilibrium.

- **Long-run macroeconomic equilibrium** occurs when real GDP = potential GDP—when *AD* = *SAS* = *LAS*.

- **Short-run macroeconomic equilibrium** occurs where *AD* = *SAS*, with *P* adjusting to achieve equilibrium.

- Economic growth results from *LAS* shifting rightward on average, due to increase in labour, capital, and technology advances.

- Persistent inflation occurs when *AD* grows faster than *LAS*—quantity theory of money says money supply growth is most likely source.

- Growth in *Y* is not steady, but goes in cycles because *AD* and *SAS* do not shift at same pace.

- Over the business cycle, short-run equilibrium may occur at

  - **Full-employment equilibrium**, where real GDP = potential GDP.

  - **Below full-employment equilibrium**— *AD* = *SAS* left of *LAS*; real GDP < potential by amount of **recessionary gap** (= **output gap**— gap between real GDP and potential GDP).

  - **Above full-employment equilibrium**— *AD* = *SAS* right of *LAS*; real GDP > potential by amount of **inflationary gap**.

- Economy fluctuates in short run because of fluctuations in *AD* and *SAS*.

- If *AD* increases so *Y* > potential, economy does not stay in above full-employment equilibrium— upward pressures on the money wage rate shifts *SAS* leftward toward long-run equilibrium.

- If factor prices increase so *SAS* shifts leftward and *Y* < potential, then **stagflation** results (inflation and falling real GDP).

Macroeconomic Schools of Thought

Economist have different views about business cycles.

- ♦ **Classical** macroeconomists believe economy is self-regulating and always at full employment.

  - **New classical** economists believe business cycles are efficient responses of economy to uneven technological change.

- ♦ **Keynesian** macroeconomists believe economy is rarely at full employment, and needs active monetary and fiscal policy.

  - **New Keynesian** economists agree with Keynesians that money wage is sticky *and* other prices are too.

- ♦ **Monetarists** believe economy is self-regulating and normally at full employment, provided monetary policy is not erratic.

HELPFUL HINTS

1 The aggregate demand and aggregate supply model introduced in this chapter (and developed throughout this book) is an insightful method of analyzing complex macroeconomic events. To sort out these complex events, it is helpful if *you always draw a graph*—even a small graph in the margin of a multiple-choice question. Graphs are powerful and effective tools for analyzing economic events.

2 When using graphs, two factors often confuse students:

   a Sometimes graphs are based on explicit numerical or algebraic models, where the intercepts, slopes, sizes of shifts, etc., have explicit values. Often these numbers are based on real-world values, but sometimes they are just "made-up" numbers that the instructor has picked to illustrate the point (although they are still economically logical). Do *not* get caught up in the exact values of the numbers. Concentrate on the basic economic results—for example, an increase in *AD* leads to an increase in the price level and real GDP.

   b One common student mistake is failing to *distinguish between a shift in a curve versus a movement along a curve*. This distinction is crucial in understanding the factors that influence *AD* and *AS*, and you can be sure that your instructor will test you on it! The slope of the *AD* curve reflects the impact of a change in the price level on aggregate demand. A change in the price level produces a *movement along* the *AD* curve. A change in one of the factors affecting the *AD* curve other than the price level *shifts* the entire *AD* curve. Similarly, a change in the price level produces a *movement along* the *SAS* or the *LAS* curve and does not lead to a shift in the curves.

3 A change in the price level will not shift the *AD* or the *AS* curves. To cement the previous point, consider Figure 26.1. The initial long-run equilibrium is at the point *a*. (For the moment, ignore the SAS_1 curve.)

What happens in our model when there is a decrease in expected future disposable income and profits (such as happened in the 1990–91 recession)? This decrease in expected income and profits leads to a decrease in consumption and investment, and a decrease in aggregate demand, shown as the shift from AD_0 to AD_1.

FIGURE **26.1**

To understand what happens next, imagine that the AD_0 and SAS_1 curves are peeled off the page (remember, we are ignoring SAS_1 for the moment). This removal leaves us with the curves SAS_0 and AD_1, and with a price level of P_0. At P_0, there is a surplus of goods and services (the quantity of real GDP supplied is Y_0 [at *a*], greater than the quantity of real GDP demanded of Y_c [at *c*]). Firms find their inventories piling up, so they cut prices and decrease production.

This decrease in price eliminates the surplus in two ways. First, as price decreases, firms supply fewer goods and services: a movement down along the *SAS* curve from *a* to *b*. (Be careful—the price change does *not* shift the *SAS* curve.) Second, the decrease in price increases the quantity demanded: a movement down along

AD_1 from *c* to *b*. (Note there is no shift in the *AD* curve as price changes.)

The result is the new, below full-employment equilibrium at *b*, with a lower price level (P_1) and a lower level of real GDP (Y_1).

4 In Figure 26.1, point *b* is a short-run, below full-employment equilibrium, but it is not a long-run equilibrium, since $Y_1 < Y_0$ (potential). There are two possible adjustments back from Y_1 to Y_0. First, the government or central bank could intervene with an expansionary fiscal or monetary policy, raising *AD* back to AD_0—the economy will move back to a full-employment, long-run equilibrium at *a* with $Y = Y_0$ (potential). Second, if the government does nothing, the unemployment at *b* will lead to downward pressures on the money wage rate and other factor prices (although this adjustment can be very slow). As the money wage rates decrease, the *SAS* curve shifts slowly rightward, eventually reaching SAS_1, with a full-employment, long-run equilibrium at *d* with $Y = Y_0$ (potential).

5 On the supply side, there is a crucial (and hard to understand) distinction between suppliers' behaviour in the short run and the long run. The short run and long run are not lengths of calendar time, but are defined in terms of whether factor prices change. In the short run, the prices of productive factors do not change; in the long run, they do.

To see what this difference implies, consider what happens when the price level increases. In the short run, factor prices stay unchanged, so that per-unit revenues are increasing, while per-unit costs are unchanged. Profit-maximizing firms react by hiring more productive resources and supplying more real GDP as the price level increases—the short-run aggregate supply curve is upward-sloping.

In the long run, factor prices adjust by the same amount as the price level, which means that the costs of each unit of production have increased by the same percentage as the revenue. These two effects offset each other, there is no change in profits, and firms do not change their supply decision as the price level increases—the long-run aggregate supply curve is vertical.

This distinction between the short run and the long run also applies to influences affecting the short-run and long-run aggregate supply curves. Since prices of productive resources are held constant for the short-run aggregate supply curve but not for the long-run aggregate supply curve, a change in the prices of productive resources will shift *SAS* but not *LAS*.

S E L F - T E S T

True/False and Explain

Aggregate Supply

1 As the price level increases, in the long run the aggregate quantity of goods and services supplied increases.

2 Any factor that shifts the short-run aggregate supply curve rightward also shifts the long-run aggregate supply curve rightward.

3 A technological advance (other things remaining unchanged) shifts the long-run aggregate supply curve rightward, but the short-run aggregate supply curve will not shift.

4 If the wage rate decreases (other things remaining unchanged), both the long-run aggregate supply curve and the short-run aggregate supply curve shift rightward.

Aggregate Demand

5 An increase in the foreign exchange value of the dollar will increase aggregate demand in Canada.

6 An increase in the expected rate of inflation will decrease aggregate demand.

7 An increase in the quantity of money increases the quantity of real GDP demanded.

8 If the price level increases, the quantity of real GDP demanded will decrease.

Explaining Macroeconomic Fluctuations

9 A shift rightward in the aggregate demand curve increases the price level, which in turn shifts the short-run aggregate supply curve rightward in the short run.

10 If the aggregate demand curve and the short-run aggregate supply curve both shift rightward at the same time, but the aggregate demand curve shifts further rightward, the price level increases.

11 An economy is initially in short-run equilibrium and then expected future profits decrease. The new short-run equilibrium will always be a below full-employment equilibrium.

12 If the economy is in an above full-employment equilibrium, the long-run aggregate supply curve will shift rightward until the economy is at full-employment equilibrium.

13 If real GDP is higher than potential GDP, the money wage rate will rise.

Macroeconomic Schools of Thought

14 If the economy slows down, a Keynesian would argue this is the efficient response of the economy to a technological shock.

15 Under the monetarist view of the business cycle, the main cause of recessions is changes in the money supply.

Multiple-Choice

Aggregate Supply

1 A technological advance will shift
  a both *SAS* and *AD* rightward.
  b both *SAS* and *LAS* leftward.
  c *SAS* rightward but leave *LAS* unchanged.
  d *LAS* rightward but leave *SAS* unchanged.
  e both *SAS* and *LAS* rightward.

2 An increase in the money wage rate will shift
  a both *SAS* and *LAS* rightward.
  b both *SAS* and *LAS* leftward.
  c *SAS* leftward, but leave *LAS* unchanged.
  d *LAS* rightward, but leave *SAS* unchanged.
  e *SAS* rightward, but leave *LAS* unchanged.

3 Long-run aggregate supply will increase for all of the following reasons *except*
  a a fall in the money wage rate.
  b a rise in human capital.
  c the introduction of new technology.
  d more aggregate labour hours.
  e more capital stock.

4 Potential GDP is the level of real GDP at which
  a aggregate demand equals short-run aggregate supply.
  b there is full employment.
  c there is a recessionary gap.
  d there is over full employment.
  e prices are sure to increase.

5 The short-run aggregate supply curve is the relationship between the price level and the quantity of real GDP supplied, holding constant
  a the wage rate only.
  b the quantities of factor inputs.
  c the level of government expenditures.
  d the price level.
  e the prices of factor inputs.

6 Consider Figure 26.2. Which graph illustrates what happens when factor prices decrease?
  a (a)
  b (b)
  c (c)
  d (d)
  e none of the above

FIGURE **26.2**

Aggregate Demand

7 Consider Figure 26.2. Which graph illustrates what happens when government expenditures increase?
  a (a)
  b (b)
  c (c)
  d (d)
  e none of the above

8 Consider Figure 26.2. Which graph illustrates what happens when the quantity of money decreases?
  a (a)
  b (b)
  c (c)
  d (d)
  e none of the above

9 Consider Figure 26.2. Which graph illustrates what happens when expected future disposable income increases?
  a (a)
  b (b)
  c (c)
  d (d)
  e none of the above

10 Which of the following is a reason for the downward slope of the aggregate demand curve?
  a   the wealth effect
  b   the expectations effect
  c   the expected inflation effect
  d   the nominal balance effect
  e   none of the above

11 Which of the following will cause the aggregate demand curve to shift rightward?
  a   an increase in interest rates (at a given price level)
  b   an increase in expected inflation
  c   an increase in taxes
  d   a decrease in the price level
  e   an increase in the price level

Explaining Macroeconomic Fluctuations

12 We observe an increase in the price level and a decrease in real GDP. Which of the following is a possible explanation?
  a   The expectation of future profits has increased.
  b   The expectation of future disposable income has increased.
  c   The price of raw materials has increased.
  d   The stock of capital has increased.
  e   The money supply has increased.

13 Short-run macroeconomic equilibrium *always* occurs when the
  a   economy is at full employment.
  b   economy is below full employment.
  c   economy is above full employment.
  d   quantity of real GDP demanded equals the quantity of real GDP supplied.
  e   *AD* curve intersects the *LAS* curve.

14 Consider the economy represented in Table 26.1. In short-run macroeconomic equilibrium, the price level is _____ and the level of real GDP is _____ billion dollars.
  a   120; 600
  b   120; 500
  c   125; 550
  d   130; 600
  e   130; 500

TABLE 26.1

Price Level	Aggregate Demand (billions of 2002 $)	Short-Run Aggregate Supply (billions of 2002 $)	Long-Run Aggregate Supply (billions of 2002 $)
100	800	300	600
110	700	400	600
120	600	500	600
130	500	600	600
140	400	700	600

15 Consider the economy represented in Table 26.1. The economy is in a(n)
  a   full-employment equilibrium and factor prices will not change.
  b   above-full-employment equilibrium, and factor prices will increase.
  c   above-full-employment equilibrium, and factor prices will decrease.
  d   below-full-employment equilibrium, and factor prices will decrease.
  e   below-full-employment equilibrium, and factor prices will increase.

16 Consider the economy represented in Table 26.1. There is
  a   an inflationary gap equal to $100 billion.
  b   an inflationary gap equal to $50 billion.
  c   a recessionary gap equal to $50 billion.
  d   a recessionary gap equal to $100 billion.
  e   no gap; the economy is at full employment.

17 The economy cannot remain at a level of real GDP above long-run aggregate supply (*LAS*) because prices of productive resources will
  a   decrease, shifting *LAS* rightward.
  b   decrease, shifting *SAS* rightward.
  c   increase, shifting *LAS* leftward.
  d   increase, shifting *SAS* leftward.
  e   increase, shifting *SAS* rightward.

18 Consider an economy starting from a position of full employment. When aggregate demand decreases, which of the following changes does *not* occur?
  a   The price level decreases.
  b   The level of real GDP decreases in the short run.
  c   A recessionary gap arises.
  d   Factor prices decrease in the long run, shifting the short-run aggregate supply curve rightward.
  e   The long-run aggregate supply curve shifts leftward to create the new full-employment equilibrium.

19 If factor prices remain constant, an increase in aggregate demand will cause a(n)

a increase in the price level and an increase in real GDP.

b increase in the price level and a decrease in real GDP.

c decrease in the price level and an increase in real GDP.

d decrease in the price level and a decrease in real GDP.

e increase in the price level but no change in real GDP.

20 Which of the graphs in Figure 26.3 illustrates a below-full-employment equilibrium?

a (a) only

b (b) only

c (c) only

d (d) only

e both (c) and (d)

FIGURE **26.3**

21 Which of the graphs in Figure 26.3 illustrates an above-full-employment equilibrium?

a (a) only

b (b) only

c (c) only

d (d) only

e both (c) and (d)

22 If real GDP is greater than potential GDP, the economy is

a not in short-run equilibrium.

b in a recessionary equilibrium.

c in an above-full-employment equilibrium.

d in a below-full-employment equilibrium.

e in full-employment equilibrium.

23 Which one of the following newspaper quotations best describes a movement along an *SAS* curve?

a "The decrease in consumer spending may lead to a recession."

b "The increase in consumer spending is expected to lead to inflation, without any increase in real GDP."

c "Recent higher wage settlements are expected to cause higher inflation this year."

d "Growth has been unusually high the last few years due to more women entering the workforce."

e "The recent tornadoes destroyed many factories in Calgary and Edmonton."

Macroeconomic Schools of Thought

24 Which of the following news quotes *best* describes a *Keynesian* view of a recession?

a "Rapid computerization is creating obsolete workers and higher unemployment."

b "The unexpectedly tight fiscal policy is raising spending and lowering unemployment."

c "The anti-inflationary policy of the Bank of Canada is increasing spending."

d "The cuts in government spending have helped lower consumer spending and created unemployment."

e "Businesses are very worried about future sales and have lowered their purchases of capital equipment."

25 Which of the following news quotes *best* describes a *new classical* view of a recession?

  a "Rapid computerization is creating obsolete workers and higher unemployment."

  b "The unexpectedly tight fiscal policy is raising spending and lowering unemployment."

  c "The anti-inflationary policy of the Bank of Canada is increasing spending."

  d "The cuts in government spending have helped lower consumer spending and created unemployment."

  e "Businesses are very worried about future sales and have lowered their purchases of capital equipment."

Short Answer Problems

1 The substitution effects imply that an increase in the price level will lead to a decrease in the aggregate quantity of goods and services demanded. Explain.

2 Why is the *LAS* curve vertical?

3 Why is the *SAS* curve positively sloped?

4 What are the most important factors in explaining the steady and persistent increases in the price level over time in Canada?

5 Suppose the economy is initially in full-employment equilibrium. Graphically illustrate the short-run effects of an increase in the money wage rate. What happens to the price level and the level of real GDP?

6 Consider an economy that is in above full-employment equilibrium due to an increase in *AD*. Prices of productive resources have not changed. With the help of a graph, discuss how the economy returns to full-employment equilibrium, with no government intervention.

7 Table 26.2 shows the aggregate demand and short-run aggregate supply schedule for an economy. Long-run aggregate supply is equal to 1.1 trillion 2002 $.

TABLE 26.2

Price Level	Aggregate Demand (trillions of 2002 $)	Short-Run Aggregate Supply (trillions of 2002 $)
100	1.3	0.9
105	1.2	1.0
110	1.1	1.1
115	1.0	1.2
120	0.9	1.3

  a Graph this economy's *AD*, *SAS*, and *LAS* curves, and show the original macroeconomic equilibrium. What kind of equilibrium is this—below full employment, above full employment, or full employment? If there is an inflationary or recessionary gap, identify how large it is.

  b Next, suppose that at every price level, the quantity of real GDP demanded falls by $200 billion. Plot the new aggregate demand curve on your graph, and show the new short-run equilibrium. What kind of equilibrium is this—below full employment, above full employment, or full employment? If there is an inflationary or recessionary gap, identify how large it is.

  c Suppose that the government does not take any action and that the cause of the decrease in aggregate demand remains unchanged. What kind of adjustments occur in the long run? Explain what happens to the price level, real GDP, *AD*, and *AS* during this adjustment, illustrating the changes on your graph.

8 With the aid of a graph, illustrate an economy that has persistent inflation and positive economic growth over a three-year period.

9 Consider an economy for which economists have estimated that last year's real GDP was $800 billion, equal to potential GDP. The price level was 105. Suppose that this year the economists estimate that potential GDP has increased by 10 percent. However, actual real GDP has decreased by 5 percent, while the price level has also decreased by 5 percent.

  Draw an *AD–AS* graph showing last year's equilibrium, as well as last year's aggregate demand, aggregate supply (short-run and long-run), price level, and real GDP level. Next, given this information, show what has happened to the price level and the level of real GDP this year (show this year's equilibrium), plus what has happened to aggregate demand, short-run aggregate supply, and long-run aggregate supply since last year.

ℂⓉ **10** In 1996, the Saguenay region of Quebec suffered some of the worst floods in memory, with many roads, towns, and buildings destroyed.

    a   Assuming that the economy was originally in full-employment equilibrium, explain what has happened to the *LAS* and *SAS* curves in the local economy as a result of the destruction of the capital stock.

    b   Assuming that the *AD* curve is constant, what might happen to the price level and real GDP in the short run as a result of the changes you have described in part **a**? Show this result on an *AD*–*SAS* graph.

    c   Several observers, especially those in the construction industry, argued that the rebuilding of the destroyed capital stock would strongly stimulate the local economy. What component of aggregate demand is affected by this rebuilding? What will happen to aggregate demand as a result of this rebuilding?

    d   Some observers implied the local economy was better off, in a purely economic sense, as a result of the floods and the resulting rebuilding process. Do you agree?

ANSWERS

True/False and Explain

1   **F**   In the long run, the money wage rates increase as well, leaving profits, real wages, and production unchanged. (626–627)

2   **F**   Changes in factor prices shift only *SAS* and not *LAS*. (628–629)

3   **F**   Anything that shifts *LAS* also shifts *SAS*. (628–629)

4   **F**   Only the *SAS* shifts in response to a wage change. (628–629)

5   **F**   Increase in value of dollar makes Canadian exports more expensive and imports

cheaper, decreasing demand for Canadian goods. (631–634)

6   **F**   If individuals expect an increased inflation rate, they will spend more today to avoid higher future prices. (631–634)

7   **T**   Higher quantity of money increases spending. (631–634)

8   **T**   Movement along the *AD* curve due to wealth and substitution effects. (630–631)

9   **F**   Increase in *P* leads to movement along *SAS* curve, not shift in it. (638–639)

10   **T**   Try drawing a graph. (638–639)

ℂⓉ **11**   **F**   Depends on where initial short-run equilibrium is relative to *LAS*, and on size of decrease in *AD* from decrease in future profits—try drawing graphs. (638–639)

12   **F**   *SAS* shifts, not *LAS*. (635–639)

13   **T**   Unemployment below the natural rate, upward pressure on the money wage rate. (638–639)

14   **F**   This is new classical argument. (640–641)

15   **T**   Monetarists believe main source *AD* shocks is change in money supply. (640–641)

Multiple-Choice

1   **e**   Technological advances means same inputs can produce more output, leading to increase in quantity supplied in both short and long run. (626–634)

2   **c**   Wage rate is held constant along given *SAS*; if money wage rate increases, production is less at every price level shifting *SAS* leftward. (628–629)

3   **a**   Changes in the money wage rates change *SAS* only, not *LAS*. (628–629)

4   **b**   Definition. (626)

5   **e**   Short run is defined as time period where factor prices are constant. (627)

6   **a**   When factor prices decrease, firms produce more at every price level shifting *SAS* rightward. (628–629)

7   **c**   Increase in government expenditures increases aggregate spending, shifting *AD* rightward. (630–634)

8 d Decrease in quantity of money decreases aggregate spending, shifting *AD* leftward. (630–634)

9 c Increase in expected future disposable income increases household consumption, shifting *AD* rightward. (630–634)

10 a **b** and **c** shift *AD* curve, **d** doesn't exist. (630–634)

11 b Answers **a** and **c** cause shift leftward; **d** and **e** movements along *AD* curve. (630–634)

⒞ 12 c Answers **a**, **b**, and **e** increase *AD* increasing real GDP, while **d** shifts *LAS* rightward, increasing real GDP. **c** shifts *SAS* leftward increasing *P* and decreasing real GDP (try drawing a graph). (638–639)

13 d Short-run macroeconomic equilibrium always occurs where *AD = SAS*; equilibrium *may* occur at answers **a–c** and **e**, but doesn't *always* occur there. (638–639)

14 c Short-run equilibrium where *AD = SAS*, at *P* = 125 and real GDP = 550—halfway between *P* = 120 and *P* = 130. (634–635)

15 d Real GDP = 550 billion < potential (full-employment) GDP of 600 billion, so unemployed workers eventually offer to work for less. (634–639)

16 c Actual real GDP = 550 billion, 50 billion less than potential GDP of 600 billion. (634–635)

17 d Above *LAS*, extra demand for resources increases their prices, increasing cost of production, so *SAS* shifts leftward. (634–639)

18 e Decrease in *AD* creates recession, decreasing factor prices, shifting *SAS* rightward, pushing economy back to *LAS*. (638–639)

19 a Rightward shift *AD* and movement up along *SAS* curve (638–639)

20 a Below-full-employment equilibrium occurs when *AD = SAS* to left of *LAS*. (634–635)

21 e Above-full-employment equilibrium occurs when *AD = SAS* to right of *LAS*. (634–635)

22 c Equilibrium is with *AD = SAS*; if *Y* is > *LAS* then an above-full-employment equilibrium. (634–635)

⒞ 23 a Decrease in consumer spending leads to shift leftward in *AD*, movement down *SAS* curve in short-run, decreasing *P* and decreasing *Y*. (634–639)

24 e Expectations (animal spirits) primary cause of recession for Keynesians. (640–641)

25 a Fluctuations in technological advances primary cause of recession for new classicals. (640–641)

Short Answer Problems

1 There are two substitution effects. First, if the prices of domestic goods increase and foreign prices remain constant, domestic goods become relatively more expensive, and so households will buy fewer domestic goods and more foreign goods. This decline in spending decreases the quantity of real GDP demanded. Thus, an increase in the price level (prices of domestic goods) decreases the aggregate quantity of (domestic) goods and services demanded.

Second, the increase in the price level increases the rate of interest, which increases saving and decreases spending. This decline in spending also decreases the quantity of real GDP demanded.

2 Long-run aggregate supply is the level of real GDP supplied when the money wage rate changes in step with the price level to achieve full employment. Since this level of real GDP equals potential GDP and is independent of the price level, the long-run aggregate supply curve is vertical. Potential GDP is the level of real GDP when factor prices freely adjust to clear resource markets.

3 The short-run aggregate supply curve is positively sloped because it holds factor prices constant. When the price level increases, firms see the prices of their output (revenues) increasing, but the prices of their input (costs) remain unchanged. With profits increasing, each firm has an incentive to increase output and so aggregate output increases.

4 The price level increases either from an increase in aggregate demand or from a decrease in aggregate supply. Both of these forces have contributed to periods of an increasing price level. The steady and persistent increases in the price level, however, have been the result of a tendency for aggregate demand to increase faster than aggregate supply, due principally to increases in the growth rate of the quantity of money.

5 In Figure 26.4, the economy is initially at point *a* on the SAS_0 curve. An increase in the money wage rate will shift the *SAS* curve leftward to SAS_1. At the new equilibrium, point *b*, the price level has increased and the level of real GDP has decreased.

FIGURE **26.4**

6 In Figure 26.5, the increase in *AD* from AD_0 to AD_1 results in above-full-employment equilibrium at point *b* and causes the price level to increase. Since money wage rates have not changed, the real cost of labour to firms decreases, profits rise, and output is stimulated as indicated by the movement along the SAS_0 curve from point *a* to point *b*. Furthermore, the purchasing power of workers' money wage rates decreases.

Workers eventually demand higher money wage rates and firms will be willing to pay them. Similarly, other prices of productive resources will increase. This increase in prices of productive resources shifts the *SAS* curve leftward, resulting in a new equilibrium. There will continue to be pressure for money wage rates and other prices of productive resources to increase until the *SAS* curve shifts all the way to SAS_1, where the purchasing power of the money wage rates and other prices of productive resources has been restored and the economy is again at full employment, point *c*.

FIGURE **26.5**

7 a The economy's AD_0, SAS_0, and *LAS* curves are graphed in Figure 26.6 (ignore the AD_1 and SAS_1 curves for now). The macro-economic equilibrium occurs where the *AD* and *SAS* curves cross, at a price level of 110 and real GDP of 1.1 trillion 2002 $. Since this level of real GDP equals potential GDP, this economy is in a full-employment equilibrium, with no type of gap.

FIGURE **26.6**

b This decrease in aggregate demand leads to a new short-run equilibrium where the new AD_1 crosses SAS_0, at a price level of 105 and real GDP of 1 trillion 2002 $. Since real GDP is less than potential GDP, the economy is in a below-full-employment equilibrium, and there is a recessionary gap (or output gap) equal to the difference between real GDP and potential GDP, a gap of $100 billion.

c Since real GDP is below potential GDP, unemployment is above the natural rate. Eventually unemployed resources start offering to work for lower factor prices, shifting the *SAS* curve rightward to SAS_1, raising aggregate supply, lowering prices even more, and leading to a new long-run equilibrium where SAS_1 crosses AD_1 and *LAS* where the price level is 100 and real GDP is back at potential GDP ($1.1 trillion).

8 In order to have these two events, long-run aggregate supply is growing (shifting rightward), and aggregate demand is shifting rightward as well, but at a faster pace. Figure 26.7 illustrates such a case, with the points *a*, *b*, and *c* showing the three years. (The *SAS* curves have been omitted from the graph for simplicity.)

FIGURE **26.7**

9 Figure 26.8 shows the original full-employment equilibrium, at last year's equilibrium price level of 105 and income level of 800.

FIGURE **26.8**

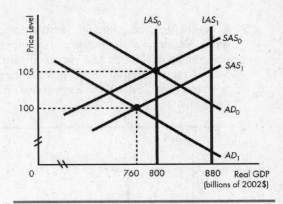

For the current year, the *LAS* curve has shifted rightward to LAS_1, a value of 880, and the *SAS* curve shifts with it to SAS_1, all else equal. The new short-run equilibrium must be along the intersection of SAS_1 and an *AD* curve. Since prices are 5 percent lower at 100, and real GDP is 5 percent lower at 760, the new *AD* curve must have shifted leftward as shown.

(*Hint:* To decide where AD_1 should be, first find the intersection of $P = 100$ and $Y = 760$ on the new *SAS* curve, and then draw in the *AD* curve to go through this point.)

10 a The destruction of towns, roads, etc., is a destruction of the capital stock, which would lower potential GDP, shifting the *LAS* and *SAS* curves leftward together.

b Figure 26.9 shows the original full-employment equilibrium at Y_0 and P_0.

FIGURE **26.9**

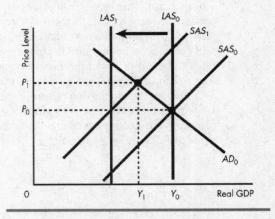

The shift leftward in the long-run aggregate supply to LAS_1 and the short-run aggregate supply to SAS_1, combined with the unchanged AD curve, leads to stagflation—a rise in the price level to P_1, accompanied by a fall in real GDP to Y_1.

c The resulting rebuilding would stimulate investment demand, and increase aggregate demand, perhaps dramatically.

d The region is worse off—higher inflation, and a lower level of potential GDP and real GDP. This recession is followed by higher growth once the new investment starts, *but* this investment is merely replacing lost capital, and is not adding new capital stock.

27

Expenditure Multipliers: The Keynesian Model

Fixed Prices and Expenditure Plans

In very short term, price level is fixed—aggregate demand determines aggregate quantity sold.

♦ To understand *AD*, we study the aggregate expenditure model.

♦ **Aggregate planned expenditure** (*AE*) = planned consumption (*C*) + planned investment (*I*) + planned government expenditures (*G*) + planned exports (*X*) – planned imports (*M*) = real GDP (*Y*).

♦ *C*, *M* depend on real GDP (*Y*), so that increases in *Y* increase *AE*, and increases in *AE* increase *Y*.

Consumption and saving depend primarily on **disposable income** (*YD*) = real GDP – net taxes (*T*).

♦ **Consumption function** shows increase in *YD* leads to increase in consumption.

♦ **Saving function** shows increase in *YD* leads to increase in saving, with $\Delta C + \Delta S = \Delta YD$.

♦ **Marginal propensity to consume** (*MPC*) = fraction of ΔYD that is consumed = $\Delta C / \Delta YD$ = slope of consumption function.

♦ **Marginal propensity to save** (*MPS*) = fraction of ΔYD that is saved = $\Delta S / \Delta YD$ = slope of saving function.

♦ $MPC + MPS = 1$.

Influences other than ΔYD *shift* the functions.

♦ Increase in *expected future disposable* income or decrease in *real interest rate* or increase in *wealth* shifts *S* function downward, *C* function upward.

♦ Consumption and saving are function of real GDP, since increase in real GDP increases in *YD*.

Import function relates imports and real GDP.

♦ **Marginal propensity to import** is fraction of ΔY spent on imports = $\Delta M / \Delta Y$.

Real GDP with a Fixed Price Level

Components of aggregate expenditure interact to determine *Y*, and *AE* is influenced by *Y*.

♦ *AE* can be represented by graph or schedule. Increase in *Y* leads to increase in *AE*.

♦ Aggregate planned expenditure has two parts:

• **Autonomous expenditure** (*A*) = part of *AE* that does *not* vary with income.

• **Induced expenditure** (*N*) = part of *AE* that *does* vary with income.

♦ Actual aggregate expenditure may not equal planned expenditure if level of real GDP is not consistent with plans.

♦ **Equilibrium expenditure** when *AE* = real GDP.

• On graph, where *AE* curve crosses 45° line.

• If real GDP is above equilibrium value, *AE* < real GDP. Firms cannot sell all their production, increasing unplanned inventories. Firms lower production, leading to decrease in real GDP and convergence to equilibrium.

- If real GDP is below equilibrium value, $AE >$ real GDP. Firms sell all production and more, leading to unplanned decrease in inventories. Firms increase production to restore inventories, leading to increase in real GDP and convergence to equilibrium.

The Multiplier

The **multiplier** is the amount by which change in autonomous expenditure is multiplied to determine change in equilibrium expenditure and real GDP.

- ♦ Increase in autonomous expenditure increases real GDP, leading to further (secondary) increase in aggregate planned expenditure, leading to further increases in real GDP, etc.

- ♦ Secondary, *induced* effects means total Δ real GDP > initial Δ autonomous expenditure.

- ♦ Multiplier = (Δ real GDP)/(Δ autonomous expenditure) = 1/(1 − slope of AE function).

  - Multiplier > 1 because of induced effects.

  - Higher slope of AE function implies larger induced effects and larger multiplier.

  - Multiplier is higher if MPC is higher, or marginal tax rate is lower, or marginal propensity to import is lower.

- ♦ Recessions and depressions begin with expenditure fluctuations magnified by multiplier effect.

The Multiplier and the Price Level

Aggregate demand curve shows relationship between real GDP demanded and price level, other things remaining the same, and can be derived from AE curve.

- ♦ Increase in price level shifts AE curve downward (due to wealth and substitution effects), lowers equilibrium real GDP, shown by movement up and to left on AD curve.

- ♦ Δ non-price variables (autonomous expenditures) shift both AE and AD curves.

- ♦ In short run, increase in AE leads to shift rightward in AD curve, increasing price level, which lowers AE somewhat, offsetting increase in Y somewhat, so multiplier is smaller.

- ♦ In long run, vertical LAS means there is large enough increase in price level to cause a decrease in AE that totally offsets initial increase, so multiplier = 0.

FIGURE **27.1**

Consider the graph of consumption and disposable income in Figure 27.1. Along the 45° line, consumption equals disposable income at all points. For example, at point a, $C = YD = $ \$300 billion.

Consider point b. Consumption is still equal to \$300 billion, but now disposable income is only \$200 billion. To the left of the 45° line, variables measured on the vertical axis (here, consumption) are greater than variables measured on the horizontal axis (here, disposable income).

Next, consider point c. Consumption is still equal to \$300 billion, but now disposable income is \$400 billion. To the right of the 45° line, variables measured on the vertical axis are less than variables measured on the horizontal axis.

To summarize, consider the consumption function (CF) shown in Figure 27.2. Using the 45° line as our reference, any point on the consumption function to the left of the 45° line has consumption greater than disposable income (and therefore saving (= $YD - C$) is negative). Any point on the consumption function to the right of the 45° line has consumption less than disposable income (and saving is positive).

FIGURE **27.2**

To make sure you understand, draw the graph of the aggregate expenditure function, with a 45° line, and identify the points on your graph where aggregate expenditure is greater than income, equal to income, or less than income. *Note:* For the consumption function, the 45° line is a pure reference line—it is possible in equilibrium for consumption to be greater than, less than, or equal to disposable income. However, for the aggregate expenditure function, the point on the 45° line where $AE = Y$ is more than just a reference point; it shows the point of *equilibrium expenditure*.

2   Aggregate demand is the relationship between the price level and the quantity of goods and services demanded; in other words, it is the relationship between the price level and the level of planned aggregate expenditure. One purpose of this chapter is to help you understand planned aggregate expenditure by separating and examining its individual components. In particular, we examine consumption expenditure, investment, and net exports—the three components of private aggregate expenditure. As you put the discussion of this chapter and the next in perspective, remember that the ultimate objective is a more complete understanding of aggregate demand (and what shifts it), which combines these expenditure

components with government expenditure on goods and services. This understanding of the components will help you in later chapters to understand the potential causes of past and future recessions.

Be sure you can distinguish the *AD* curve from the *AE* curve—they are based on different thought experiments. Each *AE* curve holds constant the price level, and represents only a single point on an *AD* curve. The *AD* curve allows the price level to vary. Changing the price level will shift the *AE* curve, but create a movement along the *AD* curve.

3   This chapter distinguishes between *autonomous* expenditure and *induced* expenditure. Autonomous expenditure is independent of changes in real GDP, whereas induced expenditure will vary as real GDP varies. In general, a change in autonomous expenditures creates a change in real GDP, which in turn creates a change in induced expenditure. As the flow graph in Figure 27.3 illustrates, these changes are at the heart of the multiplier effect.

FIGURE **27.3**

(Even though autonomous expenditure may be independent of changes in real GDP, it will not be independent of changes in other variables— for example, the price level.)

4   The concept of the multiplier is very important. It results from the interaction of the components of aggregate expenditure. An initial increase in autonomous expenditure directly increases real GDP, but that is not the end of the story. As shown in Figure 27.3, that initial increase in real GDP generates an increase in *induced* expenditure, which further increases real GDP, and induces further increases in expenditure. The total effect on real GDP is larger than the initial increase in autonomous expenditure, because there is induced expenditure. You should become thoroughly familiar with both the intuition and the mathematics behind the multiplier.

5 The multiplier shows the change in equilibrium expenditure, and the change in equilibrium real GDP, price level held constant—it shows the shift rightward or leftward in the *AD* curve. However, the price level normally will change with a shift in the *AD* curve, the size of the change depending on the *AS* curve. In the short run, the change in the price level creates an opposite change in aggregate expenditure, one that somewhat offsets the initial change in aggregate expenditure, so that the total change in real GDP is less than the initial shift in *AD* would indicate. In the long run, this offsetting effect is 100 percent.

6 The mathematical note to Chapter 27 on the algebra of the multiplier will be covered by some students' instructors, and this material is worth reviewing if you are one of those students.

To start, recall that aggregate planned expenditure (*AE*) is equal to the sum of components' planned levels:

(1) $AE = C + I + G + X - M$

Next, recall that consumption consists of autonomous consumption (*a*) and induced consumption (*bYD*), or

(2) $C = a + bYD$

Substituting in the definitions of disposable income ($YD = Y - T$) and net taxes ($T = T_a + tY$, where T_a is autonomous taxes) yields:

(3) $C = a + b(Y - T) = a - T_a + b(1 - t)Y$

Next, recall that imports also depend on real GDP.

(4) $M = mY$

Next, substitute the consumption function (equation (3)) and the import function (equation (4)) into the aggregate planned expenditure function:

(5) $AE = a - T_a + b(1 - t)Y + I + G + X - mY$

Collecting terms:

(6) $AE = [a - T_a + I + G + X] + [b(1 - t) - m]Y$

or

(6a) $AE = A + [b(1 - t) - m]Y$

A is autonomous expenditure and $[b(1 - t) - m]$ is the slope of the aggregate planned expenditure function.

Equilibrium occurs when $Y = AE$ along the 45° line:

(7) $Y^* = A + [b(1 - t) - m]Y^*$

Collecting terms and solving yields the solution:

(8) $Y^* = \dfrac{1}{1 - [b(1 - t) - m]}A$

We can use equation (8) to show the algebraic formula for the multiplier. We start with a shock to autonomous expenditure (ΔA) which creates a change in equilibrium expenditure and real GDP:

(9) $\Delta Y^* = \dfrac{1}{1 - [b(1 - t) - m]}\Delta A$

Dividing both sides of (9) by ΔA gives us the equation for the multiplier:

(10) $\dfrac{\Delta Y^*}{\Delta A} = \dfrac{1}{1 - [b(1 - t) - m]}$

$= \dfrac{1}{1 - \text{Slope of } AE \text{ function}}$

We can also use equation (9) and the definition of *A* to calculate three specific multipliers. First, we can see that a change in government expenditures implies $\Delta A = \Delta G$, so that the **government expenditures multiplier** is:

(11) $\dfrac{\Delta Y}{\Delta G} = \dfrac{1}{1 - [b(1 - t) - m]}$

Second, we can see that a change in autonomous taxes means that $\Delta A = -b\Delta T_a$, so that the **autonomous tax multiplier** is:

(12) $\dfrac{\Delta Y}{\Delta T_a} = \dfrac{b}{1 - [b(1 - t) - m]}$

Third, we can see that a simultaneous change in government expenditures and autonomous taxes means that $\Delta G = -b\Delta T_a$, so that the **balanced budget multiplier** is:

$\dfrac{1 - b}{1 - [b(1 - t) - m]}$

SELF-TEST

True/False and Explain

Fixed Prices and Expenditure Plans

1 The sum of the marginal propensity to consume and the marginal propensity to save equals 1.

2 A change in disposable income will shift the consumption function.

3 An increase in expected future disposable income will shift both the consumption and saving functions upward.

4 Net taxes increase as real GDP increases.

Real GDP with a Fixed Price Level

5 When aggregate planned expenditure exceeds real GDP, inventories will increase more than planned.

6 Equilibrium expenditure occurs when aggregate planned expenditure equals real GDP.

7 Induced expenditure is that part of aggregate expenditure that varies as real GDP varies.

8 The aggregate expenditure schedule lists the level of aggregate planned expenditure that is generated at each level of real GDP.

The Multiplier

9 If the slope of the *AE* function is 0.75, the multiplier is equal to 3.

10 If the marginal tax rate increases, the multiplier will be higher.

11 If the marginal propensity to import decreases, the multiplier will be higher.

The Multiplier and the Price Level

12 An increase in the price level shifts the aggregate expenditure curve upward.

13 An increase in autonomous expenditure always increases equilibrium real GDP in the short run.

14 An increase in autonomous expenditure always increases equilibrium real GDP in the long run.

15 The higher the marginal propensity to consume, the higher the multiplier in the long run.

Multiple-Choice

Fixed Prices and Expenditure Plans

1 The fraction of the last dollar of disposable income saved is the
a marginal propensity to consume.
b marginal propensity to save.
c marginal propensity to dispose.
d marginal tax rate.
e saving function.

2 Consider Table 27.1. Autonomous consumption is equal to
  a $0.
  b $65.
  c $100.
  d $260
  e $400.

TABLE **27.1**

Disposable Income (2002 $)	Consumption Expenditure (2002 $)
0	100
100	165
200	230
300	295
400	360

3 Consider Table 27.1. The marginal propensity to consume is
  a   0.35.
  b   0.65.
  c   1.15.
  d   1.65.
  e   not calculable with the information given.

4 In Table 27.1, at which of the following level(s) of YD is there positive saving?
  a   0
  b   100
  c   200
  d   300
  e   all of the above levels

5 Which of the following events would shift the consumption function upward?
  a   Increase in disposable income
  b   Decrease in disposable income
  c   Decrease in the real interest rate
  d   Decrease in expected future disposable income
  e   Increase in wealth

Real GDP with a Fixed Price Level

6 The aggregate expenditure curve shows the relationship between aggregate planned expenditure and
  a   disposable income.
  b   real GDP.
  c   the interest rate.
  d   consumption expenditure.
  e   the price level.

7 If there is an unplanned increase in inventories, aggregate planned expenditure is
  a   greater than real GDP and firms will increase output.
  b   greater than real GDP and firms will decrease output.
  c   less than real GDP and firms will increase output.
  d   less than real GDP and firms will decrease output.
  e   less than real GDP and firms will decrease investment.

8 If $AE = 50 + 0.6Y$ and $Y = 200$, unplanned inventory
  a   increases are 75.
  b   increases are 30.
  c   decreases are 75.
  d   decreases are 30.
  e   changes are 0 and equilibrium exists.

9 Autonomous expenditure is *not* influenced by
  a   the interest rate.
  b   the foreign exchange rate.
  c   real GDP.
  d   the price level.
  e   any variable.

10 In Figure 27.4, the marginal propensity to consume is
  a   0.3.
  b   0.6.
  c   0.9.
  d   1.0.
  e   none of the above.

FIGURE **27.4**

Note: There are no taxes in this economy.

11 In Figure 27.4, *autonomous* aggregate expenditure is
   a 10.
   b 100.
   c 150.
   d 347.
   e 375.

12 In Figure 27.4, *equilibrium* expenditure is
   a 10.
   b 100.
   c 150.
   d 347.
   e 375.

13 In Figure 27.4, at the equilibrium level of real GDP, *induced* expenditure is
   a 28.
   b 150.
   c 225.
   d 347.
   e 375.

14 In Figure 27.4, the marginal propensity to import is
   a 0.
   b 0.1.
   c 0.25.
   d 0.3.
   e 0.6.

The Multiplier

15 In Figure 27.4, the multiplier is
   a 0.25.
   b 1.
   c 1.60.
   d 2.50.
   e 10.

16 An increase in expected future disposable income leads to a(n)
   a increase in consumption and a decrease in aggregate expenditure.
   b increase in both consumption and aggregate expenditure.
   c decrease in both consumption and aggregate expenditure.
   d decrease in consumption and an increase in aggregate expenditure.
   e increase in consumption and either an increase or a decrease in aggregate expenditure, depending on what happens to saving.

17 Which of the following quotations illustrates the idea of the multiplier?
   a "The new stadium will generate $200 million in spinoff spending."
   b "Higher expected profits are leading to higher investment spending by business, and will lead to higher consumer spending."
   c "The projected cuts in government jobs will hurt the local retail industry."
   d "Taking the grain elevator out of our small town will destroy all the jobs."
   e All of the above.

18 The value of the multiplier increases with a(n)
   a increase in the marginal propensity to import.
   b increase in the marginal tax rate.
   c decrease in the marginal propensity to consume.
   d decrease in the marginal propensity to save.
   e increase in the marginal propensity to save.

The Multiplier and the Price Level

19 An increase in the price level will
   a shift the *AE* curve upward and increase equilibrium expenditure.
   b shift the *AE* curve upward and decrease equilibrium expenditure.
   c shift the *AE* curve downward and increase equilibrium expenditure.
   d shift the *AE* curve downward and decrease equilibrium expenditure.
   e have no impact on the *AE* curve.

20 A decrease in the price level will
   a increase aggregate expenditure and thus produce a movement along the aggregate demand curve.
   b increase aggregate expenditure and thus produce a rightward shift in the aggregate demand curve.
   c increase aggregate expenditure and thus produce a leftward shift in the aggregate demand curve.
   d have no effect on aggregate expenditure.
   e increase aggregate expenditure, but produce no effect on the aggregate demand curve.

21 Suppose that investment increases by $10 billion. If the multiplier is 2, the *AD* curve will
a shift rightward by the horizontal distance of $20 billion.
b shift rightward by a horizontal distance greater than $20 billion.
c shift rightward by a horizontal distance less than $20 billion.
d not be affected.
e shift upward by a vertical distance equal to $20 billion.

22 Suppose the multiplier is 2 and the short-run aggregate supply curve is positively sloped. If investment increases by $10 billion, equilibrium real GDP will
a increase by $20 billion.
b increase by more than $20 billion.
c decrease by less than $20 billion.
d be unaffected.
e increase by less than $20 billion.

23 Suppose the multiplier is 2 and investment increases by $10 billion. Starting at potential GDP, in the long run equilibrium real GDP will
a increase by $20 billion.
b increase by more than $20 billion.
c decrease by less than $20 billion.
d be unaffected.
e increase by less than $20 billion.

Mathematical Note to Chapter 27: The Algebra of the Multiplier

24 Consider Fact 27.1. What is the equation for the aggregate expenditure function of this economy?
a $AE = 16 + 0.7Y$
b $AE = 36 - 0.7Y$
c $AE = 26 + 0.8Y$
d $AE = 36 + 0.9Y$
e $AE = 36 + 0.7Y$

FACT 27.1

The economy of Beverly Hills has a consumption function of $C = 10 + 0.8Y$, investment equal to 6, government expenditures on goods and services equal to 10, exports equal to 10, and an import function of $M = 0.1Y$.

---

25 Consider Fact 27.1. What is equilibrium real GDP in this economy?
a 36
b 120
c 130
d 360
e None of the above

Short Answer Problems

1 Explain how studying the circular flow in Chapters 20 and 23 helps us to understand the multiplier process of Chapter 27.

2 Suppose aggregate planned expenditure is greater than real GDP. Explain how equilibrium expenditure is achieved.

3 Define and explain autonomous expenditure, induced expenditure, and what role each plays in the multiplier process.

4 Explain (without algebraic expressions) why the multiplier is larger if the marginal propensity to consume is higher.

5 Explain how the effects of price level changes on the *AE* curve will generate an *AD* curve.

6 Table 27.2 illustrates the consumption function for a very small economy.

TABLE 27.2

Disposable Income (2002 $)	Consumption Expenditure (2002 $)	Saving (2002 $)
0	3,000	
3,000	5,250	
6,000	7,500	
9,000	9,750	
12,000	12,000	
15,000	14,250	

a Compute the economy's saving at each level of disposable income by completing Table 27.2.

b Compute the economy's *MPC* and *MPS*.

c From the information given and computed, draw the economy's consumption and saving functions.

d Write out the equations of the consumption and saving functions.

7 Consider an economy with the following components of aggregate expenditure:
- Consumption function: $C = 20 + 0.8Y$
- Investment function: $I = 30$
- Government expenditures: $G = 8$
- Export function: $X = 4$
- Import function: $M = 2 + 0.2Y$

(There are no taxes, so $YD = Y$.)

a What is the marginal propensity to consume in this economy?

b What is the equation of the aggregate expenditure function in this economy?

c What is the slope of the AE function?

d Find this economy's equilibrium aggregate expenditure and real GDP by completing the columns of Table 27.3.

TABLE **27.3**

Y	C	I	G	X	M	AE
0						
30						
60						
90						
120						
150						
180						

e Using the equation of the aggregate function you derived in **b**, solve mathematically for the equilibrium aggregate expenditure and real GDP.

f What is the multiplier for this economy?

8 Consider an economy with the following characteristics:
- Autonomous consumption expenditure = $10 billion
- Investment = $5 billion
- Government expenditures of goods and services = $40 billion
- Exports = $5 billion
- Slope of the AE function = 0.5
- There are no autonomous imports.

(Assume that the price level is constant.)

a What is autonomous expenditure in this economy?

b What is the equation of the AE function?

c Draw a graph of the AE curve for this economy (label it AE_0) as well as a 45° line.

d What is equilibrium expenditure?

ⓒⓣ **e** What is induced expenditure in equilibrium?

9 Return to the economy of Short Answer Problem **8**. Now suppose the government increases its expenditures on goods and services to $60 billion.

a Using the graph from Short Answer Problem **8c**, draw the new AE curve and label it AE_1.

ⓒⓣ **b** What is the new equilibrium expenditure? Solve for this value using both the graphical approach and the mathematical approach.

c What is the multiplier?

ⓒⓣ **d** After the increase in government expenditures, were there increases or decreases in autonomous expenditure, induced expenditure, consumption, imports, and investment?

10 Explain carefully what an increase in expected future disposable income will do to the consumption function, the saving function, the aggregate expenditure curve, and the aggregate demand curve.

ANSWERS

True/False and Explain

1 T Last dollar of YD is either spent or saved. (652)

2 F Change in YD leads to movement along consumption function. (650–653)

3 F Shifts upward consumption function—more consumption expenditure at each level of *current YD*, but given constant current YD, this increase in consumption means less saving. (652–653)

4 T Due to induced income taxes. (653)

5 F AE > real GDP creates excess sales, leading to falling inventories. (656–657)

6 T Definition. (656–657)

7 T Definition. (655)

8 T Definition. (655)

9 F Multiplier = $1/(1 - \text{slope of } AE \text{ function}) = 1/(1 - 0.75) = 1/0.25 = 4$. (658–660)

ⓒⓣ **10 F** Higher marginal tax rate lowers slope of *AE* curve and size of multiplier. (660–661)

11 T Lower marginal propensity to import increases slope of *AE* curve and size of multiplier. (660–661)

12 F Increase in price level lowers *AE* through wealth and substitution effects. (663–665)

13 T Increase in *AE* shifts *AD* curve rightward, movement along *SAS* in short run with an increase in real GDP. (665–555)

14 F Same initial effect as for **13**, but if start at potential GDP, given vertical *LAS* curve, there is no increase in real GDP. (665–555)

15 F In long run, multiplier is zero due to vertical *LAS* curve. (665–555)

Multiple-Choice

1 b Definition. (652–652)

2 c Level of consumption when disposable income is zero. (650)

3 b $MPC = \Delta C/\Delta YD = (165 - 100)/(100 - 0) = 0.65$. (652)

4 d $YD > C$. Also true at $YD=400$. (650–537)

5 e **a** and **b** are movements along curve, **c** and **d** shift it downward. (652–653)

6 b Definition. (655)

ⓒⓣ **7 d** Increase in inventories means $AE <$ real GDP. Firms' sales decrease, so they decrease production in response. (656–657)

ⓒⓣ **8 b** $Y = 200$ implies $AE = 50 + 0.6(200) = 170$. Unplanned inventories $= Y - AE = +30$. (656–657)

9 c Definition. (655)

10 c $MPC =$ slope of consumption function $= \Delta C/\Delta Y = 90/100 = 0.9$. (652)

11 c Intercept of *AE* function. (655)

12 e Where *AE* curve crosses 45° line. (655–657)

13 c Induced $=$ aggregate $-$ autonomous $= 375 - 150 = 225$. (655–657)

ⓒⓣ **14 d** Marginal propensity to import $= MPC -$ slope of *AE* curve $= 0.9 - 0.6 = 0.3$, where slope of *AE* curve $= \Delta AE/\Delta Y = 225/375 = 0.6$. (655–657)

15 d Multiplier $= 1/(1 -$ slope of *AE* function) $= 1/(1 - 0.6) = 1/0.4 = 2.5$. (660)

16 b Increase in expected future disposable income leads to more consumption spending, less saving, and an increase in autonomous expenditure. (652–659)

17 e All of choices discuss secondary, induced effects. (658–659)

ⓒⓣ **18 d** This change raises *MPC* and multiplier. Others lower multiplier. (659–661)

19 d Increase in price level decreases aggregate expenditure due to wealth and substitution effects. New equilibrium at lower real GDP $=$ equilibrium expenditure. (663–665)

20 a Decrease in price level increases aggregate expenditure due to three effects, leading to movement along *AD* curve. (663–665)

21 a Multiplier effect raises *AE* and *Y* by 2 times original Δ autonomous expenditure, which leads to shift rightward by same amount in *AD* curve. (663–665)

22 e Multiplier effect of Question **21** is reduced by increase in price level due to positively sloped *SAS* curve. (663–555)

23 d Vertical *LAS* curve means that there is no increase in real GDP after shift rightward in *AD*. (663–555)

24 e $AE = 10 + 0.8Y + 6 + 10 + 10 - 0.1Y = 36 + 0.7Y$. (558–559)

25 b Solve $Y^* = 36 + 0.7Y^*$, which leads to $Y^*(1 - 0.7) = 36$, and therefore $Y^* = 36/0.3 = 120$. (558–559)

Short Answer Problems

1 The circular flow shows us that firms produce goods and services, sell them to consumers, investors, governments, and the rest of the world, and use the money earned to pay factors of production, who in turn buy goods and services. The circular flow thus shows us the secondary, induced effects of the multiplier process in action. An initial increase in autonomous expenditure increases sales for firms, increasing household income, increasing consumption expenditure, etc.

2 If aggregate planned expenditure is greater than real GDP, inventories decrease more than planned, and firms increase output to replenish those depleted inventories. As a result, real GDP increases. This continues as long as real GDP is less than aggregate planned expenditure. It will stop only when equilibrium is attained—when real GDP equals aggregate planned expenditure.

3   Autonomous expenditure is the part of aggregate expenditure that does not vary with real GDP, but varies as a result of changes in other variables such as the real interest rate. Induced expenditure is the part of aggregate expenditure that varies with real GDP. The multiplier process starts out with a change in autonomous expenditure that changes aggregate expenditure, which in turn changes real GDP. This change in real GDP creates secondary effects by changing induced expenditure in the same direction, which in turn changes aggregate expenditure and real GDP, leading to a total effect that is a multiple of the initial change in autonomous expenditure.

4   Any initial stimulus to autonomous expenditure generates a direct increase in real GDP. The basic idea of the multiplier is that this initial increase in real GDP generates further increases in real GDP as increases in consumption expenditure are induced. At each round of the multiplier process, the increase in spending, and thus the further increase in real GDP, are partially determined by the marginal propensity to consume. A larger marginal propensity to consume means a larger increase in real GDP at each round, so the total increase in real GDP will be greater. Thus the multiplier will be larger if the marginal propensity to consume is larger.

5   The aggregate demand curve illustrates the relationship between the price level and aggregate expenditures. The aggregate expenditure diagram shows the level of equilibrium expenditure holding the price level constant. If the price level changes, the AE curve shifts resulting in a new level of equilibrium expenditure. Thus, for each price level, there is a different level of equilibrium expenditure. These combinations of price level and corresponding aggregate expenditure are points on the aggregate demand curve. For example, if the price level increases, autonomous expenditure will decline, and the AE curve shifts downward. This shift decreases equilibrium expenditure. Since an increase in the price level is associated with a reduction in equilibrium expenditure, the AD curve is negatively sloped.

6 a   The answers to **a** are shown in Table 27.2 Solution, where saving = $YD - C$.

TABLE 27.2 SOLUTION

Disposable Income (2002 \$)	Consumption Expenditure (2002 \$)	Saving (2002 \$)
0	3,000	−3,000
3,000	5,250	−2,250
6,000	7,500	−1,500
9,000	9,750	−750
12,000	12,000	0
15,000	14,250	+750

b   The $MPC = (\Delta$ consumption)/(Δ disposable income). Using the first two entries in the table, we can see that change in consumption is 2,250, and the change in disposable income is 3,000, so that the MPC = 0.75 = 2,250/3,000.

   The $MPS = (\Delta$ saving)/(Δ disposable income). Using the first two entries in the table, we can see that Δ saving is +750, and Δ disposable income is 3,000, so that the MPS = 0.25 = 750/3,000. Using any other two adjacent entries in the table will yield the same result.

c   The consumption function is shown in Figure 27.5, and the saving function is illustrated in Figure 27.6.

FIGURE 27.5

FIGURE **27.6**

d The equation of the consumption function is based on an intercept of 3,000 and the slope (*MPC*) of 0.75. $C = 3,000 + 0.75YD$. Similarly, for the saving function, $S = -3,000 + 0.25YD$.

7 a From the consumption function equation we know this value is $0.8 = \Delta C/\Delta Y$.

b Substitute the various equations into:

$AE = C + I + G + X - M$,

$AE = 20 + 0.8Y + 30 + 8 + 4 - 2 - 0.2Y$,

$AE = 60 + 0.6Y$.

c The slope of the *AE* function comes from the equation and equals $\Delta AE/\Delta Y = 0.6$.

d The answer is presented in Table 27.3 Solution below. The table is constructed by substituting the various values of *Y* into the equations. Note that equilibrium occurs when $AE = Y$ at a value of 150.

TABLE **27.3** SOLUTION

Y	C	I	G	X	M	AE
0	20	30	8	4	2	60
30	44	30	8	4	8	78
60	68	30	8	4	14	96
90	92	30	8	4	20	114
120	116	30	8	4	26	132
150	140	30	8	4	32	150
180	164	30	8	4	38	168

e Equilibrium occurs when

$Y = AE$,

$Y^* = 60 + 0.6Y^*$,

$Y^*(1 - 0.6) = Y^*(0.4) = 60$,

$Y^* = 60/0.4 = 150$

f The multiplier $= 1/(1 - \text{slope of } AE \text{ function}) = 1/(1 - 0.6) = 1/0.4 = 2.5$.

8 a Autonomous expenditure is the sum of autonomous consumption expenditure, investment, government expenditure on goods and services, and exports. This sum is $60 billion.

b The equation is of the form $AE = A + eY$, where *A* is autonomous expenditure and *e* is the slope of the *AE* function. In this case, the equation is $AE = 60 + 0.5Y$, where units are billions of dollars.

c See the curve labelled AE_0 in Figure 27.7. The curve was drawn by noting that autonomous expenditure ($60 billion) gives the vertical intercept and the slope of the *AE* function is 0.5.

FIGURE **27.7**

d Equilibrium expenditure can be solved two ways. First, equilibrium expenditure occurs at the intersection of the AE_0 curve and the 45° line. Equilibrium expenditure is $120 billion. Second, it can be calculated by solving the $AE = Y$ equation:

$Y^* = 60 + 0.5Y^*$,
$Y^*(1 - 0.5) = 60$,
$Y^* = 60/0.5 = 120$.

e Induced expenditure = total expenditure − autonomous expenditure = 120 − 60 = 60 in this case.

9 a See the curve labelled AE_1 in Figure 27.7. The new curve reflects the fact that autonomous expenditure increases by $20 billion but the slope of the AE function remains unchanged.

b The new equilibrium expenditure is $160 billion. This answer is given by the intersection of the AE_1 curve with the 45° line, or by solving the new equilibrium condition:

$Y^* = 80 + 0.5Y^*$,
$Y^*(1 − 0.5) = 80$,
$Y^* = 80/0.5 = 160$.

c Since a $20 billion increase in autonomous expenditure generates a $40 billion increase in equilibrium expenditure, the multiplier is 2. This value can be obtained by using the formula that the multiplier = 1/(1 − slope of AE function).

d The total change in real GDP is $40 billion. First, note that the change in autonomous expenditure is just the increase in government expenditures of $20 billion, and further note:

Δ total expenditure = Δ autonomous expenditure + Δ induced expenditure

or

+$40 billion = +$20 billion + $20 billion,

so that the change in induced expenditure is also $20 billion.

Second, since real GDP has increased, this increases both consumption and imports, because they are part of induced expenditure. However, investment is autonomous, so it is not affected by the change in real GDP.

10 An increase in expected future disposable income leads to less saving (so that the saving function shifts downward at each level of disposable income) and more consumption out of current disposable income (so that the consumption function shifts upward). This is an increase in autonomous consumption, and also an increase in aggregate expenditure, leading to a shift upward in the aggregate expenditure function. This shift creates multiplier effects and a shift rightward in the aggregate demand curve at the current price level.

Chapter 28

Canadian Inflation, Unemployment, and Business Cycles

KEY CONCEPTS

Inflation Cycles

Inflation is caused by two sources in the short run.

Demand-pull inflation arises from increasing aggregate demand due to tax cuts or increases in quantity of money, government expenditures, exports, or investment.

- Short run result is increased P (inflation), increased Y, decreased unemployment to below natural rate.

- Unemployment less than natural rate creates labour shortage, increasing wages and costs. *SAS* shifts leftward, price level increases even more, but real GDP falls back to original level.

- If *AD* shifts rightward again, and wages increase again, a *demand-pull inflation spiral* may result.

- Persistent inflation requires persistent increases in quantity of money.

Cost-push inflation arises from decreasing aggregate supply, due to increases in costs (increases in money wage rates and money prices of raw materials).

- *SAS* shifts leftward, firms decrease production, creating **stagflation** (increased price level, decreased real GDP).

- If government or Bank of Canada shifts *AD* rightward in response, price level increases again, so that input owners raise input prices again, and a *cost-push inflation spiral* may result.

- If no government or Bank response—economy remains with high unemployment in the short run.

If inflation is expected, then money wages adjust to keep up with anticipated inflation, Δ price level only, no Δ real GDP or employment.

- Expected inflation creates actual inflation.

- To anticipate inflation, people must forecast it.

- People forecast inflation in different ways, including hiring specialists, who make best possible forecast on basis of all available relevant information (a **rational expectation**).

Inflation and Unemployment: The Phillips Curve

Phillips curve shows relationship between inflation and unemployment.

- **Short-run Phillips curve** (*SRPC*) shows relationship between inflation and unemployment for a given expected inflation rate and natural rate of unemployment. It is negatively sloped.

- In short run, if actual inflation > expected, then movement up and leftward along *SRPC*.

- **Long-run Phillips curve** (*LRPC*) shows relationship between inflation and unemployment when actual inflation = expected. It is vertical at the natural rate of unemployment.

- Decrease in expected inflation rate shifts *SRPC* downward.

- Increase in natural rate of unemployment shifts both *LRPC* and *SRPC* rightward.

The Business Cycle

Two approaches to understanding business cycle.

Mainstream theory states potential GDP grows steadily, but aggregate demand grows at fluctuating rate and causes cycles.

- If money wage rate sticky and if aggregate demand grows faster than potential GDP, inflationary gap results.

- If aggregate demand grows slower than potential GDP, recessionary gap results.

Four mainstream theories with different sources of aggregate demand shocks and money wage stickiness:

- **Keynesian cycle theory**—fluctuations in business confidence create fluctuations in investment and aggregate demand; money wage assumed sticky.

- **Monetarist cycle theory**—fluctuations in investment, consumption and money growth create fluctuations in aggregate demand; money wage assumed sticky.

- **New classical cycle theory**—unexpected fluctuations in aggregate demand come from incorrect expectations; money wages sticky due to incorrect expectations.

- **New Keynesian cycle theory**—unexpected fluctuations in aggregate demand come from incorrect expectations due to fact money wages were negotiated over several past dates.

Real business cycle (RBC) theory regards random fluctuations in productivity (due to Δ pace of technological change) as main source of the cycle.

- RBC recession starts with technological change that makes existing capital obsolete—temporary decrease in productivity.

- Fall in productivity decreases demand for labour and capital (which decreases real rate of interest).

- Decreasing real rate of interest decreases labour supply (intertemporal substitution effect), leading to small decrease in real wage rate, large decrease in employment—recession begins.

Critics of RBC theory argue that money wages are sticky, intertemporal substitution is weak and technological shocks are *caused by AD* fluctuations.

- Defenders of RBC theory reply that it is consistent with facts (explains both growth *and* cycles) and microeconomic theory.

HELPFUL HINTS

1 An important concept introduced in this chapter is that of a *rational expectation*—the best possible forecast on the basis of all available relevant information. Text Figure 28.5 applies this concept to forecasting the price level. The *actual* price level occurs in the short run at the intersection of the *AD* curve and the *SAS* curve, and in the long run at the intersection of the *AD* curve and the *LAS* curve. In Figure 28.5, when *AD* is expected to increase to AD_1, the best (most likely to be correct) *forecast* of the new price level is at the intersection of AD_1 and *LAS*, yielding a wage demand leading to SAS_1.

Note that the rational expectation of the price level will be at the intersection of the *expected* aggregate demand curve and the *expected short-run* aggregate supply curve in the short run, and the *expected long-run* aggregate supply curve in the long run. The *actual* equilibrium, which determines the *actual* price level, is at the intersection of the *actual* aggregate demand curve and the *actual short-run* aggregate supply curve.

2 This chapter contains competing theories for explaining real-world events. There is no dispute over the facts such as the level of prices or real GDP. The dispute centres around what changes in the economy created the facts, and what government policies might affect the economy.

To help you remember and understand these theories, use Table 28.1 on the next page. It highlights the similarities and differences between the theories, and highlight how radically different real business cycle theory is.

Theories differ based on two primary factors: the source of the cycle (*AD* versus *AS*), and the responsiveness of the labour market (sticky versus flexible wages). Be sure you can catalogue and understand these theories.

Remember, these are theories, *not* statements of facts, and their explanations could be incorrect. Only proper empirical investigation over time will cast light on their validity.

TABLE **28.1** BUSINESS CYCLE THEORIES

Labour Market Structure	Theory	Primary Source of the Cycle
Wages are sticky, U above natural rate	Keynesian	Investment (*AD* shocks)
	Monetarist	Investment, consumption, growth rate of money (*AD* shocks)
	New classical	Unexpected fluctuations in *AD*
	New Keynesian	Unexpected *and* expected fluctuations in *AD*
Wages are flexible, U = natural rate always	Real business cycle	Productivity (*AS*) shocks

S E L F - T E S T

True/False and Explain

Inflation Cycles

1   If people expect aggregate demand to increase but it does not, the price level will increase and real GDP will decrease.

2   Increases in government expenditures alone can create persistent inflation.

3   An increase in exports cannot create demand-pull inflation.

4   Inflation resulting from expansionary monetary policy is an example of cost-push inflation.

5   Stagflation occurs when real GDP decreases and the price level increases.

6   If an increase in aggregate demand is correctly anticipated, inflation will not occur.

7   A rational expectation is a forecast that is always correct.

Inflation and Unemployment: The Phillips Curve

8   The short-run Phillips curve shows that if there is an increase in the inflation rate, unemployment will decrease.

9   The long-run Phillips curve shows a tradeoff between inflation and unemployment.

10   If there is an increase in the expected rate of inflation, the long-run Phillips curve shifts rightward.

11   If there is a decrease in the natural rate of unemployment, only the long-run Phillips curve shifts.

The Business Cycle

12   Unanticipated decreases in aggregate demand cause recessions only in new Keynesian theory, not in new classical theory.

13 A decrease in aggregate demand will cause a recession in Keynesian theory.

14 Real business cycle theorists believe that wages are flexible and adjust quickly.

15 In real business cycle theory, most fluctuations in real GDP are the best possible responses of the economy to the uneven pace of technological change.

Multiple-Choice

Inflation Cycles

I Which one of the following is a cause of demand-pull inflation?
a   A sharp increase in the price of oil
b   Higher wages negotiated by unions
c   An increase in exports
d   A decrease in the money supply
e   A decrease in exports

2 Demand-pull inflation occurs when
a   aggregate demand increases.
b   aggregate supply decreases.
c   input costs increase.
d   people incorrectly forecast inflation.
e   unemployment is above the natural rate.

3 Which of the following would cause the aggregate demand curve to keep shifting rightward year after year?
a   a one-time tax cut
b   a one-time increase in government expenditures on goods and services
c   inflation
d   continuous excess wage demands
e   a positive rate of money growth

4 An increase in the price level due to an increase in the price of oil
a   will create stagflation in the short run and *will* trigger a cost-push inflation spiral.
b   will create stagflation in the short run and *may* trigger a cost-push inflation spiral.
c   will raise output above potential GDP.

d   must lead to an increase in the wage rate.
e   must lead to a decrease in the wage rate.

5 Figure 28.1 illustrates an economy initially in equilibrium at point *a*. What would cause the short-run aggregate supply curve to shift from SAS_0 to SAS_1?
a   increase in the price of oil
b   increase in the price level
c   increase in the marginal product of labour
d   increase in the demand for money
e   decrease in wages

FIGURE 28.1

6 If the *AD* curve in Figure 28.1 is correctly expected to shift from AD_0 to AD_1, what will be the new equilibrium real GDP (*Y*) and price level (*P*)?
a   *Y* = $380 billion, *P* = 125
b   *Y* = $500 billion, *P* = 150
c   *Y* = $500 billion, *P* = 100
d   *Y* = $620 billion, *P* = 125
e   *Y* = $500 billion, *P* = 125

7 If the *AD* curve in Figure 28.1 is expected to shift from AD_0 to AD_1 but, in fact, remains at AD_0, what will be the new equilibrium real GDP (*Y*) and price level (*P*)?
a   *Y* = $380 billion, *P* = 100
b   *Y* = $500 billion, *P* = 150
c   *Y* = $500 billion, *P* = 100
d   *Y* = $620 billion, *P* = 125
e   *Y* = $380 billion, *P* = 125

8 If the *AD* curve in Figure 28.1 is expected to remain at AD_0 but, in fact, shifts to AD_1, what will be the new equilibrium real GDP (*Y*) and price level (*P*)?
- **a** $Y = \$380$ billion, $P = 125$
- **b** $Y = \$500$ billion, $P = 150$
- **c** $Y = \$500$ billion, $P = 100$
- **d** $Y = \$620$ billion, $P = 125$
- **e** $Y = \$500$ billion, $P = 125$

9 Which of the following is *not* true of a rational expectation forecast?
- **a** It uses all available information.
- **b** It can be wrong.
- **c** It is always correct.
- **d** It is the best possible forecast.
- **e** Sometimes economic agents purchase their forecasts from specialists.

10 Stagflation results directly from a shift of the aggregate
- **a** demand curve leftward.
- **b** demand curve rightward.
- **c** supply curve leftward.
- **d** supply curve rightward.
- **e** demand curve rightward, followed by a shift leftward in the aggregate supply curve.

Inflation and Unemployment: The Phillips Curve

11 The short-run Phillips curve shows the relationship between
- **a** the price level and real GDP in the short run.
- **b** the price level and unemployment in the short run.
- **c** unemployment and real GDP in the short run.
- **d** inflation and unemployment, when inflation expectations can change.
- **e** inflation and unemployment, when inflation expectations do not change.

12 Figure 28.2 illustrates an economy's Phillips curves. What is the natural rate of unemployment?
- **a** 9%
- **b** 6%
- **c** 4%
- **d** depends on the actual inflation rate
- **e** cannot be determined without more information

FIGURE **28.2**

13 Figure 28.2 illustrates an economy's Phillips curves. What is the expected inflation rate?
- **a** 9%
- **b** 4%
- **c** 2%
- **d** depends on the actual inflation rate
- **e** cannot be determined without more information

14 Figure 28.2 illustrates an economy's Phillips curves. If the current inflation rate is 4 percent, what is the current unemployment rate?
- **a** 9%
- **b** 6%
- **c** 4%
- **d** 3%
- **e** cannot be determined without more information

15 If the inflation rate is lower than the expected inflation rate,
- **a** unemployment will be above the natural rate.
- **b** the natural rate of unemployment will increase.
- **c** the expected inflation rate will increase.
- **d** unemployment will be below the natural rate.
- **e** the economy must off the *SRPC*.

16 If there is a fully anticipated increase in the inflation rate,
   a unemployment will be below the natural rate.
   b unemployment will be above the natural rate.
   c the natural rate of unemployment will increase.
   d the economy must be off the *LRPC*.
   e the economy must be on the *LRPC*.

The Business Cycle

17 Which of the following news quotes *best* describes a *new Keynesian* view of a recession?
   a "Rapid computerization is creating obsolete workers and higher unemployment."
   b "The unexpectedly tight fiscal policy is raising spending and lowering unemployment."
   c "The promised anti-inflationary policy of the Bank of Canada is increasing spending."
   d "The promised cuts in government spending have helped lower consumer spending and created unemployment."
   e "Businesses are very worried about future sales and have lowered their purchases of capital equipment."

18 Which of the following news quotes *best* describes a *new classical* view of a recession?
   a "Rapid computerization is creating obsolete workers and higher unemployment."
   b "The unexpectedly tight fiscal policy is lowering spending and creating unemployment."
   c "The promised anti-inflationary policy of the Bank of Canada is lowering spending as promised."
   d "The promised cuts in government spending have helped lower consumer spending and created unemployment."
   e "Businesses are very worried about future sales and have lowered their purchases of capital equipment."

19 What is the key impulse in the Keynesian theory of the business cycle?
   a changes in expected future sales and profits
   b changes in the quantity of money
   c unanticipated changes in aggregate demand
   d anticipated changes in aggregate demand
   e changes in the pace of technological change

20 An increase in aggregate demand causes real GDP to increase by the least amount in the
   a Keynesian theory.
   b monetarist theory.
   c new Keynesian theory.
   d new classical theory.
   e real business cycle theory.

21 If the intertemporal substitution effect is weak, then RBC theory will have problems explaining
   a a large decrease in employment in a recession.
   b how a recession begins.
   c why aggregate demand decreases in a recession.
   d the automatic adjustment to full employment.
   e what creates technological change.

22 The intertemporal substitution effect states that
   a in a recession, investment is low and the capital stock increases slowly, leading to a rising marginal product of capital.
   b money wages are based on a rational expectation of the price level.
   c a decrease in productivity leads to a decrease in the demand for capital, and a decrease in the real interest rate.
   d when current real wages and real interest rates are high, people decrease their labour supply strongly.
   e when current real wages and real interest rates are high, people increase their labour supply strongly.

23 According to the real business cycle theorists, increased unemployment rate during a recession is due to an increase in the
   a deviation of the unemployment rate from the natural rate, resulting from a real wage rate too high to clear the labour market.
   b deviation of the unemployment rate from the natural rate, resulting from increased job market turnover.
   c natural rate of unemployment resulting from a real wage that is too high to clear the labour market.
   d natural rate of unemployment resulting from increased job market turnover.
   e rate of new entries into the labour market.

24 Which of the following news quotes *best* describes a *real business cycle* view of a recession?

   a "Rapid computerization is creating obsolete workers and higher unemployment."

   b "The unexpectedly tight fiscal policy is lowering spending and creating unemployment."

   c "The promised anti-inflationary policy of the Bank of Canada is lowering spending as promised."

   d "The promised cuts in government spending have helped lower consumer spending and created unemployment."

   e "Businesses are very worried about future sales and have lowered their purchases of capital equipment."

25 According to real business cycle theory, if the Bank of Canada increases the money supply when real GDP declines, real GDP

   a will increase, but only temporarily.

   b will increase permanently.

   c and the price level will both be unaffected.

   d will be unaffected, but the price level will increase.

   e will decrease due to the inefficiencies introduced into production as a result.

Short Answer Problems

1 What happens to the price level and real GDP if the government increases expenditures on goods and services and that increase is not anticipated (the price level is not expected to change)?

2 Explain how the events in Short Answer Problem **1** might lead to a demand-pull inflation spiral.

3 List the four important features of the Canadian economy that make severe depression less likely today.

4 Explain the differences between the short-run Phillips curve and the long-run Phillips curve.

5 Sometimes politicians or other commentators say: "Unemployment is a more serious economic and social problem than inflation. Increasing inflation by a small amount in order to lower unemployment is therefore worthwhile." Briefly evaluate this statement.

6 Why does inflation start? Why does it persist?

7 Table 28.2 gives data for a hypothetical economy in years 1 and 2.

TABLE **28.2**

	Year 1	Year 2
Real GDP (billions of dollars)	800	750
Price level (GDP deflator)	100	105

   a If the real business cycle theory is true, what happened to aggregate demand and aggregate supply in this economy?

   b If the new Keynesian theory is true, what happened to aggregate demand and aggregate supply in this economy?

8 Consider the labour market in the economy from Short Answer Problem **7**.

   a If the real business cycle theory is true, what happened in the labour market? Is the unemployment natural or not?

   b If the new Keynesian theory is true, what happened in the labour market? Is the unemployment natural or not?

9 Suppose that you have been selected to be the economic advisor to the prime minister, on the basis of your sterling performance in macroeconomics. You have been asked to evaluate the new Keynesian theory of the business cycle, and the real business cycle theory of the business cycle, and to explain what each theory argues should be the optimal government policy for a recession.

   a What does each theory argue is the likely cause of a recession, and why?

   b What does each theory argue is the best response to a recession? Why do the two theories differ? That is, what crucial differences in their approach to the economy leads to the different policy conclusions?

10 The country of Colditz has an expected inflation rate of 8 percent, and its recent inflation and unemployment history is summarized in Table 28.3. Originally both unemployment and inflation are each 8 percent.

   a What is Colditz's natural rate of unemployment?

   b Draw a graph of Colditz's short-run and long-run Phillips curves.

TABLE 28.3

Inflation (% per year)	Unemployment (%)
12	4
10	6
8	8
6	10
4	12

c If inflation unexpectedly increases to 12 percent per year, explain what happens to unemployment, and show it on your graph.

d Return to the original situation. If the expected inflation rate increases to 10 percent, and the actual inflation rate increases to 10 percent, explain and show on your graph what happens, *ceteris paribus*, to inflation and unemployment.

ANSWERS

True/False and Explain

1 **T** If expected increase in aggregate demand, increasing wage demands, leading to leftward shift *SAS* curve, but no Δ *AD* curve, resulting in stagflation. (684)

2 **F** Persistent inflation requires persistent increases in quantity of money. (680–681)

3 **F** Increase in exports shift *AD* rightward, which can create demand-pull inflation. (680–681)

4 **F** Cost-push inflation is due to increase in input costs. (682–683)

5 **T** Definition. (682–683)

6 **F** *AD* shifts rightward, *SAS* shifts leftward due to higher wage demands, so price level increases. (684)

7 **F** Correct on *average*. (685)

8 **T** Movement up and leftward along the *SRPC*. (686–688)

9 **F** Vertical at the natural rate of unemployment. (686–688)

10 **F** Movement upward along the *LRPC*. (686–688)

11 **F** Both SRPC and LRPC shift when natural rate shifts. (686–688)

12 **F** In both theories, unanticipated decrease means wages set too high, creating unemployment and recession. (689)

13 **T** Due to sticky money wages, SAS curve does not adjust quickly. (689)

14 **T** See text discussion. (690–693)

15 **T** See text discussion. (690–693)

Multiple-Choice

1 **c** Increase in demand. (680–681)

2 **a** Definition. (680–681)

3 **e** **a** and **b** have one-time effects, **c** caused by Δ*AD*, and **d** is supply-side effect. (680–681)

4 **b** Increase in price of oil leads to leftward shift *SAS* curve, creating cost-push inflation (stagflation), which *may* trigger cost-push inflation spiral if government raises aggregate demand. (682–683)

5 **a** Increase in price of crucial input leads to increase in costs of production, and leftward shift *SAS*. (682–683)

6 **b** Expected *P* at intersection of *LAS* and expected *AD* = *AD*$_1$, and actual new *SAS* is set here, and new equilibrium is where actual *AD* and new *SAS* cross. (684–685)

7 **e** Expected *P* at intersection of expected *AD* = *AD*$_1$, and actual new *SAS* is set here, and new equilibrium is where actual *AD* and new *SAS* cross. (684–685)

8 **d** Expected *P* at intersection of *LAS* and expected *AD* = *AD*$_1$, and actual new *SAS* is set here, and new equilibrium is where actual *AD* and new *SAS* cross. (684–685)

9 **c** Correct on *average*. (684–685)

10 **c** Definition. (682–683)

11 **e** Definition. (686)

12 **a** *LRPC* is at natural rate. (687)

13 **c** Expected inflation rate is where *SRPC* crosses *LRPC*. (687)

14 **c** Found by reading off the *SRPC*. (686–687)

15 **a** Draw a Phillips curve. (686–687)

16 e Economy just moves up *LRPC*. (686–687)

17 b One of the key impulses in new Keynesian theory is unexpected change in *AD*. (689)

18 b Key impulse in new classical theory is unexpected change in *AD*. (689)

19 a See text discussion. (689)

20 e Vertical *AS* curve. (689–693)

21 a Intertemporal substitution means Δ current real wage or real interest rate leads to big Δ labour supply. (690–693)

22 e Definition. (690–693)

23 d All unemployment is natural, and real wage rate is always correct. (690–693)

24 a Key impulse is Δ pace of technological change. (690–693)

25 d Because *LAS* is vertical. (690–693)

Short Answer Problems

1 An increase in government expenditures on goods and services shifts the aggregate demand curve rightward. If the price level is not expected to change, the short-run aggregate supply curve remains unchanged, and the increase in aggregate demand causes the price level to increase and real GDP to increase.

2 The higher price level leads to demands for higher wages, which push up the costs of production and shift the *SAS* curve leftward, leading to a further increase in the price level and a decrease in real GDP. A demand-pull inflation spiral could result *if* the government once again raises the level of their purchases or if the government continues to run a deficit (financed by printing money). *AD* will then continue to shift rightward, triggering leftward shifts in *SAS*, leading to the demand-pull inflation spiral.

3 The four important features of the Canadian economy that make severe depression less likely today are: (1) bank deposits are insured; (2) the Bank of Canada is prepared to be the "lender of last resort"; (3) taxes and government spending play a stabilizing role; and (4) multi-income families are more economically secure.

4 The short-run Phillips curve assumes that the expected inflation rate is constant, and is therefore downward-sloping. Therefore, an increase in the inflation rate (and therefore a decrease in real wages), will create a decrease in unemployment to a rate below the natural rate. The long-run Phillips curve is constructed assuming that the expected inflation rate adjusts fully to reflect changes in the actual inflation rate, and is therefore vertical at the natural rate of unemployment. If there is an increase in the actual inflation rate, there is an equivalent increase in the expected inflation rate (so that the real wage rate stays constant), and the rate of unemployment stays constant at the natural rate.

5 Partially this statement is a value judgment, based on the tradeoff of a higher cost to society from the higher inflation versus the gain to society from a lower inflation rate. In this case, we would need to evaluate the costs of inflation vis-à-vis the costs of unemployment. However, there is also an objective (positive) problem with this statement. In the short run, such a tradeoff does exist, represented by the downward-sloping short-run Phillips curve. In the long run, there is no such tradeoff. As a result, a higher inflation rate leads to a lower unemployment rate in the short run, but eventually inflation expectations will increase, shifting upward the short-run Phillips curve, and unemployment returns to the natural rate. Therefore in the long run, increasing inflation will have no impact on the unemployment rate, but will increase the costs to society that come from the higher inflation.

6 Inflation is an increase in the price level, and starts with either a shift rightward in the *AD* curve due to increases in the quantity of money, government spending, or exports (demand-pull inflation), or with a shift leftward in the *SAS* curve due to increases in wages or raw materials prices (cost-push inflation). However, the increase in the price level in either case can only persist if an inflation spiral results from the initial shock. A demand-pull or cost-push inflation spiral starts when increases in aggregate demand and shifts leftward in *SAS* chase each other up the long-run aggregate supply curve.

7 a Since real GDP has decreased, the *LAS* curve must have shifted leftward, since the only *AS* curve is a vertical *LAS* in a RBC world. For the price level to have increased, it must be the case that either the *AD* curve increased, or decreased so little that in combination with the *LAS* curve shift, the price level has increased.

b In order to get both the price level rising, and real GDP decreasing, it must be that the *SAS* curve shifted leftward by more than the shift rightward in the *AD* curve (if there was one), indicating that people anticipated an increase in *AD* (leading to an increase in wages and a shift leftward in the *SAS*), but the actual increase was less than anticipated.

8 a A real business cycle recession starts with a temporary decrease in productivity, which leads to a decrease in the marginal product of capital, and a decrease in the demand for capital (and therefore a decrease in the real interest rate), a decrease in the demand for investment, and a shift leftward in the *AD* curve. In addition, there is a decrease in the demand for labour because of the decrease in productivity, and a shift leftward in the supply of labour because of the lower real interest rate. These two shifts lead to a decrease in employment and a shift leftward in the *LAS* curve. All unemployment is natural.

b In the new Keynesian labour market, money wages are based on wrong expectations, so that real wages are too high since the increase in money wages is more than the increase in the price level. Labour supply is greater than labour demand, creating the unemployment. All the extra unemployment is cyclical, not natural.

9 a The new Keynesian theory argues the likely source of a recession is a negative shock to aggregate demand, most likely due to unanticipated, and possibly anticipated, changes in one or more of the underlying variables. The RBC theory argues that the key impulse is a change in the pace of technological change, leading to a negative shock to the *LAS*.

b The new Keynesian theory also argues that money wages are sticky, so that the labour market and the *SAS* adjust slowly—the economy is in the recession for some time unless the government increases *AD*. The RBC theory argues that the labour market has already adjusted instantly, and output is at potential GDP. Any government policy will affect *AD*, but have no impact on real variables, so no policy should be carried out.

The crucial difference is due to the impulse variable that starts the recession—in

one case it is an *AD* variable and can be counteracted by increasing *AD*, and in the other case it is a *LAS* variable, and increasing *AD* has no beneficial effect.

10 a The natural rate of unemployment is the rate of unemployment when the actual rate of inflation equals the expected rate of inflation—in this case, the natural rate of unemployment is 8 percent.

b See Figure 28.3. The long-run Phillips curve is vertical at the natural rate of unemployment. The current short-run curve is $SRPC_0$ (ignore the other short-run curve for the moment).

FIGURE 28.3

c The relevant short-run Phillips curve is $SRPC_0$, the curve for an expected inflation rate of 8 percent. From the curve (or Table 28.3), with inflation equal to 12 percent, unemployment is 4 percent at the point *a*.

d An increase in the expected inflation rate shifts the short-run Phillips curve to a new curve ($SRPC_1$), with the new curve crossing the long-run Phillips curve at the new expected inflation rate of 10 percent. (The actual shape of the curve is not clear without further information, so we are assuming the new curve is parallel to the old curve.) If the actual inflation rate is 10 percent, the unemployment rate will be 8 percent, at the natural rate, at the point *b*.

Part 9 Wrap Up
Understanding Macroeconomic Fluctuations

PROBLEM

You have been hired as an economic consultant for the premier of the country of Nova Calenia. The economy of Nova Calenia is in recession, reflected in Table P9.1.

TABLE **P9.1**

	Year 1	Year 2
Price level (GDP deflator)	125	130
Inflation Rate	7%	4%
Real GDP (billions of constant dollars)	200	190
Real wages (billions of constant dollars)	15.00	15.45
Employment (billions of hours)	100	90
Unemployment (%)	8	11

One set of advisors (who are mainstream business cycle theorists) have told the premier that the recession has been caused by an unexpected decrease in aggregate demand (due to an unexpected decrease in exports), combined with sticky wages (inflation was expected to remain constant at 7 percent).

a Explain briefly to the premier what these advisors think is happening to the market for goods and services. Explain what happens to aggregate expenditure as part of your answer. In addition, draw an *AD-AS* graph illustrating what happens in this market. Explain what happens in the labour market (just describe what is going on in the labour market, but do draw a graph of what has happened to the Phillips Curve).

Another set of advisors (real business cycle theorists) have argued that these events are due solely to an aggregate supply shock, driven by technological change.

b Explain briefly to the premier what these advisors think is happening to the market for goods and services (draw an *AD–AS* graph as part of your answer), and in the labour market (just describe what is going on, do not draw a graph of the labour market).

MIDTERM EXAMINATION

You should allocate 24 minutes for this examination (12 questions, 2 minutes per question). For each question, choose the best answer.

I The consumption function shows the relationship between consumption expenditure and
  a the interest rate.
  b the price level.
  c disposable income.
  d saving.
  e nominal income.

2 If the money wage rate decreases,
  a *AD* shifts rightward.
  b firms hire less labour.
  c only *LAS* shifts rightward.
  d only *SAS* shifts rightward.
  e both *SAS* and *LAS* shift rightward.

3 The changes represented in Figure P9.1 *must*
  a not occur in the real world, because *AD* and *SAS* cannot change at the same time.
  b create an inflationary gap.
  c create a recessionary gap.
  d create inflation.
  e do none of the above.

FIGURE **P9.1**

4 If real GDP is less than aggregate planned expenditure,
  a aggregate planned expenditure will increase.
  b real GDP will decrease.
  c the price level must decrease to restore equilibrium.
  d imports must be too large.
  e aggregate planned expenditure will decrease.

5 We observe an increase in the price level and an increase in real GDP. A possible explanation is that the
  a quantity of money has fallen.
  b expectation of future disposable income has decreased.
  c price of raw materials has increased.
  d stock of capital has increased.
  e expectation of future profits has increased.

6 What is the key impulse in the new Keynesian theory of the business cycle?
  a changes in animal spirits
  b changes in the money supply
  c unanticipated changes in aggregate demand
  d anticipated changes in aggregate demand
  e changes in the pace of technological change

7 Suppose that investment increases by $10 billion. Which of the following *reduces* the effect of this increase in autonomous expenditure on equilibrium real GDP?
  a increase in the marginal propensity to consume
  b decrease in the marginal propensity to import
  c decrease in the marginal tax rate
  d steeper *SAS* curve
  e flatter *SAS* curve

8 In a recent study, the University of Underfunded argued that it created four times as many jobs as people it hired directly. This argument illustrates the idea of
  a the marginal propensity to consume.
  b the multiplier.
  c government spending.
  d the tax multiplier.
  e universities wasting taxpayers' dollars.

9 What is the key impulse in the real business cycle theory of the business cycle?
  a changes in expected future sales and profits
  b changes in the money supply
  c unanticipated changes in aggregate demand
  d anticipated changes in aggregate demand
  e changes in the pace of technological change

10 The aggregate demand curve illustrates that, as the price level decreases, the
  a quantity of real GDP demanded increases.
  b quantity of real GDP demanded decreases.
  c quantity of nominal GDP demanded increases.
  d quantity of nominal GDP demanded decreases.
  e value of assets decrease.

11 A rise in the natural rate of unemployment is shown as a
  a rightward shift in only the long-run Phillips curve only.
  b leftward shift in only the long-run Phillips curve only.
  c rightward shift in only the short-run Phillips curve only.
  d leftward shift in both the short-run and long-run Phillips curves.
  e rightward shift in both the short-run and long-run Phillips curves.

12 Suppose OPEC unexpectedly collapses, decreasing the price of oil. This is a positive aggregate supply shock. As a result, in the short run the price level will
  a   increase and real GDP will increase.
  b   increase and real GDP will decrease.
  c   decrease and real GDP will increase.
  d   decrease and real GDP will decrease.
  e   increase and real GDP will stay the same.

ANSWERS

Problem

  a   Figure P9.2 shows the Year 1 equilibrium at a price level of 125 and real GDP of 200. The fall in exports is a fall in planned aggregate expenditure. There will be unplanned increases in inventories, and firms will reduce production in response, leading to a fall in real GDP, price level held constant. This is shown as a shift leftward in the *AD* curve to AD_1 in Figure P9.2 below. Under mainstream theory, with sticky wages and expected inflation of 7%, firms and workers had expected a price level of 134 (= 125 × 1.07), which determines the shift in the *SAS* curve to SAS_1. The resulting below-full employment equilibrium is shown in Figure P9.2.

Figure **P9.2**

The labour market has rising real wages, and rising unemployment, implying that the real wage is too high (nominal wages were based on the expected inflation of 7 percent, but since *AD* was unexpectedly low, the actual inflation is only 4 percent, creating high real wages), creating (cyclical) unemployment above the natural rate. Figure P9.3 shows the short-run and long-run Phillips Curves for this economy, assuming that the natural rate of unemployment is 8% and expected inflation was 7%.

Figure **P9.3**

  b   The real business cycle graph of the market for goods and services is shown in Figure P9.4. Note that aggregate demand is assumed constant, and that a shift leftward in long-run aggregate supply causes all the changes. This shift is due to a decrease in productivity, due to the technological change, which lowers the demand for labour and capital (lowering the real interest rate). There is also a decrease in the supply of labour, due to the lower real interest rate, creating a big decrease in labour hired, and therefore a shift leftward in the *LAS* curve. The extra unemployment is due to a rise in natural unemployment—the turnover rate has risen in the labour market.

Figure **P9.4**

Midterm Examination

1 c   Definition. (650–653)

2 d   If money wage rate decreases, cost of production decreases, firms hire more labour, supply more goods and services,

represented by (only) *SAS* shifting rightward. (634–639)

3 e   These changes could occur. Gaps cannot be determined without *LAS* curve. (638–639)

4 a   Firms' sales > production decreases inventories, leading to increased production. New equilibrium has higher real GDP = higher *AE*. (654–657)

5 e   e shifts *AD* rightward, increasing *P* and real GDP. **a** and **b** shift *AD* leftward, while **c** shifts *SAS* leftward, decreasing *Y*, and **d** shifts *LAS* rightward, decreasing *P* (draw a graph). (634–639)

6 c   Anticipated changes are not as important—see text discussion. (689–695)

7 d   Leads to more ΔP, less ΔY. All others make effect larger. (663–667)

8 b   University spending creates multiplier effects. (660–662)

9 e   See text discussion. (689–695)

10 a   *AD* curve is downward-sloping due to wealth and substitution effects. Real GDP by definition, not nominal, and asset values increase here. (630–633)

11 e   *LRPC* is vertical at new higher natural rate, and *SRPC* shifts with it since it crosses *LRPC* at natural rate. (686–688)

12 c   Fall in the cost of production and a rightward shift in *SAS*. (682–683)

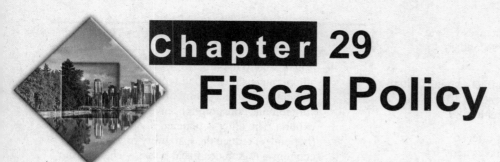

Chapter 29
Fiscal Policy

Government Budgets

Federal budget is annual statement of revenue and outlays of government of Canada (**provincial budget** is for provincial governments).

♦ Budgets finance government activities and achieve macroeconomic policy objectives (**fiscal policy**).

♦ Fiscal policy made by government and Parliament, in consultation with bureaucrats, provincial governments, and business and consumer groups.

♦ Budgetary revenues—personal income taxes, corporate income taxes, indirect taxes (GST), investment income.

♦ Budgetary outlays—transfer payments, expenditures on goods and services, debt interest payments.

♦ Budget balance = revenues – outlays

   • **Budget surplus** when revenues > outlays.

   • **Budget deficit** when revenues < outlays.

   • **Balanced budget** when revenues = outlays.

♦ **Government debt** = total borrowing by governments = sum of past deficits – sum of past surpluses.

   • Persistent deficits of the 1980s increased borrowing, which increased interest payments and increased deficit, etc.

   • Balanced budget of 1997 stopped this cycle—government debt is falling.

♦ Provincial government outlays are almost as large as federal, focused on hospitals, schools, and colleges/universities.

♦ Canada's past decade of budget surpluses unusual compared to other industrial nations.

Supply-Side Effects of Fiscal Policy

Fiscal policy may have **supply-side effects** on employment, potential GDP, and aggregate supply.

♦ Higher income taxes decrease incentives to work by creating **tax wedge** (before-tax wage rate – after-tax wage rate), decreasing labour supply and potential GDP.

♦ Taxes on consumption increase the wedge by increasing consumption taxes, lowering real wage rate and labour supply.

♦ Taxes on interest income weaken incentives to save, reduce quantity of saving (quantity supplied of loanable funds) and therefore reduce investment and growth rate of real GDP.

♦ Since nominal interest rate is taxed, extra strong impact of tax on real *after-tax* interest rate.

♦ **Laffer curve** is relationship between tax rate and tax revenue collected. Claims high tax rate may collect less taxes than a lower tax rate due to negative incentives.

♦ Most economists note incentive effects of tax cuts, but believe tax cuts will reduce tax revenues and potentially increase budget deficits.

Stabilizing the Business Cycle

Fiscal policy actions can be **discretionary** (initiated by Parliament, involves Δ government outlays, taxes), or **automatic** (triggered by state of economy).

♦ **Government expenditures multiplier** = magnified effect of Δ government expenditures on aggregate demand.

♦ Initial increase in G increases real GDP, which leads to secondary, induced effects.

♦ **Autonomous tax multiplier** = magnified effect of Δ autonomous taxes on aggregate demand.

♦ Increase in *T* decreases *YD*, decreases *C*, and decreases real GDP, leading to secondary, induced effects.

• Since some of tax change affects saving, initial $\Delta C = - MPC \times \Delta$ taxes—smaller effect than government expenditures multiplier.

♦ **Balanced budget multiplier** is effect of simultaneous, equal change in taxes and government expenditure—it is positive.

If real GDP < potential GDP, discretionary fiscal policy can be used to restore full employment.

♦ Increases in *G*, decreases in *T* increase aggregate expenditure, and shift *AD* curve rightward.

♦ Multiplier effect shifts *AD* curve even further right, movement along *SAS* curve in short run towards full employment equilibrium.

♦ Reducing government expenditures or increasing taxes reduces aggregate expenditure, shifts *AD* leftward, reducing an inflationary gap.

Discretionary fiscal policy is limited by

♦ recognition lag—recognizing fiscal policy is needed.

♦ law-making lag—slowness of the legislative process.

♦ impact lag—time it takes policy to have an impact.

Induced taxes and transfer payments are **automatic stabilizers**—mechanisms that automatically reduce fluctuations in real GDP.

♦ **Induced taxes** and induced transfer payments vary with real GDP.

♦ The larger the marginal tax rate, the smaller the multiplier effects of autonomous shocks.

Budget deficits fluctuate with business cycle due to cyclical fluctuations in net taxes.

♦ **Structural surplus or deficit** is budget balance when real GDP = potential.

♦ **Cyclical surplus or deficit** = actual balance − structural balance.

♦ Cyclical surplus or deficit is due only to fact that real GDP ≠ potential.

HELPFUL HINTS

1 It is crucial to distinguish between two types of autonomous shocks. One type adds to the instability of the economy; it includes changes in autonomous consumption, investment, and exports. The other is planned in order to (hopefully) reduce the instability of the economy; it includes fiscal policy—changes in government expenditures and taxes. Because the two shocks work through the same multiplier process, the same process that creates instability can also help to reduce instability.

2 The size of the fiscal policy multipliers depends on the sizes of the *MPC*, the marginal tax rate, and the marginal propensity to import. Figure 29.1 below shows why. A crucial part of the multiplier process is the change in induced expenditure in the second round of the multiplier. These induced expenditures are reduced as income is siphoned off for saving, to pay for taxes, or to buy imported goods!

FIGURE **29.1**

SELF-TEST

True/False and Explain

Government Budgets

1 The federal deficit is the total amount of borrowing the federal government has undertaken.

2 Only government expenditures on goods and services, not transfer payments, are crucial in analysing the federal deficit.

3 A government starts with a balanced budget. In the next year, if the percentage growth in outlays is higher than the percentage growth in revenues, the government will have a deficit.

4 Government investment income is an example of a budgetary outlay.

5 The federal government had budget deficits from 1997 to 2008.

Supply-Side Effects of Fiscal Policy
6 Cutting income taxes will shift the *AD* curve rightward, but will reduce potential GDP.

7 An increase in taxes on interest income will decrease potential GDP growth.

8 The Laffer Curve claims that a cut in the tax rate always increases tax revenue.

9 If the nominal interest rate is 10%, the tax rate is 5%, and the inflation rate is 4%, then the real after-tax interest rate is 1%.

Stabilizing the Business Cycle
10 An increase in autonomous transfer payments matched by an increase in autonomous taxes will increase real GDP by the size of the increase in transfer payments.

11 Taxes and transfer payments that vary with income act as automatic stabilizers in the economy.

12 If real GDP increases, so do autonomous taxes.

13 If an economy has a structural deficit, the budget balance at potential GDP is negative.

14 A cut in autonomous taxes will increase equilibrium real GDP in the short run.

15 An increase in government expenditures shifts the *AD* curve rightward.

Multiple-Choice

Government Budgets
1 Provincial government outlays
   a are small and irrelevant to the economy.
   b are an important source of fiscal policy.
   c are always equal to provincial government revenues.
   d are focused on transfer payments to individuals, such as employment insurance.
   e tend to fluctuate with federal outlays.

2 Which of the following would *not* increase the budget deficit?
   a an increase in interest on the government debt
   b an increase in government expenditures on goods and services
   c an increase in government transfer payments
   d an increase in indirect business taxes
   e a decrease in government investment income

3 The budget deficit grew as a percentage of GDP after 1974 because
  a government expenditures on goods and services rose, while tax revenues remained constant.
  b government expenditures on goods and services remained constant, while tax revenues fell.
  c transfer payments rose, while tax revenues remained constant.
  d debt interest payments rose, while tax revenues fell.
  e none of the above.

4 Which of the following groups does *not* influence federal fiscal policy?
  a government bureaucrats
  b provincial governments
  c Parliament
  d business and consumer groups
  e government unions

5 Which of the following is a budgetary outlay?
  a personal income taxes
  b government investment income
  c debt interest payments
  d indirect taxes
  e corporate income taxes

6 The government of Ricardia's budget lists the following projected collections and spending: $25 million in personal income taxes, $15 million in corporate income taxes, $5 million in indirect taxes, $2 million in investment income, $30 million in transfer payments, $12 million in government expenditures, and $8 million in debt interest. Ricardia has a government budget
  a surplus of $3 million.
  b surplus of $57 million.
  c surplus of $13 million.
  d deficit of $13 million.
  e deficit of $3 million.

7 The largest source of revenues for the federal government is
  a transfer payments.
  b expenditures on goods and services.
  c personal income taxes.
  d corporate income taxes.
  e indirect taxes such as the GST.

8 Compared to the other major industrial economies, in recent years Canada
  a is one of the heaviest borrowers.
  b is the only one of these economies running a surplus.
  c is the only one of these economies running a deficit.
  d is the only economy with provincial/state governments that play a significant role.
  e has borrowed only to finance the purchase of public capital.

Supply-Side Effects of Fiscal Policy

9 Which of the following quotations correctly refers to the effects of fiscal policy in the *long run*?
  a "The increase in taxes will increase real GDP."
  b "The increase in taxes will raise prices only."
  c "A change in the budget has no impact on real GDP unless it changes aggregate supply."
  d "A change in the budget has no impact on real GDP."
  e "An increase in government expenditures on goods and services will increase real GDP."

10 Which of the following quotations correctly refers to the effects of fiscal policy in the *short run*?
  a "The increase in taxes will increase real GDP."
  b "The increase in taxes will raise prices only."
  c "A change in the budget has no impact on real GDP unless it changes aggregate supply."
  d "A change in the budget has no impact on real GDP."
  e "The increase in government expenditures on goods and services will increase real GDP."

11 If the nominal interest rate is 11%, the inflation rate is 4% and the tax rate is 25%, what is the real after-tax interest rate?
  a −1.25%
  b 4.25%
  c 5.25%
  d 8%
  e 10%

12 An increase in the tax rate on interest income will lead to

a less saving, more spending and more economic growth.

b less saving, less investment, and lower economic growth.

c more saving, more investment and higher economic growth.

d a strong intertemporal substitution effect, leading to more labour supplied.

e higher real after-tax interest rates.

13 Which of the following is *not* a problem created for an economy by a higher tax wedge?

a It lowers after-tax real interest rates.

b It raises before-tax wage rates and lowers employment.

c Potential GDP decreases.

d Saving decreases.

e The government's deficit rises.

14 Which of the following would lower potential GDP?

a Increased tax rate on interest income

b Increased tax rate on consumption spending

c Increased tax rate on labour income

d All of the above

e Only **a** and **c**

15 The Laffer Curve has been criticized by mainstream economists because

a there is no theoretical possibility of higher tax rates leading to lower tax revenues.

b higher tax rates do not create negative incentive effects.

c tax cuts are just spent, not saved as predicted by the theory.

d savers look only at real interest rates, not nominal interest rates.

e empirically, tax cuts have not led to higher tax revenues.

Stabilizing the Business Cycle

16 Suppose that the autonomous tax multiplier is −2. If autonomous taxes decrease by $4 billion and incentives to work and save are affected, in the long run real GDP will

a decrease by $8 billion.

b increase by $8 billion.

c be unaffected.

d increase, but by how much is unclear.

e decrease, but by how much is unclear.

17 Short-run fiscal policy is limited by the fact that

a the *LAS* curve is vertical.

b the legislative process is slow.

c real GDP is typically not equal to potential GDP.

d the policy might shift the *SAS* curve to the right.

e the policy might shift the *SAS* curve to the left.

18 Which of the following is an example of a fiscal policy designed to counter a recessionary gap?

a increasing debt interest payments

b increasing taxes

c decreasing transfer payments

d increasing transfer payments

e decreasing government expenditures on goods and services

19 During an expansion, tax revenue

a and government outlays decline.

b declines and government outlays increase.

c increases and government outlays decline.

d and government outlays increase.

e stays constant and government outlays increase.

20 Which of the following happens *automatically* if the economy goes into a recession?

a Only government outlays increase.

b Only net taxes increase.

c The deficit increases.

d The deficit decreases.

e Both government outlays and net taxes increase, and the deficit stays the same.

21 Which of the following policies will *not* shift the *AD* curve rightward?

a increasing government expenditures on goods and services

b decreasing autonomous taxes

c increasing autonomous transfer payments

d increasing government expenditures on goods and services *and* increasing autonomous taxes by the same amount

e decreasing government expenditures on goods and services *and* decreasing autonomous taxes by the same amount

22 Consider the economy of NoTax, where the multiplier is 2.5. If the government desires to shift the *AD* curve rightward by $5 billion, the correct increase in government expenditures is

a $2 billion.

b $2.5 billion.

c $3 billion.

d $7.5 billion.

e $8.33 billion.

23 How does an increase in the marginal tax rate affect the size of the multiplier?
   a It has no impact.
   b It makes the multiplier larger.
   c It makes the multiplier smaller.
   d It makes the multiplier smaller, but only if the new tax rate is larger than the *MPC*.
   e It makes the multiplier smaller, but only if the new tax rate is smaller than the *MPC*.

24 A cyclical deficit is when
   a government outlays are greater than revenues.
   b government outlays are less than revenues.
   c there is a deficit due to the fact real GDP is greater than potential GDP.
   d there is a deficit due to the fact real GDP is less than potential GDP.
   e there is a deficit even when real GDP equals potential GDP.

25 The country of Ricardia has a budget plan with constant government outlays equal to $100 billion and taxes related positively to real GDP by the equation: Taxes = $25 billion + 0.1$Y$. If the structural deficit is $10 billion, what is potential GDP in this economy?
   a $65 billion
   b $75 billion
   c $650 billion
   d $750 billion
   e $850 billion

Short Answer Problems

1 What changes in the components of the federal government budget after 1974 were the principal causes of continuing large government deficits?

2 During the summer of 1995, Saskatchewan had a provincial election. A central plank of the Saskatchewan Liberal Party's election strategy was a promise to cut taxes dramatically, stating that these cuts would create 50,000 new jobs (about 10 percent of the labour force) over the next five years. Critics claimed that this policy would have only a small effect in Saskatchewan, that most of the new jobs from the tax cuts would show up in other provinces.
   a What economic concept underlies the Liberals' promise?
   b What economic concept underlies the critics' argument?

   c The Liberals lost the election, so we did not see if the tax cuts would have had the promised effect. What do you think would have happened?

3 Suppose you are visiting the town of Elbow, Saskatchewan, which is suffering a depressed economy due to low wheat prices. You spend $100 on accommodation and another $100 golfing and dining at the excellent local golf club.
   a What factors will influence how much extra real GDP will be generated within Elbow by your $200 of expenditure? (Treat Elbow as if it were a separate economy.)

   b What does your answer imply for the argument made by the Elbow town council that the Saskatchewan government should shift a government department to the town in order to stimulate the town's economy?

4 Explain why the multiplier effect of a tax cut on aggregate demand is smaller once we consider the aggregate supply curve. Secondly, what happens if there are incentive effects from the tax cuts?

5 Table 29.1 gives some information on the real interest rates, inflation rates, and tax rates from three different countries.

TABLE 29.1

	Ricardia	Barroland	Lafferia
Nominal interest rate	12%	10%	10%
Inflation rate	6%	5%	6%
Tax rate	40%	50%	50%
Real, before-tax interest rate			
Real, after-tax interest rate			
Tax Wedge			

   a Complete Table 29.1.

   b Assuming all other factors are equal, which country has the biggest negative incentive effects for lenders?

   c Assuming all other factors are equal, which country has the lowest costs for investors?

6 Some politicians and economists argue tax cuts are beneficial for the government budget balance, and also are beneficial for the economy in the short run *and* the long run. Explain their arguments, and evaluate them briefly.

7 You may wish to review the mathematical notes to Chapter 27 before doing this problem. Consider the expenditure functions for the following economy:

Consumption: $C = 4,000 + 0.7(Y - T) - 20P$
Investment: $I = 2,000$
Government: $G = 5,000$
Exports: $X = 400$
Imports: $M = 0.1Y$
Taxes: $T = 2,000$

where P is the price level.

a What is the equation of the aggregate expenditure function? What is autonomous expenditure in this economy? What is the slope of the AE function?

b Assume that the price level is equal to 100. Calculate equilibrium real GDP, consumption, and imports.

c If the price level is now equal to 200, what is the new equilibrium real GDP?

d Using your information from **b** and **c**, sketch the AD curve for this economy.

e Calculate the government expenditures multiplier, the autonomous tax multiplier, and the balanced budget multiplier for this economy.

f Suppose the price level is equal to 100, and government expenditures increase by 2,000. What is the resulting change in real GDP demanded, holding constant the price level?

g Suppose the change in real GDP demanded raises the price level by 100. What is the overall change in real GDP from the two effects? What is the multiplier after the two effects have worked through the economy? Why is your answer different from **e**?

8 As finance minister for the government of Adanac, you have decided that in order to get reelected next year, your government needs to raise real GDP by $200 billion.

a What possible fiscal policies would work to achieve your goal?

b Your crack team of economists has estimated the economy's government expenditures multiplier be 4. You are confident that this estimate is correct, since you threatened to exile the economists to the North Pole should they err. If you decide to change only government expenditures, how much change is required to accomplish your goal?

c Having carried out the increase in government expenditures, you find that the increase in real GDP is less than $200 billion, jeopardizing your chance for reelection. Before you exile the poor economists to the North Pole, is there any excuse for their mistake? (In other words, what went wrong?)

d You were focused on the short run, but what other factors could have been important for long run considerations in picking your appropriate policy?

9 During the fall of 2008 and early 2009, Canada faced the possibility of recession as an outcome of the credit crunch. The government of Canada and the opposition parties debated what the appropriate fiscal policy might be in face of this danger. The Conservative government was worried about the potential recession, but was also worried about the long-term effects of having a deficit, and were also worried that the proposed fiscal policies might not work well to reverse a recession.

a What are the potential dangers of having a new, larger deficit?

b Why might fiscal policy not work to prevent or reduce the effects of a recession?

c What are the dangers of *not* carrying out an anti-recessionary fiscal policy?

d Which danger do you think is higher—carrying out an anti-recessionary policy that doesn't work or creates deficits, or not carrying out such a policy?

10 In the economy of Paridisio, government outlays are related to the level of real GDP by the formula: Outlays $= 500 - 0.6Y$, while tax revenues are related to the level of real GDP by the formula: Taxes $= 100 + 0.4Y$.

a Complete Table 29.2.

TABLE 29.2

Real GDP	Outlays	Revenues	Budget Balance
0			
100			
200			
300			
400			
500			
600			

b If potential GDP is 300, what is the structural balance for Paridisio?

c If real GDP is currently 200, what are the values of the cyclical deficit, the structural deficit, and the actual deficit?

d Is the tax structure in this economy acting as an automatic stabilizer?

ANSWERS

True/False and Explain

1 F Deficit is when outlays > revenues in current year. (708–709)

2 F Government expenditures on goods, transfers payments, and interest payments all part of outlays. (708)

3 T If outlays grow faster than taxes, outlays > taxes next year and there is a deficit. (708–709)

4 F Example of revenue. (708)

5 F **It has run surpluses. (709**–713)

6 F Income tax cut raises YD and shifts AD rightward, and raises incentives to work and save, raising labour supply and *raising* potential GDP. (714–715)

7 T Due to negative incentive effects reducing investment and GDP growth. (716)

8 F Only if tax rate is high enough to be past peak of Laffer Curve. (717)

9 T Real after-tax rate = nominal rate × (1 – tax rate) – inflation rate = (10% × 0.5) – 4% = 1%. (716–717)

10 F They exactly offset each other (Δ net taxes = 0), so Δ real GDP = 0. (718)

11 T If income decreases, this decreases taxes + increases transfers, and increases disposable income, which increases aggregate expenditure, increasing income, potentially offsetting initial decrease. (720–723)

12 F Autonomous not affected by real GDP. (718)

13 T Definition. (720–723)

14 T Shifts AD rightward. (718–719)

15 T Increase in government expenditures = increase in quantity of goods and services demanded, so higher level of AD, same price level. (718–719)

Multiple-Choice

1 e May have a deficit, not really used for fiscal policy, almost as large as federal government outlays, *federal* government does employment insurance. (709–713)

2 d This is increase in revenue. (708–709)

3 c See text discussion. (709–713)

4 e See text discussion. (708)

5 c Others are sources of revenue. (708–709)

6 e Budget balance = revenue – outlays = ($25 + $15 + $5 + $2) – ($30 + $12 + $8) = –$3 million. (708–709)

7 c See text discussion. (708–709)

8 b See text discussion. (713)

9 c In the long run, changes in fiscal policy have an impact only if they change potential GDP (aggregate supply). (714–717)

10 e Shift rightward in AD increases real GDP in the short run. (714–723)

11 b 11 × (1 – 0.25) – 4 = 4.25%. (716)

12 b Lower return to saving, less saving (lower quantity supplied of loanable funds), raising before-tax real interest rate, leading to lower investment, and lower economic growth. (716–717)

13 e Deficit may or may not rise. (714–717)

14 d **a**, **b**, and **c** raise tax wedge, lowering employment and saving, lowering potential GDP. (714–717)

15 e See text discussion. (717)

16 d Only the incentive effects on potential GDP matter for long run, but size is uncertain. (714–723)

17 b Others irrelevant or not limitations. (720)

18 d Shifts *AD* curve rightward. (718–720)

19 c Increase in real GDP increases tax revenue. Decrease in unemployment decreases transfer payments. (720–723)

20 c In recession, decrease in *Y* decreases taxes and increases spending on employment insurance, etc., increasing deficit. (720–723)

21 e Decrease in *G* shifts *AD* leftward by government expenditures multiplier; decrease in taxes shifts *AD* rightward by autonomous tax multiplier, which has smaller impact. (718–720)

22 a Invert ΔY = multiplier × ΔG: $\Delta G = \Delta Y$/multiplier = 5/2.5 = 2. (718)

23 c Decreases *YD* at each stage of multiplier process, reducing amount of extra consumption spending. (720–723)

24 d Definition. (720–723)

25 c $10 billion = $G – T$ = $100 billion – $25 billion – 0.1 (potential GDP), therefore potential GDP = (100 – 25 – 10)/0.1 = $650 billion. (720–723)

Short Answer Problems

1 The deficit increased because government outlays as a percentage of GDP increased, while taxes as a percentage of GDP fell during the late 1970s and then slowly increased. The components of spending that showed the most consistent growth were transfer payments and interest payments on government debt.

2 a The Liberals are counting on the autonomous tax multiplier to boost aggregate expenditure and create new jobs.

b The critics are arguing that most of the new expenditure would be on products from outside the province—that the marginal propensity to import for a province is very high, so that the multipliers are very low.

c It is likely that fiscal policy multipliers are low for individual provinces due to high marginal propensities to import. For your information, imports in Saskatchewan were about 62 percent (= 15.14 billion/29.28 billion) of provincial real GDP in 1995. (*Source:* Statistics Canada, CANSIM matrices D21425 and D31874.)

3 a Your $200 will trigger a multiplier process—the owners of the factors of production at the golf course will spend their extra income, for example. This spending induces second-round increases in consumption expenditure, leading to a final change in real GDP in Elbow that is a multiple of $200. The size of the multiplier effect will be determined by two things. First, the larger the marginal propensity to consume in Elbow and the smaller the marginal propensity to import (from outside Elbow), the larger the multiplier will be. In a small town, the marginal propensity to import from outside the town is likely to be quite high, making the multiplier much smaller. Second, the effect is smaller if the aggregate supply curve is steeper—the increase in aggregate demand gets reduced by an increase in the price level.

b Such a shift might stimulate the town's economy, since the annual increase in government expenditures will create multiplier effects. The usefulness of this shift is limited by the factors that might reduce the size of the multiplier. (This was actual government policy in Saskatchewan until the Conservatives were defeated in 1991, at least partially because of this policy.)

4 The multiplier tells us the size of the change in real GDP (the shift in the *AD* curve) relative to the size of an initial change in government expenditure or autonomous taxes, holding constant the price level. Once we consider the *AS* curve, we know the price level will increase as aggregate demand increases—the increase in the price level being higher, the steeper the *AS* curve. This increase in the price level lowers aggregate expenditure, shown by the movement up the *AD* curve, leading to a smaller increase in real GDP.

The tax cut would reduce the tax wedge, creating incentive effects that would increase labour supply (lowering the before-tax wage rate and increasing labour demand) and the quantity supplied of loanable funds (lowering real interest rates and increasing investment). These incentive effects would increase potential GDP.

5 a Table 29.1 Solution below shows the answers. The real, after-tax interest rate is solved using the formula: Nominal rate × (1 − tax rate) − inflation rate. The tax wedge is the difference between the before-tax real rate (nominal rate − inflation rate) paid by borrowers and the after-tax real rate received by lenders.

TABLE 29.1 SOLUTION

	Ricardia	Barroland	Lafferia
Nominal interest rate	12%	10%	10%
Inflation rate	6%	5%	6%
Tax rate	40%	50%	50%
Real, before-tax interest rate	6%	5%	4%
Real, after-tax interest rate	1.2%	0%	−1%
Tax Wedge	4.8%	5%	5%

b Based on having the highest tax wedge, Lafferia and Barroland have the biggest negative incentive effect for lenders.

c Lafferia has the lowest before-tax real interest rate (4%), and therefore would have the lowest costs for investors.

6 The Laffer Curve claims a tax cut could potentially have such strong incentive effects that total tax revenues would rise, helping the government budget balance. However, when the U.S. cut its tax rates under Reagan, the result was a fall in tax revenue and a rise in the budget deficit.

With respect to the economy, a cut in taxes increases disposable income, and shifts the *AD* curve rightward in the normal multiplier manner, increasing real GDP in the short run. If the *LAS* curve does not shift, in the long run the economy will return to potential GDP. However, supply-side economists argue that tax cuts will also increase the after-tax returns to work and saving,

which in turn will increase labour supply and saving, increasing potential GDP and shifting the *AS* curves rightward. An evaluation is still somewhat premature. As the text points out, it is still a matter of political opinion whether the *AS* effects are small or large. So far, there is no hard empirical evidence one way or the other.

7 a The equation can be found by totalling the components of aggregate expenditure:

$AE = 4,000 + 0.7(Y − 2,000) − 20P + 2,000 + 5,000 + 400 − 0.1Y$, or

$AE = 10,000 − 20P + 0.6Y$

Autonomous expenditure, which does not depend on real GDP, is $10,000 − 20P$. The slope is 0.6.

b Substitute $P = 100$ into the *AE* function, and solve for $Y^* = AE$:

$Y^* = 10,000 − 20(100) + 0.6Y^*$, or

$Y^*(1 − 0.6) = 8,000$, or

$Y^* = 8,000/0.4 = 20,000$

Equilibrium consumption equals $4,000 + 0.7(20,000 − 2,000) − 20(100) = 14,600$.

Imports $= 0.1(20,000) = 2,000$.

c Substitute $P = 200$ into the *AE* function from **a**:

$Y^* = 10,000 − 20(200) + 0.6Y^*$, or

$Y^*(0.4) = 6,000$, or

$Y^* = 6,000/0.4 = 15,000$

d One point on the curve is $P = 100$, $Y = 20,000$ and another point is $P = 200$, $Y = 15,000$. These points are illustrated in Figure 29.2.

FIGURE **29.2**

e The government expenditures multiplier =

1 / (1 – slope of the *AE* function) =

1 / (1 – 0.6) = 2.5

The autonomous tax multiplier =

–*MPC* / (1 – slope of the *AE* function) =

–0.7 / (1 – 0.6) = –1.75

The balanced budget multiplier =

(1 – *MPC*) / (1 – slope of the *AE* function) =

(1 – 0.7) / (1 – 0.6) = 1.17.

f The change in real GDP demanded equals the change in government expenditures times the government expenditures multiplier, or 2,000 × 2.5 = 5,000.

g If the price level increases by 100, then autonomous expenditure decreases by 5,000, as we saw in **d**. This decrease completely offsets the increase in real GDP due to the increase in government expenditures on 2,000. Therefore the overall change in real GDP is equal to zero, and the multiplier is equal to zero. The answer is different here compared with part **f**, because the price level is allowed to adjust, which leads to the offsetting effects.

8 a You would need to increase aggregate demand, which means that you would need to either increase government expenditures

on goods and services, or increase transfer payments, or cut taxes.

b If the government expenditures multiplier equals 4, in order to raise real GDP by $200 billion you need to increase government expenditures by $50 billion = $200/4 billion.

c The multiplier effects we have been analysing are based on the assumption that the price level is constant. In the real world, the stimulation of aggregate demand that you have carried out would raise the price level, which lowers aggregate expenditure, and partially (or completely) offsets the increase in real GDP from your policy.

d If you had chosen a tax cut for your policy, this might have had positive incentive effects on labour supply and saving, leading to a higher level of potential GDP in the long run.

9 a A larger deficit increases the demand for loanable funds (see Chapter 23), and potentially increases real interest rates, crowding out private investment, and lowering long-term economic growth. In addition, a deficit increases the size of the government debt, and therefore increases the required debt payments by the government. Looking at the history of the government's deficits between 1971 and 1997, debt payments can create a vicious circle of rising debt, rising debt payments, rising deficits, rising debt, etc.

b Fiscal policy might not work due to lags in the system. The recognition lag would not be an issue (the problem was recognized!), but the law-making lag (getting the legislation passed) is a possible problem, as is the impact lag (the time it takes the policy to have an impact). If the policy arrives after the economy has started to re-adjust to full employment, we may create inflationary pressures.

c The dangers of not carrying out an anti-recessionary fiscal would be a longer and deeper recession, with more lost jobs and bankrupt businesses.

d This choice depends on your personal evaluation of the pros and cons listed above, as well as your judgement on which negatives to avoid!

10 a Table 29.2 is completed as Table 29.2 Solution below, using the two formulas plus the fact that the budget balance = revenues – outlays.

TABLE **29.2** SOLUTION

Real GDP	Outlays	Revenues	Budget Balance
0	500	100	–400
100	440	140	–300
200	380	180	–200
300	320	220	–100
400	260	260	0
500	200	300	100
600	140	340	200

b The structural balance is the surplus or deficit that would exist with the existing budget structure at potential GDP, and is equal to a deficit of 100.

c The structural deficit is still 100, the actual deficit is 200 at real GDP of 200, and the cyclical deficit = actual – structural = 100.

d Yes, since as real GDP decreases, tax revenues decrease and outlays increase, creating upward pressure on aggregate expenditure.

Chapter 30
Monetary Policy

Monetary Policy Objective and Framework

Bank of Canada Act sets out objectives of monetary policy.

- ♦ Bank controls quantity of money and interest rates to avoid inflation and prevent excessive swings in GDP growth and unemployment.

- ♦ Current policy is **inflation rate targeting**—explicit inflation rate target range (1 to 3 percent a year, trend of 2 percent), clear explanation of actions.

  - Inflation is measured by CPI, but Bank also focuses on *core inflation* (CPI excluding eight most volatile prices and indirect taxes).

  - Since range set in mid-1990s, actual inflation rate has been within target range, with minor deviations.

- ♦ Benefits of a target range are clear understanding by financial markets and as anchor for inflation expectations.

  - Critics argue Bank should pay more attention to unemployment rate and real GDP growth.

- ♦ Governing Council of Bank of Canada is responsible for conduct of monetary policy, with briefings by Bank economists.

- ♦ Governor of Bank of Canada consults with Minister of Finance.

The Conduct of Monetary Policy

Bank of Canada can control only one policy instrument: either quantity of money (monetary base) *or* exchange rate *or* short-term interest rate.

- ♦ Bank targets short-term interest rate, specifically **overnight loans rate** (interest rate on overnight loans members of LVTS make to each other).

Chosen target can be *set* either by

- ♦ **Instrument rule**—sets policy instrument at level based on current state of economy; or

- ♦ **Targeting rule**—sets policy instrument so forecast policy level equals target level. Bank of Canada uses targeting rule, announcing its target eight times a year.

Tools used to *achieve* chosen target

- ♦ **Operating band** is target overnight rate plus or minus 0.25 percentage points.

  - Top of operating band = **bank rate** (overnight rate + 0.25%)—interest rate Bank of Canada charges big banks on loans. Since a bank can always borrow at bank rate, overnight rate never goes higher than this.

  - Bottom of band = **settlement balances rate**—interest rate Bank of Canada pays for reserves banks hold at Bank of Canada. Since a bank can always earn settlement balances rate, overnight rate never goes lower than this.

  - Bank of Canada can always make overnight loans rate fall within target range.

- ♦ **Open market operations** (purchase or sale of government securities by Bank) move overnight rate to target rate.

  - If Bank of Canada buys government bonds, this increases banking system reserves (= increased supply of overnight funds), increasing loans, lowering overnight rate.

  - If Bank of Canada sells government bonds, this decreases banking system reserves (= decreased supply of overnight funds), decreasing loans, raising overnight rate.

Monetary Policy Transmission

Changing overnight rate affects aggregate demand (*AD*), real GDP growth and inflation through several channels.

- ◆ With lower overnight rate, other interest rates fall, quantity of money and supply of loanable funds increase, real interest rates fall.

  - • With lower interest rates, exchange rate falls, increasing net exports and *AD*.

  - • With lower real interest rates, consumption and investment increase, increasing *AD*.

  - • Increasing *AD* increases real GDP growth and inflation, although takes up to two years for full effects.

- ◆ Higher overnight rate has opposite effects, decreasing *AD*, real GDP growth, and inflation.

- ◆ Historical evidence shows changes in overnight rate create different effects on long-term and short-term interest rates.

  - • Because banks can easily choose between overnight loans and Treasury bills as short-term assets, they are close substitutes and two rates move together.

  - • 10-year government bond rate and long-term corporate bond rate are close substitutes (although corporate rate slightly higher on average), so these two rates move together.

  - • Short-term and long-term bond rates usually move together, but are not close substitutes, and sometimes move in different directions.

- ◆ Exchange rate responds to interest rate differential (gap between Canadian and U.S. rates), but relationship is weak since many other factors determining exchange rates.

Expenditure plans are affected by real interest rate.

- ◆ Lower real interest rate, lower opportunity cost of spending, greater autonomous consumption expenditure and investment.

- ◆ Lower real interest rate, lower Canadian dollar exchange rate, greater net exports.

Final link in transmission chain is a change in *AD* changing real GDP and price level.

- ◆ With real GDP < potential GDP, lowering overnight rate increases quantity of money and supply of loanable funds. This lowers real interest rates and increases *AD*, increasing real GDP and price level, leading to faster convergence to potential GDP.

- ◆ If real GDP > potential GDP (inflationary pressure), increasing overnight rate lowers quantity of money and supply of loanable funds, increasing real interest rate and decreasing *AD*, lowering inflationary pressure.

- ◆ Monetary policy is sometimes wrong due to time lags before policy takes effect.

- ◆ When Bank of Canada changes overnight rates, real GDP growth changes, but there is a loose link because real interest rates react to overnight rate *and* inflation expectations, and because of time lags in the adjustment process.

Alternative Monetary Policy Strategies

Bank of Canada uses inflation rate targeting rule, but has four possible alternative strategies.

- ◆ **Taylor rule** is an overnight rate instrument rule that sets target rate in response to current inflation rate and current estimate of output gap. If inflation is above target, or real GDP is above potential GDP, Taylor rule raises overnight rate.

- ◆ **McCallum rule** is a monetary base instrument rule based on quantity theory of money. Set monetary base to grow at rate equal to target inflation rate plus long-term real GDP growth minus medium-term velocity growth rate.

- ◆ Exchange rate targeting rule (could be a fixed exchange rate or a crawling peg), loses control over inflation rate. Problem is *real exchange rate* often changes unpredictably and is hard to offset.

- ◆ Friedman's ***k*-percent rule** is a money targeting rule that sets quantity of money to grow at *k* percent per year = growth rate of potential GDP. Requires a stable money demand function.

HELPFUL HINTS

1 Let's use a numerical example to review how the Bank of Canada can get the overnight rate to be in the middle of the target range. Suppose that the Bank wishes the overnight rate to be 3.5 percent, which means the operating band will be 3.25 to 3.75 percent.

How can the Bank guarantee that the overnight rate will be within the 0.5 percent target range? Two key factors keep the rate in the range. One is that the Bank of Canada is willing to lend as much money as members of the LVTS want to borrow at the bank rate (which is set at the upper end of the target, 3.75%). If the overnight rate was 4 percent, no member of the LVTS would borrow at this rate as they could borrow at the (lower) bank rate. Therefore the overnight rate is less than or equal to the bank rate. The second factor is that the Bank of Canada is willing to allow the members of the LVTS to hold as many deposits at the Bank of Canada as they want, and to earn the settlement balances rate of 3.25 percent. If the overnight rate was 3 percent, no bank would lend at this rate as they could earn 3.25 percent. Therefore, the overnight rate is greater than or equal to the settlements balances rate. In sum:

Settlement balances rate $\leq$ overnight rate $\leq$ bank rate

$3.25\% \leq$ overnight rate $\leq 3.75\%$

As long as the Bank of Canada is willing to meet all borrowing/lending requirements implied by the rates it sets, it can force the *actual* overnight rate to be in this range. However, if the actual rate gets stuck at one end, it would be difficult for the Bank to continuously accept deposits or loan out money. In that case it must use open market operations to affect the amount of reserves and the overnight rate.

2 Open market operations affect the overnight rate via their impact on banking system reserves. One liability of the Bank of Canada is banks' deposits at the Bank of Canada (which are part of the banks' reserves). In addition, the largest class of assets of the Bank of Canada is its holdings of government securities. Finally, recall that if total assets increase, due to the conventions of double-entry bookkeeping, total liabilities must increase by the same amount.

An open market purchase by the Bank of Canada of government securities is an increase in its assets paid for by an increase in its liabilities, principally an increase in the deposits of banks at the Bank of Canada. This increase in deposits at the Bank of Canada is an increase in banks' reserves, leaving them with excess reserves they will lend out, initially in the overnight market, pushing down the overnight rate.

3 Be careful to avoid a very common error working through open market operations. When the Bank of Canada buys or sells securities, private bank reserves at the Bank of Canada change. Many students automatically put the changed bank reserves at the Bank of Canada under assets in the Bank's balance sheet, because they are an asset on the *private bank balance sheet*. However, this is an error—the reserves are a deposit at the Bank of Canada, and therefore a *liability* to the Bank of Canada.

SELF-TEST

True/False and Explain

Monetary Policy Objective and Framework

1 The monetary policy objective of the Bank of Canada is to avoid inflation and prevent excessive swings in the exchange rate.

2 The Bank of Canada's current inflation target is a range of 1 to 3 percent per year for core inflation.

3 The benefits of a target range include creating an anchor for inflation expectations.

The Conduct of Monetary Policy

4 Increasing the bank rate will increase the amount of lending by the banking system.

5 Bank deposits at the Bank of Canada are an asset of the Bank of Canada and a liability of the banking system.

6 If the Bank of Canada sells government securities in the open market, bank reserves decrease.

7 If the Bank of Canada wants to decrease interest rates, it buys government securities in the open market.

Monetary Policy Transmission

8 A decrease in the overnight rate shifts the *AD* curve rightward.

9 An increase in the overnight rate decreases the exchange rate.

10 A decrease in the overnight rate reduces inflationary pressures.

11 An increase in the overnight rate will increase the quantity of money and lower money demand.

12 The overnight rate and the 10-year government bond rate move very closely together.

13 A lower real interest rate creates more consumption spending.

Alternative Monetary Policy Strategies

14 To follow Friedman's *k*-percent rule, the Bank of Canada would set the growth rate of money equal to the target inflation rate plus long-term real GDP growth minus the medium term velocity growth rate.

15 Under the Taylor rule, if real GDP is greater than potential GDP, the Bank of Canada should raise the overnight rate.

Multiple-Choice

Monetary Policy Objective and Framework

1 Why does the Bank of Canada pay close attention to the core inflation rate in addition to the overall CPI inflation rate?
   a The core rate is more volatile and therefore a better predictor of trend inflation.
   b The core rate includes taxes, while the overall CPI rate does not.
   c The core rate has a lower average value and therefore makes the Bank look better.
   d The core rate is less volatile and a better predictor of future CPI inflation.
   e The core rate excludes eight volatile prices and is therefore more likely to stay within the target band.

2 One criticism of the Bank of Canada's focus on an inflation control target is that
   a if inflation falls below the target range a recession will result.
   b if inflation edges above the target range, the Bank decreases aggregate demand and could create a recession.
   c the Bank pays too much attention to unemployment and real GDP growth and not enough to inflation control.
   d it makes setting expectations of inflation difficult.
   e the Bank rarely achieves its target.

3 Who is responsible for setting monetary policy in Canada?
  a The government of Canada.
  b The Governor of the Bank of Canada.
  c The Bank of Canada's economists.
  d The Governing Council of the Bank of Canada.
  e The Governing Council of the Bank of Canada, after consultation with the government of Canada.

The Conduct of Monetary Policy

4 If the Bank of Canada aims to lower the overnight rate, it will
  a lower the bank rate and settlement balances rate, as well as buy government securities.
  b lower the bank rate, increase the settlement balances rate, as well as buy government securities.
  c lower the bank rate and settlement balances rate, as well as sell government securities.
  d raise the bank rate and settlement balances rate, as well as buy government securities.
  e raise the bank rate and settlement balances rate, as well as sell government securities.

5 The Bank of Canada's current decision-making rule
  a uses the overnight loans rate target to affect the current state of the economy.
  b uses open market operations to affect the current state of the economy.
  c uses the overnight loans rate target to hit the inflation rate target.
  d uses open market operations to try and affect the exchange rate.
  e uses the growth rate of the monetary base to affect lending.

6 The bank rate is the interest rate
  a banks charge their very best loan customers.
  b banks pay on term deposits.
  c the Bank of Canada pays on reserves held by banks.
  d the Bank of Canada charges when it lends reserves to banks.
  e received for holding Government of Canada Treasury bills.

7 Which balance sheet in Table 30.1 shows the initial impact on the banking sector of an open market purchase by the Bank of Canada of $100 million of government securities from the banking sector?
  a (a)
  b (b)
  c (c)
  d (d)
  e none of the above

TABLE 30.1 BANKING SYSTEM BALANCE SHEET (MILLIONS)

(a)

Assets		Liabilities
Reserves	+100	
Securities	−100	

(b)

Assets		Liabilities
Reserves	−100	
Securities	+100	

(c)

Assets		Liabilities
Reserves	+100	Deposits+100

(d)

Assets	Liabilities	
	Deposits	+100
	Securities	−100

8 In an open market operation aimed at increasing expenditure, the Bank of Canada
  a sells government bonds, decreasing bank reserves, decreasing lending, decreasing the overnight rate.
  b sells government bonds, decreasing bank reserves, decreasing lending, increasing the overnight rate.
  c sells government bonds, decreasing bank reserves, increasing lending, increasing the overnight rate.
  d buys government bonds, increasing bank reserves, increasing lending, decreasing the overnight rate.
  e buys government bonds, increasing bank reserves, increasing lending, increasing the overnight rate.

9 The current overnight loans rate is 3 percent, with the Bank of Canada's operating band set at 2.75 to 3.25 percent. If the Bank of Canada lowers their operating band to 2.25 to 2.75 percent, which of the following is one of the reasons the overnight rate will fall to within this new range?

a Since the banking system can now borrow from the Bank of Canada at 2.75 percent, no bank would borrow on the overnight loan market at 3 percent.

b Since the banking system can now borrow from the Bank of Canada at 2.25 percent, no bank would borrow on the overnight loan market at 3 percent.

c Since the banking system can now earn 2.75 percent from the Bank of Canada, no bank would lend on the overnight loan market at 3 percent.

d Since the banking system can now earn 2.25 percent from the Bank of Canada, no bank would lend on the overnight loan market at 3 percent.

e There is a legal requirement that the overnight rate must be within the Bank of Canada's operating band.

10 The current overnight loans rate is 3 percent, with the Bank of Canada's operating band set at 2.75 to 3.25 percent. If the Bank of Canada lowers their operating band to 2.25 to 2.75 percent, what open market operation might be used to move the overnight rate to the middle of the target?

a Buying foreign exchange in the foreign exchange market

b Buying Canadian dollars in the foreign exchange market

c Selling foreign exchange in the foreign exchange market

d Buying government securities in the open market

e Selling government securities in the open market

Monetary Policy Transmission

11 Why is the exchange rate a key monetary variable?

a It is one of the four main policy rules.

b It is a key policy objective.

c It is a barometer of monetary policy.

d It shows how much the monetary base must be multiplied in order to measure the resulting increase in the quantity of money.

e It is part of the channel by which a change in the overnight rate affects aggregate demand.

12 The headline "The Bank of Canada Has Cut the Bank Rate" suggests that the Bank of Canada is trying to

a lower inflationary pressures.

b increase the overnight loans rate.

c stimulate aggregate demand.

d raise the value of the Canadian dollar.

e help banks make profits.

13 In a situation of unemployment, a decrease in the overnight rate will lead to a(n)

a increase in real GDP and the price level.

b increase in real GDP, but a decrease in the price level.

c increase in real GDP, but no change in the price level.

d increase in the price level, but no change in real GDP.

e decrease in the price level and real GDP.

14 Consider Figure 30.1. Which graph represents an anti-inflationary monetary policy?

a (a)

b (b)

c (c)

d (d)

e none of the above

FIGURE 30.1

(a)

(b)

(c)

(d)

15 Consider Figure 30.1. Which graph represents an attempt to lower unemployment with monetary policy?
  a (a)
  b (b)
  c (c)
  d (d)
  e none of the above

16 A monetary policy aimed at increasing domestic expenditure will
  a increase interest rates and decrease the exchange rate.
  b have no impact on interest rates, but increase the exchange rate.
  c have no impact on interest rates nor on the exchange rate.
  d decrease interest rates and increase the exchange rate.
  e decrease interest rates and the exchange rate.

17 Which of the following statements about historical evidence on monetary policy is *true*?
  a The overnight interest rate move inversely with short-term interest rates.
  b The overnight interest rate is not related to short-term interest rates.
  c When the Bank of Canada lowers the overnight rate, real GDP rises immediately.
  d When the gap between Canadian and U.S. interest rates increases, the exchange rate decreases.
  e When the gap between Canadian and U.S. interest rates increases, the exchange rate increases.

18 Which of the following statements *correctly* describes an anti-inflationary monetary policy?
  a "The Bank of Canada's purchases of government securities is stimulating the housing sector."
  b "The Bank of Canada's moves to lower interest rates are behind the decrease in the value of the Canadian dollar."
  c "The Bank of Canada's moves to increase the overnight loans rate are leading to less lending and less consumer spending."
  d "The Bank of Canada's sales of government securities are stimulating the housing sector."
  e "The Bank of Canada's moves to decrease the value of the Canadian dollar are leading to more spending in the economy."

19 If the inflation rate increases by 3 percent and the nominal interest rate increases by 2 percent,
  a the real interest rate increases.
  b money demand increases.
  c money demand decreases.
  d investment decreases.
  e consumption expenditure decreases.

20 An increase in the real interest rate will
  a decrease consumption expenditure.
  b increase investment.
  c decrease the exchange rate.
  d increase net exports.
  e decrease the nominal interest rate.

21 An increase in the overnight interest rate will
  a decrease the real interest rate, the inflation rate held constant.
  b decrease nominal interest rates.
  c decrease aggregate demand.
  d increase aggregate demand.
  e not change the nominal interest rate.

22 A higher Canadian interest rate will
  a increase the demand for Canadian dollars because more people move money into Canada to take advantage of the higher interest rate.
  b decrease the demand for Canadian dollars because more people move money out of Canada to take advantage of the higher interest rate.
  c increase the demand for Canadian dollars because more people move money out of Canada to take advantage of the higher interest rate.
  d decrease the demand for Canadian dollars because more people move money into Canada to take advantage of the higher interest rate.
  e not affect the demand for Canadian dollars.

23 Changing the overnight rate affects aggregate demand through several channels. Which of the following is *not* one of those channels?
  a Higher real interest rates lower net exports.
  b Higher real interest rates raise consumption expenditure.
  c Higher real interest rates lower investment spending.
  d Lower real interest rates raise consumption expenditure.
  e Lower real interest rates raise investment spending.

Alternative Monetary Policy Strategies

24 Suppose the Bank of Canada's current monetary policy strategy has the monetary base growing at a target rate. This is an example of a(n)

   a   Taylor rule.

   b   McCallum rule.

   c   inflation targeting rule.

   d   exchange rate target rule.

   e   monetary target rule.

25 For Friedman's *k*-percent rule to work, it requires

   a   stable long-term real GDP growth.

   b   a good estimate of the output gap.

   c   the real exchange rate to be predictable.

   d   a stable money demand function.

   e   good knowledge of the velocity growth rate.

Short Answer Problems

1 Suppose that the Bank of Canada is following an exchange rate target of a fixed exchange rate. Currently there is downward market pressure on the exchange rate.

   a   Explain how the Bank of Canada could use monetary policy to offset this downward pressure.

   b   Explain how consumption, investment and net exports are affected by this policy.

2 How does an open market purchase of government securities lead to a decrease in the overnight rate? What are the ripple effects of this policy on the different components of aggregate expenditure?

3 Consider the following balance sheets for the Bank of Canada and the Bank of Speedy Creek:

TABLE 30.2

Bank of Speedy Creek

Assets		Liabilities	
Reserves	60	Deposits	1,000
Securities	100		
Loans	840		
	1,000		

Bank of Canada

Assets		Liabilities	
Government securities	9,000	Bank of Canada notes	10,000
Loans to banks	500	Chartered banks' deposits	1,000
Other net assets	2,000	Government deposits	500
	11,500		11,500

   a   Suppose that the Bank of Canada buys all $100 of securities from the Bank of Speedy Creek. Show what happens to the balance sheets of the Bank of Speedy Creek and the Bank of Canada as a result of this action, explaining as you go. What does this action do to the reserves in the banking system?

   b   If this action is carried out at all the banks of the banking system, explain what will likely happen next in the overnight loans market.

4 Explain what the open market operation in Short Answer Problem **3** does to short-term and long-term interest rates, aggregate demand, real GDP, and the price level. Be sure to explain the channels by which the monetary policy affects aggregate demand.

5 Suppose there is an increase in the overnight rate and therefore in other interest rates. Using a graph of the aggregate demand–aggregate supply model, show what happens to the price level and the level of real GDP in the short run and in the long run.

6 Consider the following data, from the imaginary country of Sarconia:

Current inflation rate	3% per year
Current overnight rate	4% per year
Current growth rate of real GDP	3% per year
Estimated (long-term) growth rate of potential GDP	3% per year
Current unemployment rate	5%
Estimate of natural unemployment rate	7%
Current growth rate of monetary base	12% per year

a Is Sarconia suffering from an inflationary gap, a recessionary gap, or is it right at potential GDP? How do you know?

b If the Bank of Sarconia has an inflationary target of 2 to 4 percent per year, what would be the appropriate policy strategy?

c If the Bank of Sarconia follows a Taylor rule with an inflationary target of 2 to 4 percent per year, what should be its policy strategy?

d If the Bank of Sarconia follows a McCallum rule with an inflationary target of 2 to 4 percent per year, what additional information would you need to be able to figure out the appropriate policy strategy?

e If the Bank of Sarconia follows a Friedman *k*-percent rule, what would be the policy strategy?

7 In Short Answer Problem **6**, you should have found different policy conclusions for each of the rules in parts **b**, **c**, and **e**. Explain what differences in the crucial factors underlying each rule leads to the different policy conclusions.

8 "If banking system reserves are increasing, this is a sign that loans and deposits will soon expand." Evaluate this statement.

9 Consider the following "quotation" from the *Regional Post*:

Interest Rates Crash After Bank of Canada Action

by J. S. Smith

The Bank of Canada cut interest rates dramatically yesterday. ... [T]he bank cut its target for overnight rates to 3.25% from 4.00%. The major banks quickly followed suit, cutting the cost of borrowing for their best customers (the prime rate) to 5.50% from 6.25%. This change was following by reductions in other rates, including mortgage rates.

Explain the link from the overnight rate target to the prime rate that the major banks charge their best customers.

10 If the Bank of Canada wishes to reduce inflationary pressure, explain briefly what steps they will have to carry out in the overnight loans market.

ANSWERS

True/False and Explain

1 F Avoid inflation and prevent excessive swings in real GDP growth and unemployment. (732)

2 F 1 to 3 percent for overall inflation. (732–733)

3 T See text discussion. (733)

4 F Higher bank rate increases cost of borrowing reserves, so banks wish to hold more reserves, and *decrease* loans. (734–737)

5 F Asset of banking system (part of reserves) and liability of Bank of Canada (deposit at Bank). (737)

6 T People buy securities with deposits that are transferred to Bank of Canada, decreasing reserves. (737)

7 T Buying government bonds increases reserves, which increases supply of overnight funds. Banks respond by loaning out more, lowering overnight rate. (737)

8 T Lower overnight rate pushes down short-term and long-term interest rates, which increases consumption, investment and net exports, shifting *AD* curve rightward. (739)

9 F Higher overnight rate pushes up interest rates, raising Canadian interest rate differential, raising demand for Canadian dollar and therefore exchange rate. (741)

10 F Lower overnight rate pushes down short-term and long-term interest rates, increasing consumption, investment and net exports, shifting *AD* curve rightward, pushing up price level. (739–746)

11 F Higher overnight rate leads to lower bank reserves, lower loans, less deposits, and lower quantity of money. Lower quantity of money raises interest rate and lowers money demand. (741)

12 F They move together, but not that closely. See Text Figure 30.7. (739–740)

13 T Lower real rate leads to less saving and more consumption. (741)

14 F Should set it equal to growth rate of potential GDP. (747–748)

15 T See formula. (747)

Multiple-Choice

1 d See text discussion. (732)

2 b Anti-inflationary policy leads to decreased *AD*, which can lead to recession and unemployment. (732)

3 e See text discussion. (734)

4 a Lowering two rates will force overnight rate down in between these two rates (see Helpful Hint **1**), and buying securities increases banking system reserves, leading to more overnight loans, pushing rate down. (736–738)

5 c Overnight loan rate is policy instrument aimed at policy objective of inflation rate. (734–736)

6 d Definition. (736)

7 a Bank of Canada credits banking sector's reserves at central bank and in return gets securities from banking sector. (737)

8 d Buying bonds increases reserves to pay for them, which creates excess reserves, leading to increase in funds available for lending in overnight loans market, pushing down overnight rate. (737–738)

9 a Upper end of band is bank rate, rate Bank of Canada charges for borrowing from it. No profit-seeking bank will pay more than this rate to borrow, forcing down actual overnight rate to less than or equal to this rate. (736–738)

10 d They need to buy securities to raise banking system reserves in order to increase funds for lending in overnight market in order to push down overnight rate. (736–738)

11 e Δ overnight rate leads to Δ*r*, which Δ demand for Canadian dollar and exchange rate, which Δ*X*, Δ*M* and *AD*. (741)

12 c Lowering bank rate lowers costs of borrowing to replenish reserves, so banking system will maintain lower reserves, lend out more money, lowering interest rates and stimulating consumption, investment, net exports and *AD*. (739–746)

13 a Decrease in overnight rate shifts *AD* rightward, increasing real GDP and price level if initial equilibrium is left of full employment (draw a graph). (742–746)

14 b Output is above natural rate (inflationary gap). Policy attempting to reduce *AD* to reduce gap. (742–746)

15 c Output is below natural rate (recessionary gap). Policy attempting to increase *AD* to reduce gap. (742–746)

16 e Decrease in overnight rate decreases interest rates, decreasing demand for Canadian dollar and therefore exchange rate. (739–741)

17 e See text discussion. (739–746)

18 c All other changes lead to lower interest rates and higher aggregate expenditure, shifting *AD* rightward. (739–746)

19 c Nominal interest rate increases, money demand decreases. Real interest rate decreases since increase in inflation rate > increase in nominal interest rate, so investment and consumption expenditure increase. (741)

20 a Higher cost of borrowing decreases borrowing and spending. (741)

21 c Higher overnight rate increases other interest rates and decreases consumption, investment and net exports. (741)

22 a People trying to earn more on their money buy Canadian assets and must buy Canadian dollars to buy Canadian assets. (741)

23 b Higher real interest rates lower borrowing and spending. (739–746)

24 b Definition. (747–748)

25 d See text discussion. (748)

Short Answer Problems

1 a If the Bank of Canada pushes up the overnight loans rate, this would increase other interest rates in the economy. Increasing interest rates will increase the interest rate gap between Canada and other countries, increasing demand for the Canadian dollar. This increase in turn increases the exchange rate, offsetting the initial downward pressure.

b The higher exchange rate will lower net exports. The higher interest rates will push up the real interest rate, and therefore lower consumption expenditure and investment.

2 An open market purchase of government securities by the Bank of Canada increases the reserves of the banking system by increasing one of its components—banks' deposits at the Bank of Canada. When the securities are purchased from banks, the Bank of Canada pays for the securities by crediting the bank's deposit at the Bank of Canada, which directly increases their reserves. The banks now have more reserves, and will try to lend more on the overnight market (and will need to borrow less), putting downward pressure on overnight rates.

The lower overnight rates create substitution effects, pushing down other interest rates, increasing consumption expenditure and investment spending. The lower interest rates also lower demand for the Canadian dollar, which lowers the value of the exchange rate, and increases net exports.

3 a The impact of the purchase on the balance sheets is shown in Table 30.3.

The Bank of Canada increases its securities by 100, and pays for it by increasing the Bank of Speedy Creek's deposits at the Bank of Canada by 100, which is an increase in this bank's reserves by 100 (matching the decrease in security holdings). The balance sheets in Table 30.3 show the changes, and then the new positions.

The increase in banks' deposits of 100 also increases the reserves of the banking system by 100.

TABLE 30.3

(a) Changes in Balance Sheets
Bank of Speedy Creek

Assets		Liabilities	
Reserves	+100	Deposits	0
Securities	−100		
Loans	0		
	0		

Bank of Canada

Assets		Liabilities	
Government securities	+100	Bank of Canada notes	0
Loans to banks	0	Ch. banks' deposits	+100
Other net assets	0	Government deposits	0
	+100		+100

(b) Positions After the Open Market Operation
Bank of Speedy Creek

Assets		Liabilities	
Reserves	160	Deposits	1,000
Securities	0		
Loans	840		
	1,000		

Bank of Canada

Assets		Liabilities	
Government securities	9,100	Bank of Canada notes	10,000
Loans to banks	500	Ch. banks' deposits	1,100
Other net assets	2,000	Government deposits	500
	11,600		11,600

---

b The Bank of Speedy Creek now likely has excess reserves of 100, since deposits are unchanged by the operation. If this operation is carried out at all banks, other banks will also have excess reserves. They will try to lend out these excess reserves in the overnight loans market (and will need to borrow less), putting downward pressure on the overnight rate.

4 The lower overnight rate pushes down short-term interest rates, and to some degree long-term interest rates, including real interest rates. Lower real interest rates increase consumer spending (more borrowing, less saving) and investment spending. Lower interest rates also lower the exchange rate, leading to more net exports. Therefore, the aggregate demand curve shifts rightward, increasing real GDP and the price level in the short run, as in Text Figure 30.8.

5 Figure 30.2 illustrates the consequences of an increase in the overnight rates are. The economy is initially in long-run equilibrium at point a, the intersection of AD_0 and SAS_0 (and LAS). The price level is P_0 and GDP is at potential, Y^*. An increase in the overnight rate lowers consumption, investment and net exports and shifts the AD curve leftward, from AD_0 to AD_1. The new short-run equilibrium is at point b. The price level decreases to P_1 and real GDP decreases to Y_1. In the long run, however, input prices also decrease, which shifts SAS rightward, from SAS_0 to SAS_1. A new long-run equilibrium occurs at point c. In the long run, the price level decreases further to P_2, while real GDP returns to potential, Y^*.

FIGURE **30.2**

6 a Since unemployment is below the natural rate, real GDP is above potential GDP and there is an inflationary gap.

b Since inflation is exactly in the middle of the inflationary target range, the appropriate policy would be to do nothing different.

c A Taylor rule follows the following formula:

$$R = R^* + \pi + 0.5(\pi - \pi^*) + 0.5G$$

R is the overnight rate, R^* is the neutral real overnight rate (2% according to Taylor), π is the inflation rate, π^* is the target rate, and G is an estimate of the output gap. Substituting in the information from question, and assuming a value of π^* equal to the middle of the target range, we see:

$$R = 2 + 3 + 0.5(3 - 3) + 0.5G, \text{ or}$$

$$R = 5 + 0.5G$$

We do not know what G is, but if there is an inflationary gap, $G > 0$. Therefore, the overnight rate should be higher than 5 percent. Since it is currently 4 percent, it needs to be raised.

d The McCallum rule sets the growth rate of the monetary base equal to the target inflation rate (3%) plus the long-term real GDP growth rate (3%) minus the medium-term velocity growth rate. We would need to know the medium-term velocity growth rate in order to set the appropriate growth rate of the monetary base.

e The Friedman k-percent rule sets the growth rate of the quantity of money equal to the growth rate of potential GDP, which is 3 percent per year. Since the current growth rate of the monetary base is 12 percent per year, Sarconia would have to lower this growth rate dramatically by raising the overnight rate.

7 The simple inflationary rule of part **b** only focuses on the inflation target, which was currently being met, and not on any future problems. Both the Taylor rule (which also looks at the output gap as a source of future inflationary pressures) and the Friedman k-percent rule (which looks at the growth rate of the money supply as a source of future inflationary pressures) try and forecast future pressures and offset them before they occur. We do not have the correct information for the McCallum rule, but its use of medium-term velocity in its formula would also lead to a different result.

8 Banking system reserves might be increasing for two reasons, which will have opposite future effects on loans and deposits. It might be as a result of an open-market operation, where the Bank of Canada is buying securities and pumping up the reserves of the banking system. This creates *excess* reserves, which will be lent out, creating deposits expansion.

A second reason might be because the Bank of Canada has raised the overnight loan rate, making it more expensive for banks to be short of reserves. Then, banks will raise their *desired* reserves in order to avoid being short. In this case, they will be shrinking their loans (and therefore deposits) in order to increase their desired reserves.

9 The overnight rate is the rate banks in the banking system charge each other when there are shortages in reserves at the end of the day. If this rate climbs dramatically, banks will want to hold more reserves. To do this, they will call in loans to their other customers and raise loan rates, since these are substitutes for overnight loans.

10 To reduce inflationary pressure, the Bank of Canada needs to reduce aggregate demand. To do this, the Bank must reduce expenditure, and to do this, they need to raise nominal and real interest rates. To raise the overnight rate, the Bank would raise its target range for the overnight rate. In addition, they would probably carry out an open market operation. To raise the overnight rate, they would need to reduce banking system reserves by carrying out an open market sale of government securities. If they sell securities to the banking system, these securities will be paid for out of reserves, reducing the amount of reserves.

Chapter 31
International Trade Policy

KEY CONCEPTS

How Global Markets Work

Imports are goods and services we buy from other countries; **exports** are what we sell to other countries.

- ♦ Canada's major exports (imports) are motor vehicles/parts and crude petroleum (motor vehicles/parts and metals), our major trading partner is the United States.

- ♦ Trade includes trade in services, such as tourism.

National comparative advantage drives international trade—a country exports goods/services that it can produce at a lower opportunity cost than any other nation, imports goods/services that other nations can produce at a lower opportunity cost.

- ♦ For import goods, world price < pre-trade domestic price.

  - • Quantity demanded (= quantity bought) increases with international trade.

  - • Quantity supplied decreases with international trade and is lower than quantity demanded.

  - • Imports = quantity demanded – supplied > 0.

- ♦ For export goods, world price > pre-trade domestic price.

  - • Quantity supplied increases with international trade.

  - • Quantity demanded decreases with international trade and is lower than quantity supplied.

  - • Exports = quantity supplied – demanded > 0.

Different parts of economy gain or lose from international trade.

- ♦ *Lower* price for imported goods leads to *more* consumption by consumers—consumers of imported goods *gain* from international trade.

- ♦ *Lower* price for imported goods leads to *less* production by producers—producers of import-competing goods *lose* from international trade.

- ♦ Consumers' gain = producers' loss + gain from more consumption—society gains from imported goods.

For export goods, we also see overall gain to society.

- ♦ *Higher* price for exported goods leads to *less* consumption by consumers—consumers of exported goods *lose* from international trade.

- ♦ *Higher* price for exported goods leads to *more* production by producers—producers of exported goods *gain* from international trade.

- ♦ Producers' gain = consumers' loss + gain from more production—society gains from exporting.

International Trade Restrictions

Governments use four different tools to influence international trade and protect domestic industries—tariffs, import quotas, other import barriers, and export subsidies.

Tariffs are taxes on imported goods, providing revenue for government and helping the self-interest of import-competing industries.

- ♦ Higher domestic price = world price + tariff.

◆ Higher price means lower domestic quantity bought *and* higher domestic quantity produced—quantity imported shrinks.

◆ Government *gains* tariff revenue = tariff rate × quantity imported.

◆ Domestic producers *gain* from higher price and higher production.

◆ Consumers *lose* from higher price and lower consumption.

◆ Society loses:
Producers' gains + tariff revenue
< consumers' losses.

◆ Tariffs have been decreasing due to **General Agreement on Tariffs and Trade** (international treaty to limit trade restriction) and other free trade agreements.

◆ Recent attempts by the **World Trade Organization (WTO)** to lower barriers to trade via the **Doha round** of trade talks has failed due to disputes between rich and developing nations.

Import quotas restrict import quantities, with quota licences distributed to importers.

◆ New supply curve = domestic supply curve + quota amount.

◆ Domestic price higher than world price—quantity demanded and bought falls, quantity supplied rises.

◆ Consumers lose due to higher price.

◆ Domestic producers gain due to higher price.

◆ Importers gain profits from buying at world price and selling at higher domestic price.

◆ Society loses in similar manner to effects of tariffs.

Other import barriers restrict supply of imports, which increases domestic price and domestic production.

◆ Examples include health, safety and regulation barriers and voluntary export restraints (similar to a quota allocated to foreign exporters).

Export subsidies are payments from government to producers of exported goods.

◆ Export subsidies are illegal under international trade agreements, but agricultural subsidies to farmers have effect of increasing domestic production, leading to overproduction.

The Case Against Protection

Trade restrictions are used despite losses of gains from trade for two somewhat credible reasons—to protect **infant industries** as they mature and to prevent foreign companies from **dumping** their products on world markets at prices less than cost.

A country may restrict trade for the following less credible reasons:

◆ To save the jobs lost from free trade.

◆ To compete with cheap foreign labour.

◆ To penalize lax environmental standards.

◆ To prevent rich countries from exploiting developing countries.

One new worry is **offshoring** (hiring foreign labour or buying goods/services from abroad), especially **offshore outsourcing** (hiring foreign labour to produce in other countries).

◆ Lower transportation and communications costs have increased offshoring in recent years.

◆ Benefits, costs, winners, losers from offshoring are similar to those for free trade, with losers concentrated in the domestic services industry.

The biggest problem with protection is that it invites retaliation from other countries (trade wars).

◆ There are still trade restrictions due to:

• Tariff revenue is an attractive tax base for governments in developing countries.

• **Rent-seeking** (lobbying) by groups/industries that suffer disproportionately under freer trade.

◆ In Canada, employment insurance and interprovincial transfers provide some compensation for losses due to free trade, but in general losers are not compensated.

HELPFUL HINTS

I The crucial result of this chapter is the demonstration that a country gains from trading internationally, both from exporting and from importing.

A country gains from exporting because the world price is higher than the domestic price. Producers gain from selling internationally at this higher price. Even though consumers lose some (due to the higher price), the producers' gain more than outweighs this loss, so that the country gains overall.

Similarly, a country gains from importing because the world price is lower than the domestic price. Consumers gain from buying at this lower price. Even though producers lose some (due to the lower price), the consumers' gain more than outweighs this loss, and the country gains overall.

Note that this latter effect means that an importing country even gains from buying a good that is dumped at below-cost on the world market by another country. In essence, the dumping country is giving the importing country a subsidy!

2 An important economic effect of trade restrictions is that a tariff and an import quota have the same effects. A voluntary export restraint is also a form of a quota, but it is one imposed by the exporting country rather than by the importing country.

All trade restrictions raise the domestic price of the imported goods and reduce the amount of imports. The increase in price that results from each trade restriction produces a gap between the domestic price of the imported good and the foreign supply price of the good.

Alternative trade restrictions differ in which party captures this excess. With a tariff, the government receives the tariff revenue. For a quota imposed by the importing country, domestic importers who have been awarded a licence to import capture this excess through increased profit. For a voluntary export restraint, the excess is captured by foreign exporters who have been awarded licences to export by their government.

3 Given the considerable gains from free trade, why then do countries have such a strong tendency to impose trade restrictions? The key is that while free trade creates overall benefits to the economy as a whole, there are both winners and losers. The winners gain more in total than the losers lose, but the losers tend to be concentrated in a few industries.

Given this concentration, free trade will be resisted by some acting on the basis of rational self-interest. Even though only a small minority benefit while the overwhelming majority will be hurt, it is not surprising to see trade restrictions implemented. The cost of a given trade

restriction to *each* of the majority will be individually quite small, while the benefit to *each* of the few will be individually large. Thus the minority will have a significant incentive to see that restriction takes place, while the majority will have little incentive to expend time and energy in resisting trade restriction.

5 To understand the source of pressures for trade restrictions, let us summarize those who win and lose from trade restrictions.

Under the three forms of restrictions (tariffs, quotas, and voluntary export restraints) *consumers* lose, because the price of the imported good increases. *Domestic producers* of the imported good and their factors of production gain from all three, because the price of the imported good increases. *Foreign producers* and their factors of production lose under all three schemes, because their export sales decrease. Under quotas and voluntary export restraints, the *holders of import licences* gain from buying low and selling high (they may be foreign or domestic). *Government* gains tariff revenue under tariffs and, potentially, votes under other schemes.

Given this list, it is hardly surprising that the main supporters of trade restrictions are domestic producers and their factors of production.

SELF-TEST

True/False and Explain

How Global Markets Work

1 When a Canadian citizen stays in a hotel in France, Canada is exporting a service.

2 Countries will export goods and services which they can produce at a lower opportunity cost than other nations.

3 In order to export a good, the world price must be lower than the domestic price.

4 If Canada starts importing widgets, the price of widgets in Canada will fall and the quantity bought will increase.

5 All parts of society gain from being able to export goods at a higher price than the domestic price.

6 Producers gain from the introduction of imports.

7 Consumers gain from the introduction of imports.

International Trade Restrictions

8 When governments impose import quotas, they increase their country's gains from trade.

9 A tariff on a good will raise its price and reduce the quantity traded.

10 An import quota will cause the price of the imported good to decrease.

11 The government revenue plus the gain to producers offsets the losses to consumers from a tariff.

The Case Against Protection

12 Japan is dumping steel if it sells steel in Japan at a lower price than it sells it in Canada.

13 Since Mexican labour is paid so much less than Canadian labour, entering into a free trade agreement with Mexico guarantees Canada will lose jobs to Mexico.

14 Elected governments are slow to reduce trade restrictions because there would be more losers than gainers.

15 Entering a trade agreement that increases both imports and exports will decrease jobs domestically.

Multiple-Choice

How Global Markets Work

1 Which of the following is a Canadian service export?
  a A Canadian buys dinner while travelling in Switzerland.
  b A Swiss buys dinner while travelling in Canada.
  c A Canadian buys a clock made in Switzerland.
  d A Swiss buys a computer made in Canada.
  e A Canadian buys a Canadian computer in Switzerland.

2 If Canada imports widgets, it must be the case that
  a Canada has a comparative advantage in widget production.
  b widgets are cheaper in Canada than the rest of the world.
  c the Canadian supply of widgets is greater than the Canadian demand for widgets at the world price.
  d the Canadian supply of widgets is less than the Canadian demand for widgets at the world price
  e there is no tariff on widgets.

3 Table 31.1 shows Glazeland's doughnut market before international trade. Glazeland opens up to international trade. If the world price is $0.60, then Glazeland will produce _____ doughnuts and will _____ _____ doughnuts.
  a   2 million; import 3 million
  b   4 million; import 1 million
  c   4 million; export 1 million
  d   5 million; import 3 million
  e   5 million; export 3 million

TABLE 31.1 Glazeland's Doughnut Market

Price (dollars per doughnut)	Glazeland's Supply (millions)	Glazeland's Demand (millions)
0.20	1	10
0.30	2	8
0.40	3	6
0.50	4	4
0.60	5	2
0.70	6	0

4 Table 31.1 shows Glazeland's doughnut market before international trade. Glazeland opens up to international trade. If the world price is $0.40, then Glazeland will produce _____ doughnuts and will _____ _____ doughnuts.
  a   3 million; import 3 million
  b   3 million; export 3 million
  c   4 million; import 1 million
  d   4 million; export 1 million
  e   6 million; export 3 million

5 If Canada starts exporting gadgets, then the domestic price of gadgets
  a   decreases, leading to a decline in production and imports fill the gap.
  b   decreases, leading to a decline in demand and the different is exported.
  c   stays the same, but Canada increases production in response to the world demand.
  d   increases, demand declines and production increases and the difference is exported.
  e   increases, demand increases too and imports fill the gap.

6 If the widget market enters the world market, and the world price is higher than the domestic price, then the
  a   higher price will make consumers better off.
  b   higher price will make producers worse off.
  c   increased production will make consumers better off.
  d   decreased production will make producers worse off.
  e   amount of exports will be positive.

7 Figure 31.1 shows an export market. At the world price, domestic production is _____ units and domestic consumption is _____ units.
  a   100; 175
  b   100; 125
  c   125; 175
  d   175; 125
  e   175; 100

Figure **31.1**

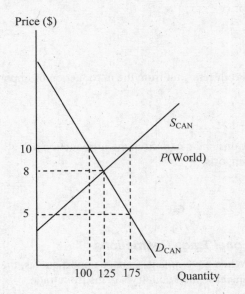

8 Figure 31.1 shows an export market. At the world price, producers have gained ___ per unit sold, and exports are ___ units.
  a $2; 25
  b $2; 50
  c $2; 75
  d $5; 50
  e $5; 75

9 Figure 31.2 shows an import market. At the world price, domestic production is _____ units and domestic consumption is _____ units.
  a   4,000; 14,000
  b   7,000; 12,000
  c   7,000; 10,000
  d   10,000; 14,000
  e   14,000; 4,000

Figure **31.2**

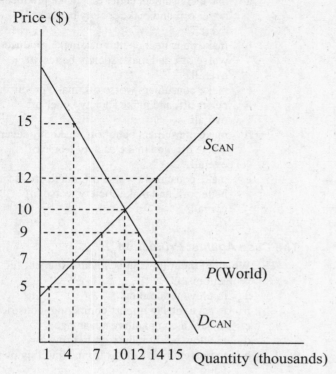

10 Figure 31.2 shows an import market. At the world price, consumers have gained ___ per unit sold, and imports are ___ units.
- **a** $2; 10,000
- **b** $2; 5,000
- **c** $2; 4,000
- **d** $3; 10,000
- **e** $3; 4,000

International Trade Restrictions

11 Figure 31.2 shows an import market. A tariff of $2 would lead to domestic production of ___ units and imports of ___ units.
- **a** 12,000; 5,000
- **b** 12,000; 2,000
- **c** 7,000; 5,000
- **d** 10,000; 2,000
- **e** 15,000; 14,000

12 Figure 31.1 shows an import market. Under an import quota of 5,000 units, what is the new domestic price?
- **a** $5
- **b** $7
- **c** $9
- **d** $10
- **e** $12

13 When an *import quota* is imposed, the gap between the domestic price and the export price is captured by
- **a** consumers in the importing country.
- **b** the domestic producers of the good.
- **c** the government of the importing country.
- **d** foreign exporters.
- **e** the importers of the good.

14 When a *voluntary export restraint* agreement is reached, the gap between the domestic import price and the export price is captured by
- **a** consumers in the importing country.
- **b** the domestic producers of the good.
- **c** the government of the importing country.
- **d** foreign exporters.
- **e** the domestic importers of the good.

15 When a *tariff* is imposed, the gap between the domestic price and the export price is captured by
- **a** consumers in the importing country.
- **b** the domestic producers of the good.
- **c** the government of the importing country.
- **d** foreign exporters.
- **e** the domestic importers of the good.

16 A tariff on watches which are imported by Atlantis will cause the domestic price of watches to
- **a** decrease and imports to increase.
- **b** increase and watch production in Atlantis to increase.
- **c** increase and watch production in Atlantis to decrease.
- **d** decrease and watch production in Atlantis to increase.
- **e** decrease and watch production in Atlantis to decrease.

17 Table 31.2 shows the Canadian supply of and demand for widgets. Widgets are available on the world market for $7. If the Canadian government imposes a tariff of $1, the selling price will be ____ and quantity bought will be ____.

a $6; 48 million
b $7; 44 million
c $8; 16 million
d $8; 24 million
e $8; 40 million

TABLE **31.2** Canada's Market for Widgets

Price (dollars per widgets)	Canadian Supply (millions)	Canadian Demand (millions)
5	12	52
6	16	48
7	20	44
8	24	40
9	28	36
10	32	32
12	36	28

18 Table 31.2 shows the Canadian supply of and demand for widgets. Widgets are available on the world market for $7. If the Canadian government imposes a tariff of $1, how much will be imported by Canada?
a 32 million
b 24 million
c 16 million
d 24 million
e 40 million

19 Table 31.2 shows the Canadian supply of and demand for widgets. Widgets are available on the world market for $7. Canadian widget producers convince their government that there is a need to protect the domestic industry from cheap imports. In response, the Canadian government sets an import quota of 8 million widgets. The resulting price of a widget in Canada will be _____, and domestic production will be ____.
a $6; 40 million
b $7; 36 million
c $8; 32 million
d $9; 28 million
e $10; 32 million

20 The introduction of a tariff will
a make consumers better off, make producers better off, and make society better off overall.
b make consumers better off, make producers worse off, and make society better off overall.
c make consumers worse off, make producers better off, and make society better off overall.
d make consumers better off, make producers worse off, and make society worse off overall.
e make consumers worse off, make producers better off, and make society worse off overall.

The Case Against Protection

21 Which of the following is *not* an argument for protectionism?
a to prevent dumping
b to save jobs in import-competing industries
c to gain a comparative advantage
d to allow infant industries to grow
e to prevent rich nations from exploiting poor nations

22 The biggest problem with protection is that
a it invites retaliation from trading partners.
b losers are not compensated.
c it worsens environmental standards.
d it can worsen national security.
e it lowers wages.

23 Why is international trade restricted?
a because government revenue is costly to collect via tariffs
b in order to get higher consumption possibilities
c to realize the gains from trade
d due to rent-seeking
e because free trade creates economic losses on average

24 The effects of offshoring from opening up call centres in India are similar to the effects from
a free trade.
b tariffs.
c import quota.
d voluntary export restraints.
e export subsidies.

25 In Canada, when international trade hurts producers and reduces jobs in import-competing industries, the government response is
a to introduce tariffs.
b to do absolutely nothing.
c to fully compensate all losers.
d to guarantee every job loser retraining.
e to allow employment insurance to help job losers with temporary relief.

Short Answer Problems

1 Suppose that Atlantis and Beltran both domestically produce widgets and watches, but currently do not trade with each other. If trade opens up between, what conditions must hold for *both* parties involved to gain from international trade?

2 Suppose Atlantis imposes a tariff on its imports of watches. How does the tariff affect the domestic price of watches, the quantity imported, and the quantity of watches produced domestically?

3 It is often argued by union leaders that tariffs are needed to protect domestic jobs. In light of your answers to Short Answer Problem **2**, evaluate this argument.

4 In a recent case, the U.S. government investigated Chinese bra manufacturers for suspected "dumping" of bras in the United States. The U.S. Department of Trade determined that the cost of making a bra in China was equivalent to $12 per bra, although they were being sold in the U.S. for $11 each. They then imposed dumping duties (tariffs) on Chinese bras of $1 per bra.

a Define dumping, and explain whether this is a case of dumping.

b Dumping duties are put in place to protect the U.S. economy from the "unfair" low price of the dumped imports. Did the dumping duties on bras make the U.S. economy better off?

5 Consider a simple world in which there are two countries, Atlantis and Beltran, each producing and consuming gadgets. The Atlantean gadget market is shown in Table 31.3, and the Beltranian market is given in Table 31.4. Both countries use the dollar as their currency.

TABLE 31.3 Atlantis' Market for Gadgets

Price (dollars per gadgets)	Atlantean Supply (millions)	Atlantean Demand (millions)
0	0	240
10	50	210
20	100	180
30	150	150
40	180	120
50	210	90
60	240	60
70	270	30
80	300	0

TABLE 31.4 Beltran's Market for Gadgets

Price (dollars per gadgets)	Beltran Supply (millions)	Beltran Demand (millions)
0	0	200
10	25	190
20	50	180
30	75	170
40	100	160
50	120	150
60	140	140
70	160	130
80	180	120

a Do the conditions exist for the two countries to trade in gadgets? Explain briefly.

b If they do trade, who will be the exporter and who will be the importer?

c Using the information in the tables, find the trading price of gadgets, and indicate how much will be exported from one country to another, and how much will be imported.

6 Suppose that Atlantis and Beltran engage in trade. (You should have been able to show in Short Answer Problem **5** that Atlantis will export gadgets to Beltran.) In a graph, show the Atlantis market for gadgets, indicating the pre-trade equilibrium and the free trade equilibrium. Indicate the winners and losers in Atlantis from free trade.

7 Suppose that Atlantis and Beltran engage in trade. (You should have been able to show in Short Answer Problem **6** that Atlantis will export gadgets to Beltran.) In a graph, show the Beltran market for gadgets, indicating the pre-trade equilibrium and the free trade equilibrium. Identify the winners and losers in Beltran from free trade.

8 Continue the analysis of Atlantis and Beltran trading gadgets. Suppose that the importing country (Beltran) introduces a tariff of $10. Show on your graph from Short Answer Problem 31 what this will do to the quantity demanded in Beltran, quantity produced, and amount imported. Indicate in words who will gain and who lose from the tariff in Beltran. How much is the tariff revenue for Beltran?

ⓒⓣ **9** Continue the analysis of Atlantis and Beltran trading gadgets. What will the impact of the tariff introduced by Beltran be on the quantity exported from Atlantis, and what will be the impact on the domestic price of gadgets, quantity produced, quantity demanded in Atlantis? Indicate in words who will gain and who lose from the tariff in Atlantis. (It is likely easier to work with Table 31.3 instead of doing this graphically.)

10 Rich countries are often worried about the impact of offshoring of services (such as call centres for computers or software) to developing countries such as India. Suppose that Canada was to ban the use of off-shoring for call centres. Explain in words who would gain and lose from this ban in Canada, and in India.

A N S W E R S

True/False and Explain

I **F** Canada is importing (using) a service. (758)

2 **T** Definition of national comparative advantage. (758)

3 **F** Must be higher to generate needed profits. (760)

4 **T** See Text Figure 31.1. (759)

5 **F** Consumers lose from higher price. (761)

6 **F** Introducing imports lowers prices for import-competing goods, hurting producers. (761)

7 **T** Introducing imports lowers prices for import-competing goods, benefiting consumers. (761)

8 **F** Trade restrictions reduce gains from trade. (762–764)

9 **T** Tariff raises price paid inside the country, which decreases quantity traded. (762–764)

10 **F** Quota decreases supply, which increases price—see Text Figure 31.4. (764)

II **F** Loss to consumers more than offsets gains to producers + tariff revenue because of higher cost domestic production. (764)

12 **F** Dumping would be selling in Canada at lower price than in Japan. (767)

13 **F** We must also examine the productivity of workers in each country, and Canadian workers are more productive. (768)

14 **F** They will be slow because losers' losses are individually much greater than winners' gains. (770)

15 **F** More imports will likely decrease jobs, but more exports will increase them—net outcome is not clear. (768)

Multiple-Choice

I **b** **a** and **c** are imports, **d** and **e** are exports of a *good*. (758)

2 **d** If we import, world price is lower and our supply is therefore too low compared to demand. Could still have a tariff. (759)

3 **e** Price = $0.60 implies supply of 5 million, demand only 2 million, so 3 million exported. (759–760)

4 **a** Price = $0.40 implies supply of 3 million, demand 6 million, so 3 million imported. (759–760)

5 **d** See Text Figure 31.2. (760)

6 **e** Higher price and higher production benefits producers and hurts consumers. (761)

7 **e** Read off demand and supply curves at world price. (760)

8 **c** Difference between domestic price (where *D* and *S* cross) and world price; quantity supplied – quantity demanded. (760–761)

9 **a** Read off demand and supply curves at world price. (759)

10 **d** Difference between domestic price (where *D* and *S* cross) and world price; quantity supplied – quantity demanded. (759–761)

11 c   New price = $9 (world price + tariff)—
quantity produced is read off supply curve,
quantity demanded off demand curve,
imports = difference. (762–764)

12 c   Add 5,000 units to the supply curve and see
where it crosses demand curve. (764–766)

13 e   Under quota, domestic government allocates
the licence to import. (764)

14 d   Because they have right to export. (766)

15 c   They collect tariff revenue = import price –
world price. (762–764)

16 b   Tariff increases domestic price = export
price + tariff, and domestic production
increases in response. (762–764)

17 e   New price is $1 + $7 = $8, so quantity
bought is 40 million off demand curve.
(762–764)

18 c   Difference between quantity demanded and
supplied at $8. (762–764)

19 d   Equilibrium is price where quota of 8
million = import demand = quantity
demanded – quantity supplied. (764–765)

20 e   See text discussion. (764)

21 c   See text discussion. (767–771)

22 a   See text discussion. (767–771)

23 d   See text discussion. (767–771)

24 a   Similar affect on domestic price of good,
domestic production, imports, and winners
and losers. (769)

25 e   See text discussion. (770–771)

Short Answer Problems

1   For two potential trading partners to be willing to
trade, they must have different comparative
advantages, so that they have different
equilibrium market prices in their respective
markets pre-trade. For example, if Atlantis' pre-
trade price of widgets is lower than Beltran's
price ($P_{ATL} < P_{BEL}$), then Atlantis can gain from
exporting widgets at a higher price (see Text
Figure 31.2) and Beltran gains from importing
widgets at a lower price (see Text Figure 31.1).
This requires $P_{ATL} < P_{TRADE} < P_{BEL}$.

2   A tariff on an imported good will *raise its price
to domestic consumers* by an amount equal to the
tariff. As the domestic price of the good
increases, the quantity of the good demanded
decreases. The increase in the domestic price
will also lead to an *increase in the quantity of the
good supplied domestically*. The lower quantity
demanded and higher quantity supplied means
that the quantity imported (= quantity supplied –
quantity demanded) decreases.

3   This argument has some truth to it. As Short
Answer Problem **2** shows, the tariff will lead an
increase in domestic production of the protected
good, which will lead to an increase in jobs in
that industry. However, the same tariff could
trigger a trade war (tariffs imposed by other
countries on Atlantis' exports), which would
reduce foreign purchases of Atlantis' goods,
reducing exports and export production,
reducing jobs in the export industry. The net
effect on jobs is unclear.

4 a   Dumping occurs when a foreign firm sells
its exports at a lower price than the cost of
production. Since the cost of production is
higher than the export price, this is indeed a
case of dumping.

b   The dumping duties are exactly like a tariff,
and as shown in Text Figure 31.3, the effect
of a tariff is to increase the domestic price of
bras, reduce domestic bra consumption (and
hurt consumers) and increase domestic bra
production (and help producers), and hurt
the U.S. economy overall.

5 a   The pre-trade price of gadgets in Atlantis
would be $30, while the pre-trade price in
Beltran would be $60. If a trading price
between $30 and $60 could come about,
both sides would gain. Therefore, the
appropriate conditions exist for trade.

b   The exporter would be Atlantis, with the
lower price, and Beltran would be the
importer with the higher price.

c   We can find the trading price ($40) in a
variety of manners. We could combine the
two supply schedules into a "world" supply
schedule, and combine the two demand
schedules into a "world" demand schedule,
and find the equilibrium world price. Such a
schedule is shown below in Table 31.5, and
world equilibrium occurs with a quantity of
280 million and price of $40.

We can also find the trading price ($40) by
looking at Tables 31.3 and 31.4, and noting
that at a price of $40, supply in Atlantis

exceeds demand by 60 million, while supply in Beltran is short of demand by 60 million, indicating that sending 60 million from Atlantis to Beltran would create equilibrium. In summary, Atlantis exports 60 million gadgets and Beltran imports 60 million.

TABLE **31.5** "World" Market for Gadgets

Price (dollars per gadgets)	World Supply (millions)	World Demand (millions)
0	0	440
10	75	400
20	150	360
30	225	320
40	280	280
50	330	240
60	380	200
70	430	160
80	480	120

6   Figure 31.3 shows the Atlantean market. The initial pre-trade equilibrium occurs at a price of $30 and a quantity traded of 150 million. We have established the world price will be $40. At this price, Atlantis will demand only 120 million gadgets (read off the demand curve), and will produce 180 million gadgets (read off the supply curve), and will export the surplus of 60 million gadgets.

FIGURE **31.3**

Producers will gain from the higher price and the higher production. Consumers will lose from the higher price and the lower consumption. Since producers gain what the consumers lose *and* gain from exporting, there is an overall gain to Atlantis.

7   Figure 31.4 shows the Beltran market. The initial pre-trade equilibrium occurs at a price of $60 and a quantity traded of 140 million. We have established the world price will be $40. At this

price, Beltran will demand 160 million gadgets (read off the demand curve), and will produce only 100 million gadgets (read off the supply curve), and will import the shortage of 60 million gadgets.

Producers will lose from the lower price and the lower production. Consumers will gain from the lower price and the higher consumption. Since consumers gain what the producers lose *and* gain from importing, there is an overall gain to Beltran.

FIGURE **31.4**

8   Figure 31.5 shows the impact of the tariff on Beltran's market. The tariff adds $10 to the world price, leading to a domestic price of $50. At this price, demand is only 150 million gadgets, and supply increases to 120 million gadgets, leading to a decreased amount of imports at 30 million units.

FIGURE **31.5**

The introduction of the tariff hurts consumers, due to the higher price and lower consumption. Producers gain from the higher price and higher production. The government gains tariff revenue ($10 × 30 million gadgets imports), but overall Beltran is worse off—the producers' gains and tariff revenue do not compensate for the losses to consumers.

9   The answer to this question is complicated by the fact that we are attempting to use a simple model to answer a slightly more complex question, so only an approximate answer is possible. Beltran is now importing only 30 million gadgets from Atlantis, instead of the previous 60 million units. Therefore, Atlantis will export only 30 million units. Looking at Table 31.3, we can see that this will occur at some price between $30 and $40 (where we cannot exactly tell without a mathematical model incorporating the tax, which is beyond the complexities of this model). Therefore, the impact of the Beltran tariff is to reduce the world price somewhat. Since the price received by Atlantean sellers will fall, they will lose some producer surplus. Since the price paid by Atlantean consumers will fall, they will gain some consumer surplus. The overall impact of the fall in world price for Atlantis will be a reduction in exports, and therefore a reduction in the gains to Atlantean producers (and a reduction in the loss to Atlantean consumers), and a reduction in the overall gain to Atlantis from exporting.

10   If a Canadian company "offshores" a call centre to India, this is essentially the company importing a service from India. All the gains and losses to individuals and the overall economy are identical to the normal case of an import, as we saw in Text Figure 31.1. The company as an importer gains the less expensive service, which means lower costs and presumably more profits for the Canadian company (and potentially lower prices for its buyers). The losers are the potential sellers in Canada (people who operate or work in call centres), who lose from a lower price in Canada for what they sell. Overall, Canada gains from being to import the cheaper product.

Similarly, for India, this is an export of a service, and as in Text Figure 31.2, we can see that the Indian suppliers of the call centre services gain from being able to sell more at a higher price, Indian consumers lose from the higher Indian price, and overall India gains from being able to export this service.

If the use of off-shore call centres is banned, then all these gains and loses are reversed. The Canadian buyers of call centre services lose (they face higher costs). The Canadian import-competing call centres gain back from the now-higher Canadian prices, but overall Canada is worse off from the ban (just like a tariff makes Canada worse off). For India, the Indian suppliers lose the higher prices, the Indian consumers gain from the lower prices, and overall India is worse off.

Understanding Macroeconomic Policy

PROBLEM

Due to a recession in the United States, the Canadian economy now has a large recessionary gap. You are working as a special economic advisor to the Prime Minister. She has two policy options to evaluate.

a The Governor of the Bank of Canada suggests carrying out an anti-recessionary *monetary* policy. The Prime Minister would like you to explain such a policy. Give an example of the changes to the overnight rate target and the type of open market operation the Bank of Canada would carry out. Show what happens to the balance sheets of the Bank of Canada and the banking sector as a result of the initial impacts of the operation. What is the overall impact of expansionary monetary policy on bank reserves and the overnight rate? Explain what this policy will do to real interest rates, consumption, investment, net exports, aggregate demand, the price level and real GDP in the short run.

b The Minister of Finance suggests carrying out an anti-recessionary *fiscal* policy. The Prime Minister would like you to explain how this policy would work. Give an example of the changes to taxes and/or government expenditures that would be needed to make this work. (The government currently has a balanced budget.) Explain how this policy would work through the economy to affect government expenditures, consumption, investment (hint: think of the impact on real interest rates), net exports, aggregate demand, the price level and real GDP in the short run.

c Now that you have explained the two policies, the Prime Minister has to pick between them. She turns to you, and asks you to give her a quick summary of some of the potential indirect impacts of each policy on the economy, as well as issues around loose links, and timing lags. Which policy would you recommend?

Midterm Examination

You should allocate 16 minutes for this examination (8 questions, 2 minutes per question). For each question, choose the best answer.

1 An attempt to stimulate the economy by using the overnight rate target would
  a lower the bank rate and the settlement balances rate, creating more excess reserves, creating more loans and lower interest rates on loans.
  b raise the bank rate and the settlement balances rate, creating more excess reserves, creating more loans and lower interest rates on loans.
  c raise the bank rate and the settlement balances rate, creating less excess reserves, creating less loans and higher interest rates on loans.
  d lower the bank rate and the settlement balances rate, creating less excess reserves, creating less loans and higher interest rates on loans.
  e lower the bank rate and the settlement balances rate, creating more excess reserves, creating more loans and higher interest rates on loans.

2 An increase in autonomous taxes leads to a
  a rightward shift in the *AD* curve equal to the autonomous tax multiplier times the tax increase.
  b leftward shift in the *AD* curve equal to the autonomous tax multiplier times the tax increase.
  c leftward shift in the *SAS* curve.
  d decrease in *Y* equal to the autonomous tax multiplier times the tax increase, in the short run.
  e decrease in *Y* equal to the autonomous tax multiplier times the tax increase, in the long run.

3 An open market purchase of government securities by the Bank of Canada will
  a increase bank reserves and increase the overnight rate.
  b decrease bank reserves and decrease the overnight rate.
  c increase bank reserves and decrease the overnight rate.
  d decrease bank reserves and increase the overnight rate.
  e decrease bank reserves but increase the overnight rate if banks have excess reserves.

4 An increase in the tax rate on wages will lead to
  a less labour hired, more production and higher potential GDP.
  b less saving, less investment, and lower economic growth.
  c more labour hired, more production and higher potential GDP.
  d a strong intertemporal substitution effect, leading to more labour supplied.
  e higher real before-tax wage rates.

5 Which of the following quotations *correctly* describes the impact of monetary policy on the economy?
  a "House sales are down a lot, due to the lower interest rates."
  b "The lower interest rates created by the central bank are creating lower exports."
  c "The tightening of monetary policy is helping sell goods abroad."
  d "Businesses are investing more, now that interest rates have become higher."
  e "The lower interest rates created by the central bank are creating more jobs."

6 When induced taxes are added to an economy with only autonomous taxes,
  a fiscal policy multipliers are made stronger.
  b discretionary fiscal policy is eliminated.
  c there will always be a structural deficit.
  d there will always be a cyclical deficit.
  e fluctuations in aggregate expenditure are reduced.

7 Whenever the inflation rate is above the target, or there is a positive output gap, the Bank of Sarconia raises the overnight rate target. The Bank of Sarconia is following a(n)
  a inflation targeting rule.
  b McCallum rule.
  c Taylor rule.
  d exchange rate target rule.
  e monetary target rule.

8 Which of the following is *not* a source of budgetary revenues?
  a personal income taxes
  b transfer payments
  c corporate income taxes
  d indirect taxes
  e investment income

ANSWERS

Problem

  a The Bank of Canada wants to lower interest rates, and will do so by lowering the overnight target range (lowering the bank rate and the settlements balance rate) and by purchasing government securities. The Bank of Canada buys these securities from private banks and pays for them by crediting the banks' deposits at the Bank of Canada (which are reserves). The result of such a purchase is shown in Table P10.1.

TABLE **P10.1**

| Bank of Canada | | Banking System | |
Assets	Liabilities	Assets	Liabilities
Government securities (+)	Bank deposits (+)	Reserves (+)	
		Government securities (−)	

The lower overnight target rate and the open market operation lead to excess reserves in the banking system. The banks will try to increase their overnight lending and reduce their overnight borrowing, which pushes down overnight rates. The banks also will lend out their excess reserves, leading to an expansion of loans, deposits and therefore the money supply.

The lower overnight rates create substitution effects, lowering other interest rates. The increase in loanable funds also lowers real interest rates in the short run, which increases consumption expenditure and investment, and decreases the demand for Canadian dollars and therefore decreases the value of the Canadian dollar and increases net exports.

The increase in consumption, investment and net exports increases aggregate demand, which translates into a shift rightward in the *AD* curve, which increases the price level, triggering a movement along the short-run aggregate supply curve, increasing real GDP.

b   An appropriate tax policy would be a tax cut. This would increase disposable income, which would increase consumption expenditure and therefore aggregate demand. An increase in government expenditures would lead directly to an increase in aggregate demand.

The increase in consumption or government expenditures increases aggregate demand, which translates into a shift rightward in the aggregate demand curve, which increases the price level, triggering a movement along the short-run aggregate supply curve, increasing real GDP.

One complication is that the fiscal policy, by either cutting taxes or raising government expenditures, would create a budget deficit. A budget deficit increases the demand for loanable funds, and increases real interest rates. The higher real interest rates will lower investment spending. The higher real interest rates will also increase the demand for the Canadian dollar, increasing the exchange rate, lowering exports and raising imports. The decrease in investment and net exports will somewhat offset the impact of the original increase in aggregate demand.

c   Indirect impacts on the economy might flow from two factors. First, the budget deficit and higher interest rates will potentially lower investment and therefore have a negative impact on capital accumulation and economic growth. Second, if tax cuts are used for the fiscal policy, this would reduce the tax wedge and potentially have positive incentive effects, helping increase potential GDP.

Fiscal policy suffers from three potential lags: the recognition lag (not an issue in this case), the law-making lag (the changes to tax or spending policy must pass Parliament) and the impact lag (the policies take time to have an impact on the economy). Monetary policy also suffers from timing lags in the monetary policy transmission process. In addition, monetary policy affects aggregate demand via the real interest rate, which is affected by a variety of other factors, including inflation expectations. Therefore, monetary policy only has a "loose link" to aggregate demand.

Your policy recommendation depends on your judgement of the speed and effectiveness of each policy. It's a value judgment!

MIDTERM EXAMINATION

1 a   Decrease in bank rate and settlement balances rate decreases cost of borrowing from central bank, decreasing desired reserves, creating excess reserves, creating increase in loans, etc. (734–738)

2 b   Multiplier calculation holds constant the price level. (718)

3 c   Bank of Canada pays for securities by crediting banks' reserves, which creates excess reserves and more lending, lowering the overnight rate. (737)

4 b   Lower return to working, lower quantity supplied of labour, raising before-tax wage rates, reducing labour hired, production, and therefore potential GDP. (716–717)

5 e   Decrease in r leads to increase in C (so **a** wrong), increase in I (so **d** wrong), increase in NX (so **b** and **c** wrong), and all increase AD, which creates more jobs. (739–746)

6 e   Induced taxes act as automatic stabilizer. Multipliers are weaker, can still do discretionary policy, and there may or may not be a cyclical/structural deficit depending on other factors. (720–723)

7 c   See Taylor rule formula. Other formulas ignore output gap. (747–749)

8 b   Outlay. (708–709)